UP, DOWN, ALL-AROUND
STITCH DICTIONARY

More than 150 stitch patterns to knit top down,
bottom up, back and forth, and in the round

WENDY BERNARD

Photography by THAYER ALLYSON GOWDY
Prop and wardrobe styling by KAREN SCHAUPETER

STC CRAFT | A Melanie Falick Book | New York

Published in 2014 by Stewart, Tabori & Chang
An imprint of ABRAMS

Text copyright © 2014 by Wendy Bernard
Photographs copyright © 2014 by Thayer Allyson Gowdy

Library of Congress Control Number: 2013945660

ISBN: 978-1-61769-099-0

Editor: Liana Allday
Designer: Anna Christian
Technical Editor: Sue McCain
Production Manager: True Sims
Prop and Wardrobe Stylist: Karen Schaupeter
Hair and Makeup: Preston Nesbit for Aubri Balk Inc.
Yarn Supplier: Blue Sky Alpacas

The text of this book was composed in Loire.

Printed and bound in China

10 9 8 7 6 5 4 3 2

Stewart, Tabori & Chang books are available at special discounts when
purchased in quantity for premiums and promotions as well as fundraising or
educational use. Special editions can also be created to specification.
For details, contact specialsales@abramsbooks.com or the address below.

THE ART OF BOOKS SINCE 1949
115 West 18th Street
New York, NY 10011
www.abramsbooks.com

CONTENTS

INTRODUCTION

As knitters, we love our stitch dictionaries. They are tomes that many of us treasure as if they were family heirloom cookbooks, providing hundreds, and probably thousands, of stitch pattern possibilities. But, if you have ever wanted to use a stitch pattern in a piece that is worked in the round or from the top down, you've probably had to re-chart your stitch pattern. Why's that, you ask? Because all of the instructions in stitch dictionaries are typically written so the pattern can be reproduced back and forth in rows from the bottom up—but not in the round, and certainly not top-down. As knitters, however, there are many situations in which we need to use stitch patterns in several different directions. For instance, if you're knitting a top-down cardigan with an allover pattern, you will need to know how to work the pattern top to bottom/flat (for the body), and top to bottom/in the round (for the sleeves). This means that you would need to work your stitch pattern two different ways, first working it flat, as written, and then converting it to in the round. Doing these calculations is not always that straightforward. And although almost

all patterns out there *can* be converted, there are some outliers that are stubborn, refusing to make the change unless you cajole them a little . . . or a lot.

As I have written the Custom Knits series in my upstairs office over the past several years, I have converted many a flat stitch pattern to top down and in the round—and in each of the three volumes in the Custom Knits series, I spent a little time talking about how to convert stitch patterns so that they suit whatever it is that you're knitting—but, as I have researched the topic and read online knitting forums over the years, I have come to realize that I'm not the only one wishing stitch dictionaries would offer instructions for knitting in more ways than bottom up and flat.

Since not everyone has time to re-chart stitch patterns, I thought I would go ahead and make your life a little easier by doing the work for you. In this book, I present 157 of my favorite stitch patterns, all of them ready to knit in more than one direction (meaning you have nearly 400 stitch pattern options at the ready). You'll find them not only in their traditional state (worked flat, bottom up), but also in the round. In almost all cases, a stitch pattern will look exactly the same whether you are working it top to bottom or bottom up, but when a pattern is obviously directional, like the eyelet Hearts on page 130, you'll see that I also provided instructions on how to reproduce the stitch pattern as closely as possible in the opposite direction. I say "as closely as possible" because there are times, especially in the textured and lace chapters, when you will have to use a k2tog instead of an ssk or skp when switching from bottom up to top down. Not all stitch patterns look exactly the same when

flipped, but in almost all cases, they look pretty darn close and you'll have fantastic results.

To give you a little bit of everything, I have included my favorite stitch patterns from the eight basic categories: knits and purls; ribs; slipped, textured, and fancy stitches; yarnovers and eyelets; cables; lace; colorwork; and hems and edgings. Plus you'll find both written-out instructions and charts for nearly every stitch pattern, because I know we all have our preferences.

These stitch patterns are perfect for using in top-down and bottom-up sweaters, as well as all manner of accessories, like socks, hats, and mittens. To help you start thinking about ways to incorporate stitch patterns into garments, I've provided a pattern with each chapter—though with these converted stitch patterns at your fingertips, it's a cinch to swap out one stitch pattern for another in any written pattern (check out the tutorial on page 16). And if designing from scratch is more your thing, you'll find three formulas on page 274—for a hat, a scarf, and mittens—each of which are great opportunities to learn how to incorporate stitch patterns and knit a custom-designed piece using any yarn and at any gauge you like.

With the *Up, Down, All-Around Stitch Dictionary*, you have at your fingertips endless opportunities for knitting in any direction you please with any stitch pattern you like. My hope is that these stitch patterns will allow you to spend less time converting patterns on graph paper and more time knitting. And most of all, I hope that this book gives you the tools you need to customize your knitting and take another step toward creating truly unique knitted items—no matter which direction you choose to knit them.

HOW TO USE THE STITCH PATTERNS

Stitch dictionaries can be big-time sources of creativity. You may be on the hunt for the perfect stitch pattern to incorporate into a garment you're designing. Or you may just want to modify an existing pattern by swapping out one stitch pattern for another you like better, or adding a motif to an otherwise plain design. No matter what your end goal, the simplest way for you to go about choosing and using the stitch patterns from this book is to swatch with the yarn you want to use for your project. Swatching will help you decide if you like the way the stitch pattern looks (and if you like working the stitch pattern enough to repeat it over and over). But not only that—you'll want to swatch the pattern in the direction you will be using it to make extra sure that your gauge is correct and the pattern looks the way you want it to.

SWATCHING BASICS

Think about it: If you don't swatch a stitch pattern before you start knitting a project, will you know how the stitch pattern will look after your project is finished? Are you willing to rip it out? If you are using fuzzy yarn or something that isn't easy to rip out, what would you do? In my opinion, casting on and knitting with confidence is a lot more fun than casting on and hoping for the best, so in order to avoid the dreaded Rrrrripp!, I strongly suggest you make a swatch.

The larger your swatch, the easier it will be to accurately read how many stitches and rows appear within each unit of measurement. Most of the time, your instructions will give you a gauge that assumes you've swatched a four-inch (10-cm) square, so try to knit a gauge swatch around this size, if at all possible. And if your project has sections that are worked both flat and in the round, it's wise to swatch both ways and compare the results.

FLAT SWATCHES

If you plan to work your project back and forth in rows, it's best to work a flat swatch. To do this, choose the needles and yarn suggested in your pattern and cast on the number of stitches you think you'll need for four inches (10 cm) worth of stitches, plus a few extra stitches on each end like I did with the swatches in this book. (Note that the written and charted stitch patterns do not include the Garter stitches that are shown in the pictures.) Work the first few rows in Garter stitch, or another nonrolling edge, and then begin your stitch pattern. Make sure to knit those "extra stitches" at the edges in Garter stitch, too (you might find it helpful to place markers so you'll remember where your extra stitches begin). When you've worked your stitch pattern for four inches (10 cm), work a few rows in Garter stitch and bind off.

IN-THE-ROUND SWATCHES

Many knitters find that their gauge changes when they work in the round. The best way to find out if your gauge changes is to swatch a few different stitch patterns in the round and compare them to flat swatches of the same stitch pattern. Personally, I tend to knit a little tighter when knitting in the round. With practice, I have learned that I can swatch flat for projects I plan to work in the round and expect to get approximately one extra stitch over four inches (10 cm) than I would normally get when knitting flat. Once you've swatched a few stitch patterns in the round, you'll likely see a trend emerge, too. If your gauge is slightly different, you can adjust your needle size or simply check the schematic and confirm whether or not it's okay if what you're knitting comes out a little tighter than what is indicated (as can be the case with sleeves or hats, for example).

There are a number of ways you can knit a gauge swatch in the round, and neither is ideal, but they do work. One way is to cast on approximately four inches (10 cm) of stitches (enough for a few multiples of your stitch pattern) onto three or four double-pointed needles and join to work in the round. Knit a tube at least four inches (10 cm) long, bind off, then wash and block the swatch. Lay the tube flat and carefully count the number of stitches and rounds per inch (see Blocking and Measuring, at right). Another way to swatch in the round is to cast on about four inches (10 cm) of stitches onto two double-pointed needles. Knit across one row; when you get to the end of the row, instead of turning to work a wrong side row, slide your stitches back to the right-hand side of the needle. With the right side facing, draw the yarn loosely behind the stitches on the needles and work the next row in the stitch pattern. Continue in this manner and bind off. Then, snip the floated yarn strands behind the work and lay your swatch flat.

THE IMPORTANCE OF SWATCHING

I can hear you sighing all the way from over here . . . I truly can. But there's no excuse to avoid swatching. Doing a proper gauge swatch before starting will not only give you close-to-final gauge, but it will also tell you how the stitch pattern will look and behave with your yarn and how it will drape. Plus, you'll have a chance to practice that cable or eyelet pattern you want to use, giving you the confidence to move ahead to the next step in your project—casting on. And at the very least, you can use your leftover swatches to make coasters or blankets, use them as Frisbees, post them on inspiration boards, or use them as wall decor. Still not convinced? Here are a few more situations in which it makes sense to swatch:

► Do you have new needles made out of fancy schmancy slippery wood? Swatch.

► Never used the yarn before? Swatch.

► Cable pattern you've never tried before? Swatch.

► Do you usually use straight needles but plan to use circulars? Swatch.

► Are you in a bad mood? Swatch. (Or re-check your gauge if you cast on while jolly.)

► You've knit the pattern flat before but are planning to knit in the round this time? Swatch.

► Using fluffy yarn and smooth yarn in the same gauge and in the same project? Swatch both.

► Had a cocktail? Swatch. (Then, re-swatch tomorrow.)

► Using super expensive fiber and don't want to waste it? Swatch anyway. (But save it just in case you need to unravel it if you run out of yarn.)

Again, carefully wash and block your swatch, and lay the piece flat to count the number of stitches and rounds per inch. With this method, you will be able to measure a wider section of the pattern piece, giving more reliable results than with the tube method.

BLOCKING AND MEASURING

After binding off, I recommend washing and lightly blocking your swatches. I like to soak my swatches in a bit of wool wash and water, then rinse and roll it in a towel. Lay out a dry towel and place the damp swatch on top, pinning it to the towel if it is unruly. When the swatch is dry, it's time to measure.

Measure your swatch on a flat surface. You can use a stitch gauge tool or a tape measure. Try to measure at least four inches (10 cm) worth of stitches and compare the stitch count to the one in the pattern to see if your gauge is correct. If you have too few stitches compared to the gauge in the pattern, then you'll have to go up a needle size or two. If you have too many, then you'll need to go down a needle size or two. Note that it's just as important to achieve row gauge, especially if you're working from a knitting pattern or chart that specifies how many rows or rounds you must knit instead of knitting to a particular measurement.

SWAPPING OUT STITCH PATTERNS

Have you ever fallen in love with a garment pattern but wanted to swap out the stitch pattern for one that's more to your liking? If so, then this section is for you. Here is a quick lesson (and a few examples) that walk you through the steps of swapping out stitch patterns.

Once you've selected a stitch pattern and the yarn you want to use, you'll need to swatch it to make sure the gauge matches what's used in the pattern. When you're satisfied with the gauge and how it looks, check the multiple of stitches in the pattern and compare it to your chosen swapped stitch pattern. (To find "compatible" stitch patterns for swapping out, check the stitch multiple index on page 284.) If the one in your existing pattern is, for instance, a multiple of 10 stitches, and your new one is the same, then you have no math to do. Knit on! If your new pattern is a multiple of six stitches, however, a little math is in order. Here are a number of different scenarios you may encounter when swapping out stitch patterns, along with examples of how to work the math.

The vest shown at right uses both Big and Little Cables (page 145) and Four-Stitch Cables (page 142).

EXAMPLE #1

Swap out a stitch pattern in a seamed sweater.

Let's say you're working a sweater with an all-over stitch pattern in pieces and flat, and the number of stitches across the Front in your size is 140 (a multiple of 10 repeated 14 times). If you want to swap out the existing stitch pattern with one that has a multiple of six, you will need to adjust the number of stitches to a multiple that is closest to 140. In this case, you will be able to adjust your stitch count to 138 (a multiple of 6 repeated 23 times), and then add two stitches to either side for stitching seams. (Just work these side stitches in Stockinette stitch, and you'll essentially maintain the size of the garment with a difference of only those two side stitches that will be eaten up after you've finished seaming the garment together.)

EXAMPLE #2

Swap out a sleeve edging in a top-down, in-the-round pullover.

If you're swapping out a sleeve edging in a top-down, circularly-knit pullover, you'll need to begin by swatching your edging. Check your gauge and how the pattern looks knit up in your yarn, and, if necessary, alter the stitch count to accommodate the multiple of stitches required in your new stitch pattern.

EXAMPLE #3

Swap out a panel of stitches in a top-down, in-the-round pullover.

Let's say you are working an in-the-round sweater from the top down (like the vest shown at right) and have chosen stitch patterns with different multiples than the original panel, which is centered down the Front. You'll need to know the total number of stitches in the Front section, decide how wide your center panel will be (and how many times you'll repeat the multiple), and subtract that number of total panel stitches from the total Front stitches. Divide the "free" stitches in half and voilà— you'll now know how many stitches you'll need on each side of your panel to center it perfectly down the front of your pullover. Note that this method also works great for inserting panels of stitchwork in the sleeves of otherwise plain top-down sweaters.

The Royal Cable Vest (page 172) provides a perfect opportunity to swap out the central cable, as explained in Example 3 (at left).

HOW TO WORK WITH CHARTS

Finally, before you begin using the stitch patterns in this book, I encourage you to read through this section on how to work with the charts. Since the charts are meant to be used for knitting bottom up, top down, flat, and in the round, there are a few special considerations to keep in mind as you work the patterns.

A chart shows you what the stitch pattern will look like from the right side of the work. Ideally, the symbols that are used should look like the actual stitches worked, so that when you look at the chart, you are able to see where you are in the pattern. Charts are numbered on the edges to help you keep track of what row of the pattern you're on. When you're working back and forth, the numbers on the right edge of the chart indicate right-side rows, and the numbers on the left indicate wrong-side rows. Row 1 indicates the first row of the chart that you will work. When Row 1 is on the left side of the chart, that means you start with a wrong-side row. For right-side rows, you will always work the chart from right to left. For wrong-side rows, you work from left to right. For a chart that shows a stitch pattern that is worked in the round, there will only be numbers on the right side, since you only work right-side rounds. If a chart shows both the flat and in-the-round stitch pattern (see Little Flames Top-Down Flat and in the Round, page 37), you will only have numbers on the right side; the rows that aren't numbered will be wrong-side rows when working flat.

The symbols always represent how the stitch(es) will look on the right side, so when you're working a wrong-side row, you have to work the symbol so that it will appear correctly on the right side. For instance, a blank white square indicates a knit stitch. So you will knit that stitch on the right side, but purl it on the wrong side. The chart key will always tell you how the stitch is to be worked; if it is to be worked differently depending on which side of the work you are on, that will be indicated as well. For instance, to produce a decrease that looks like a k2tog on the right side when you're working it on a wrong-side row, you will need to work a p2tog on the wrong side. So the key will say "K2tog on RS, p2tog on WS."

Cable and Eyelet Rib Flat

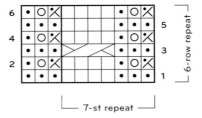

Cable and Eyelet Rib in the Round

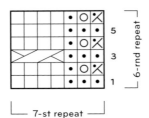

The stitch repeats are indicated below the chart, and the row/round repeats are shown to the right. In many cases, the repeat takes up the entire chart (see Cable and Eyelet Rib in the Round, above). Often, when working flat, there will be one or more extra stitches on either side (or both sides) of the main pattern repeat. This is so that the end of the stitch pattern mirrors the beginning (see Cable and Eyelet Rib Flat, above). In Cable and Eyelet Rib Flat, you will work the 7-stitch repeat the appropriate number of times, then end with the last three stitches to mirror the pattern. There is no need to mirror the stitch pattern when the piece is worked in the round, so you will rarely see extra stitches on an in-the-round chart. By the same token, you will occasionally have one or more set-up rows or rounds at the beginning of a chart that are worked before the main stitch pattern begins. You will usually work these rows/rounds once only, then repeat the designated pattern rows. If the repeat doesn't take up the entire chart, there will be a heavy vertical line before and/or after the repeat.

Occasionally a pattern repeat will shift a few stitches to the right or left to accommodate stitches within the pattern (like a decrease worked at the end of a repeat, or a cable that overlaps into the following repeat).

Wild Oats,
page 160

For instance, in Wild Oats Flat (see chart below), the repeat shifts 1 stitch to the left on Row 7 to accommodate the cable. In Diamond Eyelets Flat (page 125), the repeat shifts

2 stitches to the left on Row 5, to accommodate the 2-stitch decrease and its accompanying yarnover, then shifts 2 stitches back to the right on the following row. If the repeat doesn't shift back right away, it will when you work the first row of the chart again. This will be indicated by the location of the heavy vertical line.

With some stitch patterns that are worked in the round, the pattern might be worked across the beginning-of-the-round marker, beginning or ending one or more stitches before or after the marker (see Wild Oats in the Round, at left). The symbols and chart key will indicate how to work these extra stitches. You may need to shift the marker to keep the pattern flowing properly.

Occasionally you will see a gray-shaded square in a chart; this is a no-stitch square, and you should skip over that stitch and not work it. No-stitch squares are inserted into the chart in two instances. One is to indicate that a stitch is no longer available because a decrease has been worked without an increase to replace the stitch. This is the case in the Kick Pleat

Wild Oats Flat

8-row repeat
4-st repeat

Wild Oats in the Round

8-rnd repeat
4-st repeat

On last repeat of 1/2 LC on Rnd 7, work 1/2 LC on last 2 sts of Rnd 7 and first st of Rnd 8; reposition beginning-of-rnd marker to before last st of 1/2 LC.

On first repeat of Rnd 8, omit this st; it was worked with last 2 sts of Rnd 7. Work as knit st on subsequent repeats.

Edging bottom-up charts (below). On Rows/ Rounds 5, 9, and 13, you work a p2tog, so you are decreasing one stitch on each of those rows. The second instance where a no-stitch square is used is when there will be an increase later in the chart, and the no-stitch square is holding a place for it. In the Kick Pleat Edging Top-Down Charts (below), two no-stitch squares are inserted at the beginning of the chart, and you will see that on Rows/Rounds 5 and 9, a stitch is increased, replacing the no-stitch square. These squares allow the chart to be presented with stitches properly stacked above one another as they appear in the finished piece.

If you are working from both the text pattern and the chart, you may notice that sometimes they do not match each other. The end result will always match, but they may differ in how the repeats are set up on some of the rows. With a written pattern, you can shift where the pattern repeat is on each row for the most efficient (and easy-to-memorize) way of working it. For instance, in Waving Rib Flat (see page 63), on Row 1, the pattern repeat is p2, k4, which is very easy to memorize. When you get to Row 5, the pattern repeat shifts 3 stitches to the left. You begin with k3, then work the pattern repeat of p2, k4 to the last

Kick Pleat Edging Bottom-Up Flat

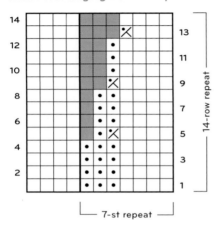

7-st repeat

Kick Pleat Edging Bottom-Up in the Round

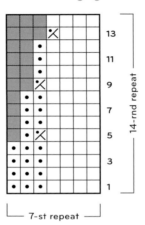

7-st repeat

Kick Pleat Edging Top-Down Flat

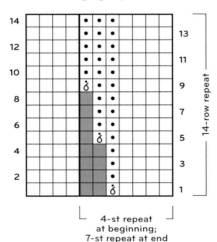

4-st repeat
at beginning;
7-st repeat at end

Kick Pleat Edging Top-Down in the Round

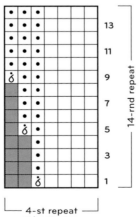

4-st repeat
at beginning;
7-st repeat at end

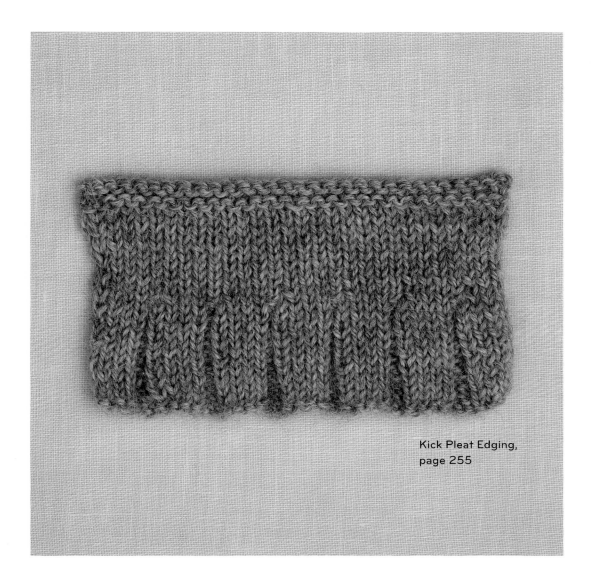

Kick Pleat Edging,
page 255

5 stitches, and finish the row. If we were to make the chart match the text, the heavy vertical repeat line would have to shift to the left on Row 5. We can do that, but it's easier to read the chart if the repeat line stays in the same place. If we were to make the text match the chart, Row 5 would read as follows: "*K3, p2, k1; repeat from * to last 2 sts, k2. That is definitely workable, but it doesn't flow as easily as working the 3 knit stitches at the beginning and then working the p2, k4 pattern repeat

that you've been working in all the other rows. Because a chart is a visual representation of the pattern, and is intended to be presented in the most clear manner possible, the pattern repeat is usually confined within the vertical repeat lines or sides of the chart (unless shifting is necessary as discussed above). In the end, the finished pattern will be exactly the same whether you work it from the text or the chart, and which you choose is entirely a matter of personal preference.

KNITS
AND PURLS

You've probably heard many knitters say, "After all, knitting is just two stitches: knits and purls!" and it's pretty much the truth. Simple knit-purl combinations like the ones in this chapter create beautiful, unique textures. Some are straightforward and familiar, like Garter Stitch on page 25, and some are more complex, like Diamond Brocade on page 28. When choosing yarns for knit-purl combinations, be sure to use solid or semi-solid colors as these stitch patterns rely on the shadowy interplay between knits and purls in order to make the pattern pop. If you use multicolor or variegated yarns, your hard work won't be as visible. It's always a good idea to swatch before you cast on to make sure your knits and purls shine and don't play second fiddle to the yarn.

Stitch patterns using a combination of knits and purls usually have a wrong side and a right side, and in some cases, like Seed Stitch on page 25, the pattern is reversible. That said, when choosing a stitch pattern for a project, look at both sides of your swatch and ask yourself if it will bother you if the wrong side shows. Knit-and-purl combinations that look good on both sides are great for everything from lightweight stoles and scarves to warmer accessories made with heavier yarns. The Interrupted Cowl on page 46 uses a chunky yarn that shows off the knit and purl stitches to full effect and makes a statement.

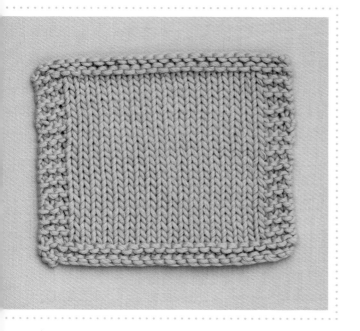

STOCKINETTE STITCH

FLAT

(any number of sts; 2-row repeat)

Row 1 (RS): Knit.
Row 2: Purl.
Repeat Rows 1 and 2 for Stockinette Stitch Flat.

IN THE ROUND

(any number of sts; 1-rnd repeat)

All Rnds: Knit.

REVERSE STOCKINETTE STITCH

FLAT

(any number of sts; 2-row repeat)

Row 1 (RS): Purl.
Row 2: Knit.
Repeat Rows 1 and 2 for Reverse Stockinette Stitch Flat.

IN THE ROUND

(any number of sts; 1-rnd repeat)

All Rnds: Purl.

GARTER STITCH

SEED STITCH

FLAT (REVERSIBLE)

(any number of sts; 1-row repeat)

All Rows: Knit.

IN THE ROUND (REVERSIBLE)

(any number of sts; 2-rnd repeat)

Rnd 1: Knit.
Rnd 2: Purl.
Repeat Rnds 1 and 2 for Garter Stitch in the Round.

FLAT (REVERSIBLE)

(even number of sts; 2-row repeat)

Row 1 (RS): *K1, p1; repeat from * to end.
Row 2: *P1, k1; repeat from * to end.
Repeat Rows 1 and 2 for Seed Stitch Flat.

IN THE ROUND (REVERSIBLE)

(odd number of sts; 2-rnd repeat)

Rnd 1: *K1, p1; repeat from * to last st, k1.
Rnd 2: Knit the purl sts and purl the knit sts as they face you.
Repeat Rnd 2 for Seed Stitch in the Round.

DIAMOND SEED BROCADE

FLAT

(multiple of 12 sts + 1; 12-row repeat)

Row 1 (RS): *K1, p1, k9, p1; repeat from * to last st, k1.
Row 2: K1, *p1, k1, p7, k1, p1, k1; repeat from * to end.
Row 3: *[K1, p1] twice, k5, p1, k1, p1; repeat from * to last st, k1.
Row 4: P1, *[p1, k1] twice, p3, k1, p1, k1, p2; repeat from * to end.
Row 5: *K3, p1, [k1, p1] 3 times, k2; repeat from * to last st, k1.
Row 6: P1, *p3, k1, [p1, k1] twice, p4; repeat from * to end.
Row 7: *K5, p1, k1, p1, k4; repeat from * to last st, k1.
Row 8: Repeat Row 6.
Row 9: Repeat Row 5.
Row 10: Repeat Row 4.
Row 11: Repeat Row 3.
Row 12: Repeat Row 2.
Rep Rows 1–12 for Diamond Seed Brocade Flat.

IN THE ROUND

(multiple of 12 sts; 12-rnd repeat)

Rnd 1: *K1, p1, k9, p1; repeat from * to end.
Rnd 2: *P1, k1, p1, k7, p1, k1; repeat from * to end.
Rnd 3: *[K1, p1] twice, k5, p1, k1, p1; repeat from * to end.
Rnd 4: *K2, p1, k1, p1, k3, [p1, k1] twice; repeat from * to end.
Rnd 5: *K3, p1, [k1, p1] 3 times, k2; repeat from * to end.
Rnd 6: *K4, p1, [k1, p1] twice, k3; repeat from * to end.
Rnd 7: *K5, p1, k1, p1, k4; repeat from * to end.
Rnd 8: Repeat Rnd 6.
Rnd 9: Repeat Rnd 5.
Rnd 10: Repeat Rnd 4.
Rnd 11: Repeat Rnd 3.
Rnd 12: Repeat Rnd 2.
Repeat Rnds 1–12 for Diamond Seed Brocade in the Round.

Flat

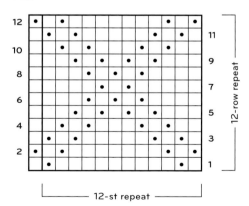

12-row repeat · 12-st repeat

In the Round

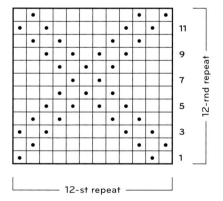

12-rnd repeat · 12-st repeat

DIAMOND BROCADE

FLAT

(multiple of 8 sts + 1; 8-row repeat)

Row 1 (RS): *P1, k7; repeat from * to last st, p1.
Row 2: P1, *k1, p5, k1, p1; repeat from * to end.
Row 3: *K2, p1, k3, p1, k1; repeat from * to last st, k1.
Row 4: P1, *p2, k1, p1, k1, p3; repeat from * to end.
Row 5: *K4, p1, k3; repeat from * to last st, k1.
Row 6: Repeat Row 4.
Row 7: Repeat Row 3.
Row 8: Repeat Row 2.
Repeat Rows 1–8 for Diamond Brocade Flat.

IN THE ROUND

(multiple of 8 sts; 8-rnd repeat)

Rnd 1: *P1; k7; repeat from * to end.
Rnd 2: *K1, p1, k5, p1; repeat from * to end.
Rnd 3: *K2, p1, k3, p1, k1; repeat from * to end.
Rnd 4: *K3, p1, k1, p1, k2; repeat from * to end.
Rnd 5: *K4, p1, k3; repeat from * to end.
Rnd 6: Repeat Rnd 4.
Rnd 7: Repeat Rnd 3.
Rnd 8: Repeat Rnd 2.
Repeat Rnds 1–8 for Diamond Brocade in the Round.

Flat

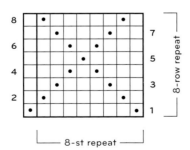

In the Round

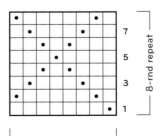

CHEVRON SEED STITCH

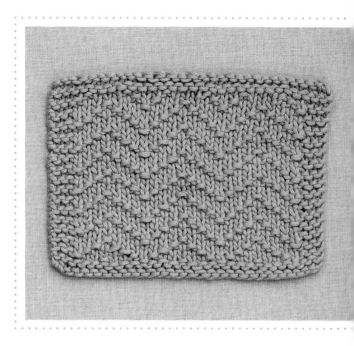

FLAT

(multiple of 8 sts + 1; 4-row repeat)

Row 1 (RS): *P1, k3; repeat from * to last st, p1.
Row 2: P1, *k1, p5, k1, p1; repeat from * to end.
Row 3: *K2, p1, k3, p1, k1; repeat from * to last st, k1.
Row 4: P1, *p2, k1, p1, k1, p3; repeat from * to end.
Repeat Rows 1–4 for Chevron Seed Stitch Flat.

IN THE ROUND

(multiple of 8 sts; 4-rnd repeat)

Rnd 1: *P1, k3; repeat from * to end.
Rnd 2: *K1, p1, k5, p1; repeat from * to end.
Rnd 3: *K2, p1, k3, p1, k1; repeat from * to end.
Rnd 4: *K3, p1, k1, p1, k2; repeat from * to end.
Repeat Rnds 1–4 for Chevron Seed Stitch in the Round.

Flat

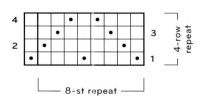

In the Round

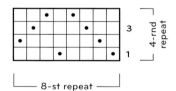

MOSS STITCH

FLAT (REVERSIBLE)

(even number of sts; 4-row repeat)

Row 1 (RS): *K1, p1; repeat from * to end.
Row 2: Repeat Row 1.
Rows 3 and 4: *P1, k1; repeat from * to end.
Repeat Rows 1–4 for Moss Stitch Flat.

IN THE ROUND (REVERSIBLE)

(even number of sts; 4-rnd repeat)

Rnds 1 and 2: *K1, p1; repeat from * to end.
Rnds 3 and 4: *P1, k1; repeat from * to end.
Repeat Rnds 1–4 for Moss Stitch in the Round.

SEEDED COLUMNS

FLAT

(multiple of 3 sts +2; 2-row repeat)

Row 1 (RS): Knit.
Row 2: P2, *k1, p2; repeat from * to end.
Repeat Rows 1 and 2 for Seeded Columns Flat.

IN THE ROUND

(multiple of 3 sts; 2-rnd repeat)

Rnd 1: Knit.
Rnd 2: *K2, p1; repeat from * to end.
Repeat Rnds 1 and 2 for Seeded Columns
in the Round.

DIAGONAL SEED STITCH

FLAT

(multiple of 5 sts; 10-row repeat)

Row 1 (RS): *K4, p1; repeat from * to end.
Row 2: *P1, k1, p3; repeat from * to end.
Row 3: *K2, p1, k2; repeat from * to end.
Row 4: *P3, k1, p1; repeat from * to end.
Row 5: *P1, k4; repeat from * to end.
Row 6: *K1, p4; repeat from * to end.
Row 7: *K3, p1, k1; repeat from * to end.
Row 8: *P2, k1, p2; repeat from * to end.
Row 9: *K1, p1, k3; repeat from * to end.
Row 10: *P4, k1; repeat from * to end.
Repeat Rows 1–10 for Diagonal Seed Stitch Flat.

IN THE ROUND

(multiple of 5 sts; 5-rnd repeat)

Rnd 1: *K4, p1; repeat from * to end.
Rnd 2: *K3, p1, k1; repeat from * to end.
Rnd 3: *K2, p1, k2; repeat from * to end.
Rnd 4: *K1, p1, k3; repeat from * to end.
Rnd 5: *P1, k4; repeat from * to end.
Repeat Rnds 1–5 for Diagonal Seed Stitch in the Round.

Flat

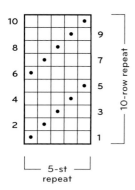

In the Round

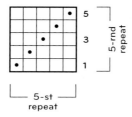

BASIC CHEVRON

FLAT (REVERSIBLE)

(multiple of 8 sts + 1; 16-row repeat)

Row 1 (RS): *P1, k7; repeat from * to last st, p1.
Row 2: K1, *p7, k1; repeat from * to end.
Row 3: P2, *k5, p3; repeat from * to last 7 sts, k5, p2.
Row 4: K2, *p5, k3; repeat from * to last 7 sts, p5, k2.
Row 5: P3, *k3, p5; repeat from * to last 6 sts, k3, p3.
Row 6: K3, *p3, k5; repeat from * to last 6 sts, p3, k3.
Row 7: P4, *k1, p7; repeat from * to last 5 sts, k1, p4.
Row 8: K4, *p1, k7; repeat from * to last 5 sts, p1, k4.
Row 9: Repeat Row 2.
Row 10: Repeat Row 1.
Row 11: Repeat Row 4.
Row 12: Repeat Row 3.
Row 13: Repeat Row 6.
Row 14: Repeat Row 5.
Row 15: Repeat Row 8.
Row 16: Repeat Row 7.
Repeat Rows 1–16 for Basic Chevron Flat.

IN THE ROUND (REVERSIBLE)

(multiple of 8 sts; 16-row repeat)

Rnds 1 and 2: *P1, k7; repeat from * to end.
Rnds 3 and 4: *P2, k5, p1; repeat from * to end.
Rnds 5 and 6: *P3, k3, p2; repeat from * to end.
Rnds 7 and 8: *P4, k1, p3; repeat from * to end.
Rnds 9 and 10: *K1, p7; repeat from * to end.
Rnds 11 and 12: *K2, p5, k1; repeat from * to end.
Rnds 13 and 14: *K3, p3, k2; repeat from * to end.
Rnds 15 and 16: *K4, p1, k3; repeat from * to end.
Repeat Rnds 1–16 for Basic Chevron in the Round.

Flat

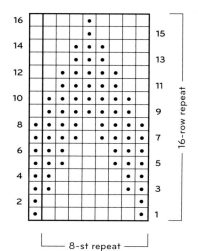

In the Round

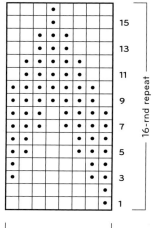

INTERRUPTED
GARTER STITCH

FLAT

(multiple of 5 sts + 1; 6-row repeat)

Row 1 (RS): Knit.
Row 2: Purl.
Row 3: Knit.
Row 4: Purl.
Row 5: *K1, p4; repeat from * to last st, k1.
Row 6: P1, *k4, p1; repeat from * to end.
Repeat Rows 1–6 for Interrupted Garter Stitch Flat.

IN THE ROUND

(multiple of 5 sts; 6-rnd repeat)

Rnds 1–4: Knit
Rnds 5 and 6: *K1, p4; repeat from * to end.
Repeat Rnds 1–6 for Interrupted Garter Stitch in the Round.

Flat

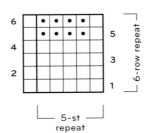

In the Round

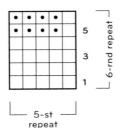

DIAMOND
MOSS STITCH

FLAT

(multiple of 6 sts; 12-row repeat)

Row 1 (RS): *K1, p1, k4; repeat from * to end.
Row 2: *P4, k1, p1; repeat from * to end.
Row 3: *P1, k1, p1, k3; repeat from * to end.
Row 4: *P3, k1, p1, k1; repeat from * to end.
Rows 5 and 6: Repeat Rows 1 and 2.
Row 7: *K4, p1, k1; repeat from * to end.
Row 8: *P1, k1, p4; repeat from * to end.
Row 9: *K3, p1, k1, p1; repeat from * to end.
Row 10: *K1, p1, k1, p3; repeat from * to end.
Rows 11 and 12: Repeat Rows 7 and 8.
Repeat Rows 1–12 for Diamond Moss Stitch
Flat.

IN THE ROUND

(multiple of 6 sts; 12-rnd repeat)

Rnds 1 and 2: *K1, p1, k4; repeat from * to end.
Rnds 3 and 4: *P1, k1, p1, k3; repeat from * to
end.
Rnds 5 and 6: Repeat Rnd 1.
Rnds 7 and 8: *K4, p1, k1; repeat from * to end.
Rnds 9 and 10: *K3, p1, k1, p1; repeat from * to
end.
Rnds 11 and 12: Repeat Rnd 7.
Repeat Rnds 1–12 for Diamond Moss Stitch
in the Round.

Flat and in the Round

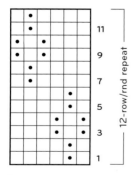

6-st repeat

LITTLE FLAMES

BOTTOM-UP FLAT

(multiple of 8 sts; 10-row repeat)

Row 1 (RS): Knit
Row 2: *P7, k1; repeat from * to end.
Row 3: *P2, k6; repeat from * to end.
Row 4: *P5, k3; repeat from * to end.
Row 5: *P4, k4; repeat from * to end.
Row 6: *P3, k5; repeat from * to end.
Row 7: *K1, p4, k3; repeat from * end.
Row 8: *P3, k3, p2; repeat from * to end.
Row 9: *K3, p2, k3; repeat from * to end.
Row 10: *P3, k1, p4; repeat from * to end.
Repeat Rows 1-10 for Little Flames Bottom-Up Flat.

BOTTOM-UP IN THE ROUND

(multiple of 8 sts; 10-rnd repeat)

Rnd 1: Knit.
Rnd 2: *P1, k7; repeat from * to end.
Rnd 3: *P2, k6; repeat from * to end.
Rnd 4: *P3, k5; repeat from * to end.
Rnd 5: *P4, k4; repeat from * to end.
Rnd 6: *P5, k3; repeat from * to end.
Rnd 7: *K1, p4, k3; repeat from * end.
Rnd 8: *K2, p3, k3: repeat from * to end.
Rnd 9: *K3, p2, k3; repeat from * to end.
Rnd 10: *K4, p1, k3; repeat from * to end.
Repeat Rnds 1-10 for Little Flames Bottom-Up in the Round.

TOP-DOWN FLAT

(multiple of 8 sts; 10-row repeat)

Row 1 (RS): Knit.
Row 2: *P3, k1, p4; repeat from * to end.
Row 3: *K3, p2, k3; repeat from * to end.
Row 4: *P3, k3, p2; repeat from * to end.
Row 5: *K1, p4, k3; repeat from * end.
Row 6: *P3, k5; repeat from * to end.
Row 7: *P4, k4; repeat from * to end.
Row 8: *P5, k3; repeat from * to end.
Row 9: *P2, k6; repeat from * to end.
Row 10: *P7, k1; repeat from * to end.
Repeat Rows 1-10 for Little Flames Top-Down Flat.

TOP-DOWN IN THE ROUND

(multiple of 8 sts; 10-rnd repeat)

Rnd 1: Knit.
Rnd 2: *K4, p1, k3; repeat from * to end.
Rnd 3: *K3, p2, k3; repeat from * to end.
Rnd 4: *K2, p3, k3; repeat from * to end.
Rnd 5: *K1, p4, k3; repeat from * to end.
Rnd 6: *P5, k3; repeat from * to end.
Rnd 7: *P4, k4; repeat from * to end.
Rnd 8: *P3, k5; repeat from * to end.
Rnd 9: *P2, k6; repeat from * to end.
Rnd 10: *P1, k7; repeat from * to end.
Repeat Rnds 1-10 for Little Flames Top-Down in the Round.

Bottom-Up Flat and in the Round

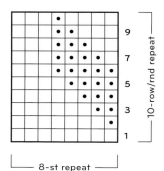

10-row/rnd repeat
8-st repeat

Top-Down Flat and in the Round

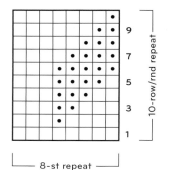

10-row/rnd repeat
8-st repeat

BASKET WEAVE

FLAT

(multiple of 8 sts + 5; 8-row repeat)

Row 1 (RS): Knit.
Row 2: K5, *p3, k5; repeat from * to end.
Row 3: *P5, k3; repeat from * to last 5 sts, p5.
Row 4: Repeat Row 2.
Row 5: Knit.
Row 6: K1, *p3, k5; repeat from * to last 4 sts, p3, k1.
Row 7: P1, *k3, p5; repeat from * to last 4 sts, k3, p1.
Row 8: Repeat Row 6.
Repeat Rows 1–8 for Basket Weave Flat.

IN THE ROUND

(multiple of 8 sts; 8-rnd repeat)

Rnd 1: Knit.
Rnds 2-4: *K3, p5; repeat from * to end.
Rnd 5: Knit.
Rnds 6-8: *P4, k3, p1; repeat from * to end.
Repeat Rnds 1–8 for Basket Weave in the Round.

Flat

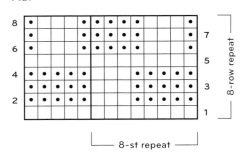

In the Round

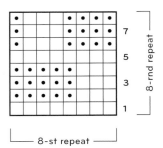

GIANT DIAMONDS

FLAT (REVERSIBLE)

(multiple of 15 sts; 14-row repeat)

Row 1 (RS): *P1, k13, p1; repeat from * to end.
Row 2: *K2, p11, k2; repeat from * to end.
Row 3: *P3, k9, p3; repeat from * to end.
Row 4: *K4, p7, k4; repeat from * to end.
Row 5: *P5, k5, p5; repeat from * to end.
Row 6: *P1, k5, p3, k5, p1; repeat from * to end.
Row 7: *K2, p5, k1, p5, k2; repeat from * to end.
Row 8: Repeat Row 3.
Row 9: Repeat Row 7.
Row 10: Repeat Row 6.
Row 11: Repeat Row 5.
Row 12: Repeat Row 4.
Row 13: Repeat Row 3.
Row 14: Repeat Row 2.
Repeat Rows 1–14 for Giant Diamonds Flat.

Flat and in the Round

[knitting chart: 15-st repeat wide, 14-row/rnd repeat; rows numbered 1, 3, 5, 7, 9, 11, 13]

15-st repeat

IN THE ROUND (REVERSIBLE)

(multiple of 15 sts; 14-rnd repeat)

Rnd 1: *P1, k13, p1; repeat from * to end.
Rnd 2: *P2, k11, p2; repeat from * to end.
Rnd 3: *P3, k9, p3; repeat from * to end.
Rnd 4: *P4, k7, p4; repeat from * to end.
Rnd 5: *P5, k5, p5; repeat from * to end.
Rnd 6: *K1, p5, k3, p5, k1; repeat from * to end.
Rnd 7: *K2, p5, k1, p5, k2; repeat from * to end.
Rnd 8: *K3, p9, k3; repeat from * to end.
Rnd 9: Repeat Row 7.
Rnd 10: Repeat Row 6.
Rnd 11: Repeat Row 5.
Rnd 12: Repeat Row 4.
Rnd 13: Repeat Row 3.
Rnd 14: Repeat Row 2.
Repeat Rnds 1–14 for Giant Diamonds in the Round.

POLKA DOTS

FLAT

(multiple of 10 sts; 24-row repeat)

Row 1 (RS): Knit.
Row 2: *P4, k2, p4; repeat from * to end.
Row 3: *K3, p4, k3; repeat from * to end.
Row 4: *P2, k6, p2; repeat from * to end.
Row 5: *K2, p6, k2; repeat from * to end.
Row 6: Repeat Row 4.
Row 7: Repeat Row 3.
Row 8: Repeat Row 2.
Row 9: Knit.
Row 10: Purl.
Row 11: Knit.
Row 12: Purl.
Row 13: Knit.
Row 14: *K1, p8, k1; repeat from * to end.
Row 15: Repeat Row 4.
Row 16: Repeat Row 3.
Row 17: *P3, k4, p3: repeat from * to end.
Row 18: Repeat Row 3.
Row 19: Repeat Row 4.
Row 20: Repeat Row 14.
Row 21: Knit.
Row 22: Purl.
Row 23: Knit.
Row 24: Purl.
Repeat Rows 1-24 for Polka Dots Flat.

IN THE ROUND

(multiple of 10 sts; 24-rnd repeat)

Rnd 1: Knit.
Rnd 2: *K4, p2, k4; repeat from * to end.
Rnd 3: *K3, p4, k3; repeat from * to end.
Rnds 4-6: *K2, p6, k2; repeat from * to end.
Rnd 7: Repeat Rnd 3.
Rnd 8: Repeat Rnd 2.
Rnds 9-13: Knit.
Rnd 14: *P1, k8, p1; repeat from * to end.
Rnd 15: *P2, k6, p2; repeat from * to end.
Rnds 16-18: *P3, k4, p3; repeat from * to end.
Rnd 19: *Repeat Rnd 15.
Rnd 20: *Repeat Rnd 14.
Rnds 21-24: Knit.
Repeat Rnds 1-24 for Polka Dots in the Round.

Flat and in the Round

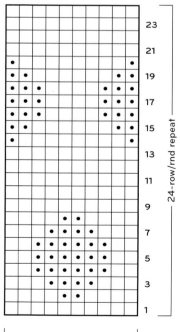

24-row/rnd repeat

10-st repeat

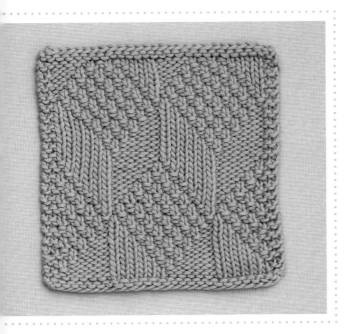

MOSS DIAMONDS AND LOZENGES

FLAT (REVERSIBLE)

(multiple of 12 sts; 44-row repeat)

Row 1 (RS): *K6, p6; repeat from * to end.
Row 2: Repeat Row 1.
Rows 3 and 4: *P1, k5, p5, k1; repeat from * to end.
Rows 5 and 6: *K1, p1, k4, p4, k1, p1; repeat from * to end.
Rows 7 and 8: *P1, k1, p1, k3, p3, k1, p1, k1; repeat from * to end.
Rows 9 and 10: *[K1, p1] twice, k2, p2, [k1, p1] twice; repeat from * to end.
Rows 11 and 12: *P1, k1; repeat from * to end.
Rows 13 and 14: *K1, p1; repeat from * to end.
Rows 15 and 16: *[P1, k1] twice, p2, k2, [p1, k1] twice; repeat from * to end.
Rows 17 and 18: *K1, p1, k1, p3, k3, p1, k1, p1; repeat from * to end.
Rows 19 and 20: *P1, k1, p4, k4, p1, k1; repeat from * to end.
Rows 21 and 22: *K1, p5, k5, p1; repeat from * to end.

Rows 23 and 24: *P6, k6; repeat from * to end.
Rows 25 and 26: *P5, k1, p1, k5; repeat from * to end.
Rows 27 and 28: *P4, [k1, p1] twice, k4; repeat from * to end.
Rows 29 and 30: *P3, [k1, p1] 3 times, k3; repeat from * to end.
Rows 31 and 32: *P2, [k1, p1] 4 times, k2; repeat from * to end.
Rows 33 and 34: *P1, k1; repeat from * to end.
Rows 35 and 36: *K1, p1; repeat from * to end.
Rows 37 and 38: *K2, [p1, k1] 4 times, p2; repeat from * to end.
Rows 39 and 40: *K3, [p1, k1] 3 times, p3; repeat from * to end.
Rows 41 and 42: *K4, [p1, k1] twice, p4; repeat from * to end.
Rows 43 and 44: *K5, p1, k1, p5; repeat from * to end.
Repeat Rows 1–44 for Moss Diamonds and Lozenges Flat.

Flat and in the Round

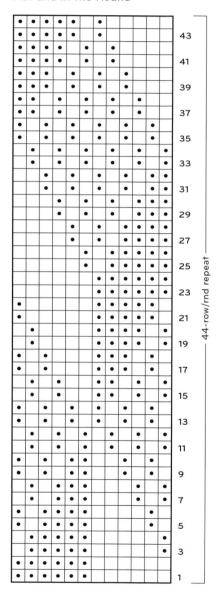

43
41
39
37
35
33
31
29
27
25
23
21
19
17
15
13
11
9
7
5
3
1

44-row/rnd repeat

12-st repeat

IN THE ROUND (REVERSIBLE)

(multiple of 12 sts; 44-rnd repeat)

Rnds 1 and 2: *K6, p6; repeat from * to end.

Rnds 3 and 4: *P1, k5, p5, k1; repeat from * to end.

Rnds 5 and 6: *K1, p1, k4, p4, k1, p1; repeat from * to end.

Rnds 7 and 8: *P1, k1, p1, k3, p3, k1, p1, k1; repeat from * to end.

Rnds 9 and 10: *[K1, p1] twice, k2, p2, [k1, p1] twice; repeat from * to end.

Rnds 11 and 12: *P1, k1; repeat from * to end.

Rnds 13 and 14: *K1, p1; repeat from * to end.

Rnds 15 and 16: *[P1, k1] twice, p2, k2, [p1, k1] twice; repeat from * to end.

Rnds 17 and 18: *K1, p1, k1, p3, k3, p1, k1, p1; repeat from * to end.

Rnds 19 and 20: *P1, k1, p4, k4, p1, k1; repeat from * to end.

Rnds 21 and 22: *K1, p5, k5, p1; repeat from * to end.

Rnds 23 and 24: *P6, k6; repeat from * to end.

Rnds 25 and 26: *P5, k1, p1, k5; repeat from * to end.

Rnds 27 and 28: *P4, [k1, p1] twice, k4; repeat from * to end.

Rnds 29 and 30: *P3, [k1, p1] 3 times, k3; repeat from * to end.

Rnds 31 and 32: *P2, [k1, p1] 4 times, k2; repeat from * to end.

Rnds 33 and 34: *P1, k1; repeat from * to end.

Rnds 35 and 36: *K1, p1; repeat from * to end.

Rnds 37 and 38: *K2, [p1, k1] 4 times, p2; repeat from * to end.

Rnds 39 and 40: *K3, [p1, k1] 3 times, p3; repeat from * to end.

Rnds 41 and 42: *K4, [p1, k1] twice, p4; repeat from * to end.

Rnds 43 and 44: *K5, p1, k1, p5; repeat from * to end.

Repeat Rnds 1–44 for Moss Diamonds and Lozenges in the Round.

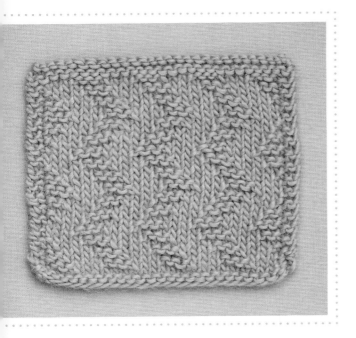

GARTER STITCH ZIGZAG

FLAT

(multiple of 6 sts; 12-row repeat)

Row 1 and all RS Rows (RS): Knit.
Row 2: *K3, p3; repeat from * to end.
Row 4: K2, *p3, k3; repeat from * to last 4 sts, p3, k1.
Row 6: K1, *p3, k3; repeat from * to last 5 sts, p3, k2.
Row 8: *P3, k3; repeat from * to end.
Row 10: Repeat Row 6.
Row 12: Repeat Row 4.
Repeat Rows 1–12 for Garter Stitch Zigzag Flat.

IN THE ROUND

(multiple of 6 sts; 12-rnd repeat)

Rnd 1 and all Odd-Numbered Rnds: Knit.
Rnd 2: *K3, p3; repeat from * to end.
Rnd 4: *P1, k3, p2; repeat from * to end.
Rnd 6: *P2, k3, p1; repeat from * to end.
Rnd 8: *P3, k3; repeat from * to end.
Rnd 10: Repeat Rnd 6.
Rnd 12: Repeat Rnd 4.
Repeat Rnds 1–12 for Garter Stitch Zigzag in the Round.

Flat and in the Round

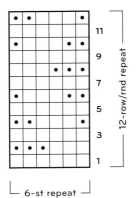

6-st repeat

12-row/rnd repeat

KNITS AND PURLS

SLANTED DIAMONDS

FLAT (REVERSIBLE)

(multiple of 10 sts; 6-row repeat)

Row 1 (RS): *K5, p5; repeat from * to end.
Row 2: K4, *p5, k5; repeat from * to last 6 sts, p5, k1.
Row 3: P2, *k5, p5; repeat from * to last 8 sts, k5, p3.
Row 4: K2, *p5, k5; repeat from * to last 8 sts, p5, k3.
Row 5: P4, *k5, p5; repeat from * to last 6 sts, k5, p1.
Row 6: *P5, k5; repeat from * to end.
Repeat Rows 1–6 for Slanted Diamonds Flat.

IN THE ROUND (REVERSIBLE)

(multiple of 10 sts; 6-rnd repeat)

Rnd 1: *K5, p5; repeat from * to end.
Rnd 2: *P1, k5, p4; repeat from * to end.
Rnd 3: *P2, k5, p3; repeat from * to end.
Rnd 4: *P3, k5, p2; repeat from * to end.
Rnd 5: *P4, k5, p1; repeat from * to end.
Rnd 6: *P5, k5; repeat from * to end.
Repeat Rnds 1–6 for Slanted Diamonds in the Round.

Flat and in the Round

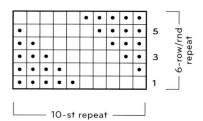

10-st repeat

INTERRUPTED COWL

Chunky and spunky, this cowl can be thrown on to add a bit of warmth and style. Use the pattern that follows as written, or substitute another in-the-round stitch pattern from this chapter to switch it up. "Fitted" cowls are usually a similar circumference as your head, about 22 inches (56 centimeters), but fiddle with the measurements if you want a more dramatic look.

STITCH PATTERN

Interrupted Garter Stitch in the Round
(multiple of 5 sts; 6-rnd repeat)

Rnds 1-4: Knit

Rnds 5 and 6: *K1, p4; repeat from * to end.

Repeat Rnds 1-6 for Interrupted Garter Stitch in the Round.

COWL

Cast on 95 sts. Join for working in the rnd, being careful not to twist sts; pm for beginning of rnd. Begin Interrupted Garter Stitch in the Rnd; work Rnds 5 and 6 once, then Rnds 1-6 seven times. BO all sts knitwise.

FINISHING

Block as desired.

SIZES

Average Adult

FINISHED MEASUREMENTS

Approximately 27 ¼" (69 cm) in circumference x 8 ¼" (21 cm) long

YARN USED

Blue Sky Alpacas Worsted Hand Dyes (50% royal alpaca / 50% merino; 100 yards / 100 grams): 2 hanks #2012 Cranberry

NEEDLES

One 24" (60 cm) long circular (circ) needle size US 9 (5.5 mm)

Change needle size if necessary to obtain correct gauge.

NOTIONS

Stitch marker

GAUGE

14 sts and 21 rows = 4" (10 cm) in Interrupted Garter Stitch in the Round

RIBS

Anyone who has knit a sweater or a cap knows the purpose of ribbing. Essentially, ribbing adds a stretchy border that makes a garment snug, or prevents curling edges. In this chapter, I have included the simple "one-by-one" and "two-by-two" ribbing patterns that we all know and love, but I have also included lots of novelty ribbings that vary in shape and appearance. Whenever you're using a new-to-you rib pattern, be sure to swatch first. Some have more elasticity than others and some aren't elastic at all, functioning more like pretty borders than snug edgings. When choosing a rib for a project, it's helpful to know exactly how much stretch you want and whether or not the ribbing is functional or for show. For instance, with gloves, ribbing around a wrist needs to be tight, but on the cuff of a belled sleeve, the ribbing can be loose and treated more like a finishing detail.

Many patterns will instantly tell you to go down a needle size when knitting ribs, but feel free to experiment with this. You might find that a loose and not-so-stretchy rib would look great as an allover pattern on a sweater. When choosing a rib, know that many of them look good on both sides and would work for scarves, blankets, and wraps. In fact, I think a non-elastic rib pattern, like Italian Chain Rib on page 54, would work up as a fantastic lap blanket in a fingering-weight yarn.

1×1 RIB

FLAT (REVERSIBLE)
(even number of sts; 1-row repeat)

All Rows: *K1, p1; repeat from * to end.

IN THE ROUND (REVERSIBLE)
(even number of sts; 1-rnd repeat)

All Rnds: *K1, p1; repeat from * to end.

2×2 RIB

FLAT (REVERSIBLE)
(multiple of 4 sts; 1-row repeat)

All Rows: *K2, p2; repeat from * to end.

IN THE ROUND (REVERSIBLE)
(multiple of 4 sts; 1-rnd repeat)

All Rnds: *K2, p2; repeat from * to end.

SEEDED RIB

FLAT (REVERSIBLE)

(multiple of 4 sts + 3; 2-row repeat)

Row 1 (RS): *K3, p1; repeat from * to last 3 sts, k3.
Row 2: K1, *p1, k3; repeat from * to last 2 sts, p1, k1.
Repeat Rows 1 and 2 for Seeded Rib Flat.

IN THE ROUND (REVERSIBLE)

(multiple of 4 sts; 2-rnd repeat)

Rnd 1: *K3, p1; repeat from * to end.
Rnd 2: *P1, k1, p2; repeat from * to end.
Repeat Rnds 1 and 2 for Seeded Rib in the Round.

TWIN RIB

FLAT (REVERSIBLE)

(multiple of 6 sts; 2-row repeat)

Row 1 (RS): *K3, p3; repeat from * to end.
Row 2: *K1, p1; repeat from * to end.
Repeat Rows 1 and 2 for Twin Rib Flat.

IN THE ROUND (REVERSIBLE)

(multiple of 6 sts; 2-rnd repeat)

Rnd 1: *K3, p3; repeat from * to end.
Rnd 2: *K1, p1; repeat from * to end.
Repeat Rnds 1 and 2 for Twin Rib in the Round.

DIAGONAL RIB

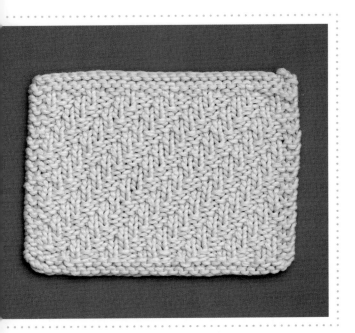

FLAT (REVERSIBLE)

(multiple of 4 sts; 8-row repeat)

Rows 1 (RS): *K2, p2; repeat from * to end.
Row 2: Repeat Row 1.
Row 3: K1, *p2, k2; repeat from * to last 3 sts, p2, k1.
Row 4: P1, *k2, p2; repeat from * to last 3 sts, k2, p1.
Rows 5 and 6: *P2, k2; repeat from * to end.
Row 7: Repeat Row 4.
Row 8: Repeat Row 3.
Repeat Rows 1-8 for Diagonal Rib Flat.

IN THE ROUND (REVERSIBLE)

(multiple of 4 sts; 8-rnd repeat)

Rnds 1 and 2: *K2, p2; repeat from * to end.
Rnds 3 and 4: *K1, p2, k1; repeat from * to end.
Rnds 5 and 6: *P2, k2; repeat from * to end.
Rnds 7 and 8: *P1, k2, p1; repeat from * to end.
Repeat Rnds 1-8 for Diagonal Rib in the Round.

Flat and in the Round

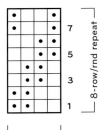

BABY CABLE RIB

FLAT

(multiple of 4 sts + 2; 4-row repeat)

Row 1 (RS): *P2, k2; repeat from * to last 2 sts, p2.
Row 2: K2, *p2, k2; repeat from * to end.
Row 3: *P2, RT; repeat from * to last 2 sts, p2.
Row 4: Repeat Row 2.
Repeat Rows 1–4 for Baby Cable Rib Flat.

IN THE ROUND

(multiple of 4 sts; 4-rnd repeat)

Rnds 1 and 2: *K2, p2; repeat from * to end.
Rnd 3: *RT, p2; repeat from * to end.
Rnd 4: Repeat Rnd 1.
Repeat Rnds 1–4 for Baby Cable Rib in the Round.

Flat

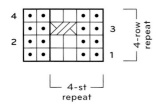

In the Round

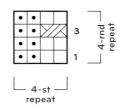

ITALIAN CHAIN RIB

FLAT

(multiple of 6 sts + 2; 4-row repeat)

Note: Pattern begins with a WS row.
Row 1 (WS): K2, *p4, k2; repeat from * to end.
Row 2: *P2, k2tog, [yo] twice, ssk; repeat from * to last 2 sts, p2.
Row 3: K2, *p1, [p1, p1-tbl] into double yo, p1, k2; repeat from * to end.
Row 4: *P2, yo, ssk, k2tog, yo; repeat from * to last 2 sts, p2.
Repeat Rows 1–4 for Italian Chain Rib Flat.

IN THE ROUND

(multiple of 6 sts; 4-rnd repeat)

Rnd 1: *P2, k4; repeat from * to end.
Rnd 2: *P2, k2tog, [yo] twice, ssk; repeat from * to end.
Rnd 3: *P2, *k1, [k1-tbl, k1] into double yo, k1; repeat from * to end.
Rnd 4: *P2, yo, ssk, k2tog, yo; repeat from * to end.
Repeat Rnds 1–4 for Italian Chain Rib in the Round.

Flat

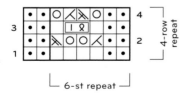

Note: Chart begins with a WS row.

In the Round

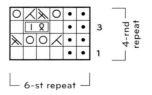

| I Ⴒ | On RS, [k1-tbl, k1] into double yo; on WS, [p1, p1-tbl] into double yo. |

CABLE AND EYELET RIB

FLAT

(multiple of 7 sts + 3; 6-row repeat)

Row 1 (RS): *P3, k4; repeat from * to last 3 sts, p3.
Row 2: K1, yo, k2tog, *p4, k1, yo, k2tog; repeat from * to end.
Row 3: *P3, C4B; repeat from * to last 3 sts, p3.
Row 4: Repeat Row 2.
Rows 5 and 6: Repeat Rows 1 and 2.
Repeat Rows 1–6 for Cable and Eyelet Rib Flat.

IN THE ROUND

(multiple of 7 sts; 6-rnd repeat)

Rnd 1: *P3, k4; repeat from * to end.
Rnd 2: *P2tog, yo, p1, k4; repeat from * to end.
Rnd 3: *P3, C4B; repeat from * to end.
Rnd 4: Repeat Rnd 2.
Rows 5 and 6: Repeat Rnds 1 and 2.
Repeat Rnds 1–6 for Cable and Eyelet Rib in the Round.

Flat

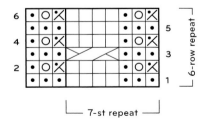

In the Round

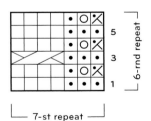

BRIOCHE RIB

FLAT (REVERSIBLE)

(even number of sts; 1-row repeat)

Set-Up Row: Knit.
Row 1: *K1, k1b; repeat from * to last 2 sts, k2.
Repeat Row 1 for Brioche Rib Flat.

IN THE ROUND (REVERSIBLE)

(even number of sts; 2-rnd repeat)

Set-Up Rnd: *K1, p1; repeat from * to end.
Rnd 1: *K1b, p1; repeat from * to end.
Rnd 2: *K1, p1b; repeat from * to end.
Repeat Rnds 1 and 2 for Brioche Rib in the Round.

SLIPPED RIB

FLAT

(even number of sts + 1; 2-row repeat)

Row 1 (RS): *K1, slip 1 purlwise wyif; repeat from * to last st, k1.
Row 2: Purl.
Repeat Rows 1 and 2 for Slipped Rib Flat.

IN THE ROUND

(even number of sts; 2-rnd repeat)

Rnd 1: *K1, slip 1 purlwise wyif; repeat from * to end.
Rnd 2: Knit.
Repeat Rnds 1 and 2 for Slipped Rib in the Round.

SPIRAL RIB

FLAT

(multiple of 9 sts + 3; 4-row repeat)

Row 1 (RS): *P3, [RC] 3 times; repeat from * to last 3 sts, p3.
Row 2: K3, *p6, k3; repeat from * to end.
Row 3: *P3, k1, [RC] twice, k1; repeat from * to last 3 sts, p3.
Row 4: Repeat Row 2.
Repeat Rows 1–4 for Spiral Rib Flat.

IN THE ROUND

(multiple of 9 sts; 4-rnd repeat)

Rnd 1: *P3, [RC] 3 times; repeat from * to end.
Rnd 2: *P3, k6; repeat from * to end.
Rnd 3: *P3, k1, [RC] twice, k1; repeat from * to end.
Rnd 4: Repeat Rnd 2.
Repeat Rnds 1–4 for Spiral Rib in the Round.

Flat

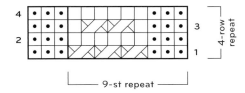

In the Round

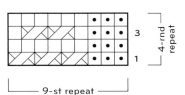

RICKRACK RIB

FLAT

(multiple of 3 sts + 1; 2-row repeat)

Row 1 (RS): *P1, LC; repeat from * to last st, p1.
Row 2: K1, *RC, k1; repeat from * to end.
Repeat Rows 1 and 2 for Rickrack Rib Flat.

IN THE ROUND

(multiple of 3 sts; 2-rnd repeat)

Rnd 1: *P1, LC; repeat from * to end.
Rnd 2: *P1, RC; repeat from * to end.
Repeat Rnds 1 and 2 for Rickrack Rib
in the Round.

Flat

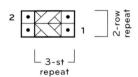

In the Round

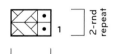

HERRINGBONE LACE RIB

FLAT

(multiple of 7 sts + 1; 2-row repeat)

Row 1 (RS): *K1, p1, k1, yo, p2tog, k1, p1; repeat from * to last st, k1.
Row 2: P1, *k2, yo, p2tog, k2, p1; repeat from * to end.
Repeat Rows 1 and 2 for Herringbone Lace Rib Flat.

Flat

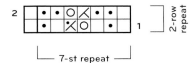

IN THE ROUND

(multiple of 7 sts; 2-rnd repeat)

Rnd 1: *K1, p1, k1, yo, p2tog, k1, p1; repeat from * to end.
Rnd 2: *K1, p2, k2tog, yo, p2; repeat from * to end.
Repeat Rnds 1 and 2 for Herringbone Lace Rib in the Round.

In the Round

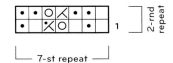

CROSS STITCH RIB

FLAT

(multiple of 4 sts + 2; 2-row repeat)

Row 1 (RS): *P2, RC; repeat from * to last 2 sts, p2.
Row 2: K2, *p2, k2; repeat from * to end.
Repeat Rows 1 and 2 for Cross Stitch Rib Flat.

IN THE ROUND

(multiple of 4 sts; 2-rnd repeat)

Rnd 1: *P2, RC; repeat from * to end.
Rnd 2: *P2, k2; repeat from * to end.
Repeat Rnds 1 and 2 for Cross Stitch Rib in the Round.

Flat

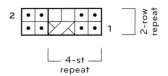

In the Round

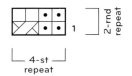

DOUBLE CROSS RIB

FLAT

(multiple of 5 sts + 2; 2-row repeat)

Row 1 (RS): *P2, RC, k1; repeat from * to last 2 sts, p2.
Row 2: K2, *RC, p1, k2; repeat from * to end.
Repeat Rows 1 and 2 for Double Cross Rib Flat.

Flat

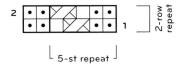

IN THE ROUND

(multiple of 5 sts; 2-rnd repeat)

Rnd 1: *P2, RC, k1; repeat from * to end.
Rnd 2: *P2, k1, RC; repeat from * to end.
Repeat Rnds 1 and 2 for Double Cross Rib in the Round.

In the Round

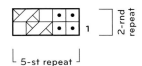

RIPPLE RIB STITCH

FLAT (REVERSIBLE)
(multiple of 4 sts; 16-row repeat)

Row 1 (RS): *P2, k2; repeat from * to end.
Row 2: Repeat Row 1.
Row 3: P1, *k2, p2; repeat from * last 3 sts, k2, p1.
Row 4: K1, *p2, k2; repeat from * last 3 sts, p2, k1.
Rows 5 and 6: *K2, p2; repeat from * to end.
Row 7: Repeat Row 4.
Row 8: Repeat Row 3.
Rows 9 and 10: Repeat Row 1.
Row 11: Repeat Row 4.
Row 12: Repeat Row 3.
Rows 13 and 14: Repeat Row 5.
Row 15: Repeat Row 3.
Row 16: Repeat Row 4.
Repeat Rows 1–16 for Ripple Rib Stitch Flat.

IN THE ROUND (REVERSIBLE)
(multiple of 4 sts; 16-rnd repeat)

Rnds 1 and 2: *P2, k2; repeat from * to end.
Rnds 3 and 4: *P1, k2, p1; repeat from * to end.
Rnds 5 and 6: *K2, p2; repeat from * to end.
Rnds 7 and 8: *K1, p2, k1; repeat from * to end.
Rnds 9 and 10: Repeat Rnd 1.
Rnds 11 and 12: Repeat Rnd 7.
Rnds 13 and 14: Repeat Rnd 5.
Rnds 15 and 16: Repeat Rnd 3.
Repeat Rnds 1–16 for Ripple Rib Stitch in the Round.

Flat and in the Round

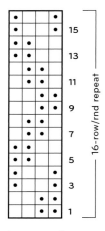

WAVING RIB

FLAT

(multiple of 6 sts + 2; 8-row repeat)

Row 1 (RS): *P2, k4; repeat from * to last 2 sts, p2.

Row 2: K2, *p4, k2; repeat from * to end.

Rows 3 and 4: Repeat Rows 1 and 2.

Row 5: K3, *p2, k4; repeat from * to last 5 sts, p2, k3.

Row 6: P3, *k2, p4; repeat from * to last 5 sts, k2, p3.

Rows 7 and 8: Repeat Rows 5 and 6.

Repeat Rows 1–8 for Waving Rib Flat.

IN THE ROUND

(multiple of 6 sts; 8-rnd repeat)

Rnds 1-4: *K4, p2; repeat from * to end.
Rnds 5-8: *K1, p2, k3; repeat from * to end.
Repeat Rnds 1–8 for Waving Rib in the Round.

Flat

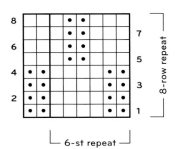

In the Round

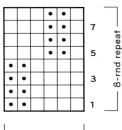

WAVING RIB WATCH CAP

Here's a simple cap made using the in-the-round Waving Rib stitch pattern from page 63. Notice how the wrong side of this stitch pattern looks when the brim is turned up? This is a perfect example of why swatching is so great: Had I not swatched this stitch pattern first, I wouldn't have discovered that the wrong side of Waving Rib is so attractive and I might not have known I could use it for this flip-up cap design.

STITCH PATTERN

Waving Rib in the Round
(see page 63 for chart)
(multiple of 6 sts; 8-rnd repeat)

Rnds 1-4: *K4, p2; repeat from * to end.

Rnds 5-8: *K1, p2, k3; repeat from * to end.

Repeat Rnds 1–8 for Waving Rib in the Round.

CAP

Using circular needle, CO 96 (102) sts. Join for working in the rnd, being careful not to twist sts; pm for beginning of round. Begin Waving Rib in the Round; work Rnds 1–8 six (7) times, then Rnd 1 once.

Shape Crown

Note: Change to dpns when necessary for number of sts on needle.

Decrease Rnd 1: *K2, k2tog, p2; repeat from * to end—80 (85) sts remain. Work even for 1 rnd.

Decrease Rnd 2: *K3, p2tog; repeat from * to end—64 (68) sts remain. Work even for 1 rnd.

Decrease Rnd 3: *K2tog, k1, p1; repeat from * to end—48 (51) sts remain. Work even for 1 rnd.

Decrease Rnd 4: *K2tog, p1; repeat from * to end—32 (34) sts remain. Work even for 1 rnd.

Decrease Rnd 5: *K2tog; repeat from * to end—16 (17) sts remain. Work even for 1 rnd.

Decrease Rnd 6: K0 (1), *k2tog; repeat from * to end—8 (9) remain. Work even for 1 rnd.

Cut yarn, leaving an 8" (20.5 cm) tail. Thread tail through remaining sts, pull tight, and fasten off.

FINISHING

Block as desired.

SIZES

Youth/Adult Small (Adult Average)

19 ¼ (20 ½)" [49 (52) cm] circumference

Note: To adjust size up or down, add or subtract in multiples of 6 sts.

YARN

Blue Sky Alpacas Suri Merino (60% baby suri alpaca / 40% merino wool; 164 yards / 100 grams): 1 hank #416 Meadow

NEEDLES

One 16" (40 cm) long circular (circ) needle size US 5 (3.75) mm

One set of five double-pointed needles (dpn) size US 5 (3.75 mm)

Change needles size if necessary to obtain correct gauge.

NOTIONS

Stitch marker

GAUGE

20 sts and 26 rnds = 4" (10 cm) in Waving Rib in the Round

TEXTURED,
SLIPPED,
AND FANCY

In this chapter, you'll find some unusual stitch patterns, many of them featuring slipped or twisted stitches and exquisitely textured surfaces. When working slipped stitches, especially in the round, pay close attention to where your yarn should be held—in either the front or back of your work—while slipping. And, unless otherwise noted, slip all stitches as if to purl. In some cases, like Linen Stitch on page 82, the stitch pattern can be easily memorized, but in others, like Overlapping Leaves on page 83, you'll want to keep careful track of rows or rounds until you get the rhythm down. Also note that when working slipped stitch patterns, you may move quickly, but the fabric you're producing will be denser than, say, a lace or eyelet stitch pattern, so patience is key.

    The stitch patterns in this chapter are versatile, and in almost all cases, they have a definite right and wrong side. These patterns work great for caps, mittens, allover patterning on a sweater, cowls, and socks—pretty much any garment that has an inside and an outside.

TRINITY STITCH

FLAT

(multiple of 4 sts + 2; 4-row repeat)

Row 1 (RS): Purl.
Row 2: K1, *[k1, p1, k1] into next st, p3tog; repeat from * to last st, k1.
Row 3: Purl.
Row 4: K1, *p3tog, [k1, p1, k1] into next st; repeat from * to last st, k1.
Repeat Rows 1–4 for Trinity Stitch Flat.

IN THE ROUND

(multiple of 4 sts; 4-rnd repeat)

Rnd 1: Purl.
Rnd 2: *[P1, k1, p1] into next st, k3tog; repeat from * to end.
Rnd 3: Purl.
Rnd 4: *K3tog, [p1, k1, p1] into next st; repeat from * to end.
Repeat Rnds 1–4 for Trinity Stitch in the Round.

GRANITE STITCH

FLAT

(even number of sts; 4-row repeat)

Note: St count is halved on Row 2; original st count is restored on Row 3.
Row 1 (RS): Knit.
Row 2: *K2tog; repeat from * to end.
Row 3: *[K1, p1] into next st; repeat from * to end.
Row 4: Purl.
Repeat Rows 1–4 for Granite Stitch Flat.

IN THE ROUND

(even number of sts; 4-rnd repeat)

Note: St count is halved on Rnd 2; original st count is restored on Rnd 3.
Rnd 1: Knit.
Rnd 2: *P2tog; repeat from * to end.
Rnd 3: *[K1, p1] into next st; repeat from * to end.
Rnd 4: Knit.
Repeat Rnds 1–4 for Granite Stitch in the Round.

TEXTURED, SLIPPED, AND FANCY

PEBBLE STITCH

FLAT

(even number of sts; 4-row repeat)

Note: Do not count sts after Row 3; original st count is restored on Row 4.

Row 1 (RS): Knit.
Row 2: Purl.
Row 3: K1, *k2tog; repeat from * to last st, k1.
Row 4: K1, *k1 in horizontal bar before next st, k1; repeat from * to last st, k1.
Repeat Rows 1–4 for Pebble Stitch Flat.

IN THE ROUND

(even number of sts; 4-rnd repeat)

Note: St count is halved on Rnd 3; original st count is restored on Rnd 4.

Rnds 1 and 2: Knit.
Rnd 3: *K2tog; repeat from * to end.
Rnd 4: *P1 in horizontal bar before next st, p1; repeat from * to end.
Repeat Rnds 1–4 for Pebble Stitch in the Round.

RUCHING STITCH

FLAT

(any number of sts; 14-row repeat)

Note: Pattern begins with a WS row. St count doubles on Row 8; original st count is restored on Row 14.

Row 1 and all WS Rows (WS): Purl.
Rows 2, 4, and 6: Knit.
Row 8: *K1-f/b; repeat from * to end.
Rows 10 and 12: Knit.
Row 14: *K2tog; repeat from * to end.
Repeat Rows 1–14 for Ruching Stitch Flat.

IN THE ROUND

(any number of sts; 14-rnd repeat)

Note: St count doubles on Rnd 8; original st count is restored on Rnd 14.

Rnds 1–7: Knit.
Rnd 8: *K1-f/b; repeat from * to end.
Rnds 9–13: Knit.
Rnd 14: *K2tog; repeat from * to end.
Repeat Rnds 1–14 for Ruching Stitch in the Round.

TEXTURED, SLIPPED, AND FANCY

TWISTED BASKET WEAVE

FLAT

(multiple of 8 sts + 5; 8-row repeat)

Row 1 (RS): *P5, T3R; repeat from * to last 5 sts, p5.
Row 2: K5, *p3, k5; repeat from * to end.
Rows 3 and 4: Repeat Rows 1 and 2.
Row 5: P1, *T3R, p5; repeat from * to last 4 sts, T3R, p1.
Row 6: K1, *p3, k5; repeat from * to last 4 sts, p3, k1.
Rows 7 and 8: Repeat Rows 5 and 6.
Repeat Rows 1–8 for Twisted Basket Weave Flat.

IN THE ROUND

(multiple of 8 sts; 8-rnd repeat)

Note: If working top-down, twists will flow downwards and to the left.
Rnd 1 (RS): *P5, T3R; repeat from * to end.
Rnd 2: *P5, k3; repeat from * to end.
Rnds 3 and 4: Repeat Rnds 1 and 2.
Rnd 5: *P1, T3R, p4; repeat from * to end.
Rnd 6: *P1, k3, p4; repeat from * to end.
Rnds 7 and 8: Repeat Rnds 5 and 6.
Repeat Rnds 1–8 for Twisted Basket Weave in the Round.

Flat

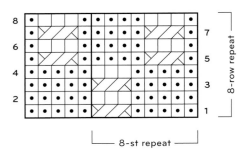

8-row repeat

8-st repeat

In the Round

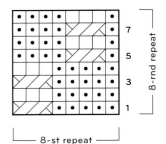

8-rnd repeat

8-st repeat

Knit into the third stitch on the left-hand needle, then the second, then the first, slip all 3 stitches from left-hand needle together.

WOVEN LADDERS

FLAT

(multiple of 8 sts + 1; 8-row repeat)

Row 1 (RS): *K5, slip 3 wyif; repeat from * to last st, k1.
Row 2: P1, *slip 3 wyib, p5; repeat from * to end.
Row 3: Repeat Row 1.
Row 4: Purl.
Row 5: K1, *slip 3 wyif, k5; repeat from * to end.
Row 6: *P5, slip 3 wyif; repeat from * to last st, p1.
Row 7: Repeat Row 5.
Row 8: Purl.
Repeat Rows 1–8 for Woven Ladders Flat.

IN THE ROUND

(multiple of 8 sts; 8-rnd repeat)

Rnds 1-3: *Slip 3 wyif, k5; repeat from * to end.
Rnd 4: Knit.
Rnds 5-7: *K4, slip 3 wyif, k1; repeat from * to end.
Rnd 8: Knit.
Repeat Rnds 1–8 for Woven Ladders in the Round.

Flat

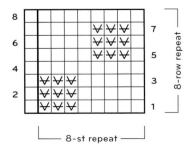

In the Round

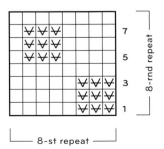

SMOCKING

FLAT

(multiple of 8 sts + 2; 8-row repeat)

Note: Pattern begins with a WS row.
Work Smocking: Insert right-hand needle from front to back between sixth and seventh sts on left-hand needle and draw up a loop, place loop on left-hand needle, k2tog (loop together with next st on left-hand needle), k1, p2, k2.
Row 1 (WS): K2, *p2, k2; repeat from * to end.
Row 2: *P2, k2; repeat from * to last 2 sts, p2.
Row 3: Repeat Row 1.
Row 4: *P2, work smocking; repeat from * to last 2 sts, p2.
Rows 5 and 6: Repeat Rows 1 and 2.
Row 7: Repeat Row 1.
Row 8: P2, k2, *p2, work smocking; repeat from * to last 6 sts, p2, k2, p2.
Repeat Rows 1–8 for Smocking Flat.

IN THE ROUND

(multiple of 8 sts; 2-rnd repeat)

Work Smocking: Insert right-hand needle from front to back between sixth and seventh sts on left-hand needle and draw up a loop, place loop on left-hand needle, k2tog (loop together with next st on left-hand needle), k1, p2, k2.
Rnds 1-3: *P2, k2; repeat from * to end.
Rnd 4: *P2, work smocking; repeat from * to end.
Rnds 5 and 6: Repeat Rnd 1.
Rnd 7: *P2, k2; repeat from * to last 2 sts; last 2 sts will be worked at beginning of Rnd 8.
Rnd 8: *Work smocking, slipping beginning-of-rnd marker as you come to it on first repeat only, p2; repeat from * to last 2 sts, k2.
Repeat Rnds 1–8 for Smocking in the Round.

Flat

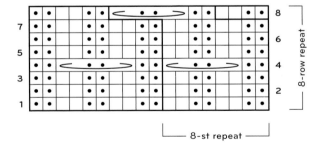

Note: Chart begins with a WS row.

In the Round

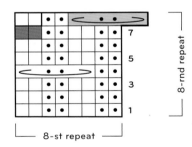

 On final repeat of Rnd 7 only, end repeat 2 sts before beginning-of-rnd marker.

Work smocking: Insert right-hand needle from front to back between sixth and seventh sts on left-hand needle and draw up a loop, place loop on left-hand needle, k2tog (loop together with next st on left-hand needle), k1, p2, k2.

On first repeat of Rnd 8, work smocking on last 2 sts of Rnd 7 and first 4 sts of Rnd 8.
Note: Leave beginning-of-rnd marker in place.

PLEATS

FLAT

(multiple of 8 sts + 6; 16-row repeat)

Set-Up Rows 1-9: Work 9 rows in St st, beginning with a knit row.

Row 1 (WS): P5, *[with right-hand needle, pick up purl bump of st 7 rows below next st on left-hand needle and place on left-hand needle, making sure st is not twisted, p2tog (picked-up purl bump together with next st on left-hand needle)] 4 times, p4; repeat from * to last st, p1.

Rows 2-8: Work in St st, beginning with a knit row.

Row 9: P1, [pick up purl bump and p2tog as before] 4 times, *p4, [pick up purl bump and p2tog as before] 4 times; repeat from * to last st, p1.

Rows 10-16: Work in St st, beginning with a knit row.

Repeat Rows 1–16 for Pleats Flat.

IN THE ROUND

(multiple of 8 sts; 16-rnd repeat)

Set-Up Rnds 1-9: Knit.

Rnd 1: *K4, [with right-hand needle, and picking up from WS, pick up purl bump of st 7 rows below next st on left-hand needle and place on left-hand needle, making sure st is not twisted, k2tog (picked-up purl bump together with next st on left-hand needle)] 4 times; repeat from * to end.

Rnds 2-8: Knit.

Rnd 9: *[Pick up purl bump and k2tog as before] 4 times, k4; repeat from * to end.

Rnds 10-16: Knit.

Repeat Rnds 1–16 for Pleats in the Round.

ROSETTE STITCH

FLAT

(even number of sts; 4-row repeat)

Work Rosette: P2tog, but do not drop sts from left-hand needle, k2tog same 2 sts, slip both sts from left-hand needle together.
Rows 1 (RS): Knit.
Row 2: *Work Rosette; repeat from * to end.
Row 3: Knit.
Row 4: P1; *work Rosette; repeat from * to last st, p1.
Repeat Rows 1–4 for Rosette Stitch Flat.

IN THE ROUND

(even number of sts; 4-rnd repeat)

Work Rosette: P2tog, but do not drop sts from left-hand needle, k2tog same 2 sts, slip both sts from left-hand needle together.
Note: Pattern results in a spiral and beginning-of-rnd marker moves forward one st every other rnd.
Rnd 1: Knit.
Rnd 2: *Work Rosette; repeat from * to end.
Rnd 3: Knit.
Rnd 4: Slip 1, *work Rosette; repeat from * to last st, work Rosette (working on last st of rnd and first st of next rnd; reposition beginning-of-rnd marker to after Rosette).
Repeat Rnds 1–4 for Rosette Stitch in the Round.

FLAT

(multiple of 10 sts; 24-row repeat)

Row 1 (RS): *LI, k3, ssk, k5; repeat from * to end.

Row 2 and all WS Rows: Purl.

Row 3: K1, *LI, k3, ssk, k5; repeat from * to last 9 sts, LI, k3, ssk, k4.

Row 5: K2, *LI, k3, ssk, k5; repeat from * to last 8 sts, LI, k3, ssk, k3.

Row 7: K3, *LI, k3, ssk, k5; repeat from * to last 7 sts, LI, k3, ssk, k2.

Row 9: K4, *LI, k3, ssk, k5; repeat from * to last 6 sts, LI, k3, ssk, k1.

Row 11: *K5, LI, k3, ssk; repeat from * to end.

Row 13: *K5, k2tog, k3, RLI; repeat from * to end.

Row 15: K4, *k2tog, k3, RLI, k5; repeat from * to last 6 sts, k2tog, k3, RLI, k1.

Row 17: K3, *k2tog, k3, RLI, k5; repeat from * to last 7 sts, k2tog, k3, RLI, k2.

Row 19: K2, *k2tog, k3, RLI, k5; repeat from * to last 8 sts, k2tog, k3, RLI, k3.

Row 21: K1, *k2tog, k3, RLI, k5; repeat from * to last 9 sts, k2tog, k3, RLI, k4.

Row 23: *K2tog, k3, RLI, k5; repeat from * to end.

Rnd 24: Purl.

Repeat Rows 1–24 for Zigzag Ribbon Stitch Flat.

Flat and in the Round

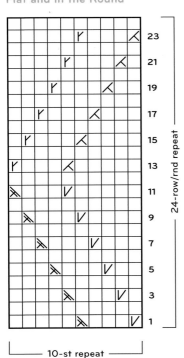

10-st repeat

24-row/rnd repeat

23 21 19 17 15 13 11 9 7 5 3 1

IN THE ROUND

(multiple of 10 sts; 24-rnd repeat)

Rnd 1: *LI, k3, ssk, k5; repeat from * to end.
Rnd 2 and all Even-Numbered Rnds: Knit.
Rnd 3: *K1, LI, k3, ssk, k4; repeat from * to end.
Rnd 5: *K2, LI, k3, ssk, k3; repeat from * to end.
Rnd 7: *K3, LI, k3, ssk, k2; repeat from * to end.
Rnd 9: *K4, LI, k3, ssk, k1; repeat from * to end.
Rnd 11: *K5, LI, k3, ssk; repeat from * to end.
Rnd 13: *K5, k2tog, k3, RLI; repeat from * to end.
Rnd 15: *K4, k2tog, k3, RLI, k1; repeat from * to end.
Rnd 17: *K3, k2tog, k3, RLI, k2; repeat from * to end.
Rnd 19: *K2, k2tog, k3, RLI, k3; repeat from * to end.
Rnd 21: *K1, k2tog, k3, RLI, k4; repeat from * to end.
Rnd 23: *K2tog, k3, RLI, k5; repeat from * to end.
Rnd 24: Knit.
Repeat Rnds 1–24 for Zigzag Ribbon Stitch in the Round.

TEXTURED, SLIPPED, AND FANCY

WOVEN TRANSVERSE HERRINGBONE

FLAT

(multiple of 4 sts + 2; 24-row repeat)

Row 1 (RS): *K2, slip 2 wyif; repeat from * to last 2 sts, k2.

Row 2: P1, *slip 2 wyib, p2; repeat from * to last st, slip 1 wyib.

Row 3: *Slip 2 wyif, k2; repeat from * to last 2 sts, slip 2 wyif.

Row 4: Slip 1 wyib, *p2, slip 2 wyib; repeat from * to last st, p1.

Rows 5-12: Repeat Rows 1–4.

Row 13: Repeat Row 3.

Row 14: Repeat Row 2.

Row 15: Repeat Row 1.

Row 16: Repeat Row 4.

Rows 17-24: Repeat Rows 13–16.

Repeat Rows 1–24 for Woven Transverse Herringbone Flat.

IN THE ROUND

(multiple of 4 sts; 24-rnd repeat)

Rnd 1: *K2, slip 2 wyif; repeat from * to end.

Rnd 2: Slip 1 wyif, *k2, slip 2 wyif; repeat from * to last 3 sts, k2, slip 1 wyif.

Rnd 3: *Slip 2 wyif, k2; repeat from * to end.

Rnd 4: K1, *slip 2 wyif, k2; repeat from * to last 3 sts, slip 2 wyif, k1.

Rnds 5-12: Repeat Rnds 1–4.

Rnd 13: Repeat Rnd 3.

Rnd 14: Repeat Rnd 2.

Rnd 15: Repeat Rnd 1.

Rnd 16: Repeat Rnd 4.

Rnds 17-24: Repeat Rnds 13–16.

Repeat Rnds 1–24 for Woven Transverse Herringbone in the Round.

Flat

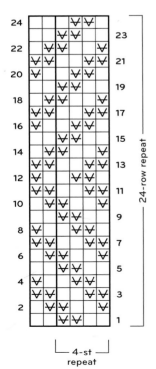

4-st repeat

In the Round

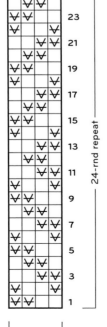

4-st repeat

HERRINGBONE

FLAT

(multiple of 7 sts + 1; 4-row repeat)

Row 1 (RS): *K2tog, k2, RLI, k3; repeat from * to last st, k1.
Row 2: Purl.
Row 3: K1, *k2, RLI, k3, k2tog; repeat from * to end.
Row 4: Purl.
Repeat Rows 1–4 for Herringbone Flat.

IN THE ROUND

(multiple of 7 sts; 4-rnd repeat)

Rnd 1: *K2tog, k2, RLI, k3; repeat from * to end.
Rnd 2: Knit.
Rnd 3: K1, *k2, RLI, k3, k2tog; repeat from * to last 6 sts, k2, RLI, k3, k2tog (last st of rnd together with first st of next rnd). Reposition beginning-of-rnd marker to before k2tog.
Rnd 4: Knit.
Repeat Rnds 1–4 for Herringbone in the Round.

Flat

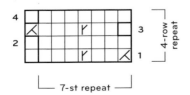

In the Round

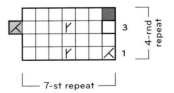

On final repeat of Rnd 3 only, work k2tog on last st of Rnd 3 and first st of Rnd 4; reposition beginning-of-rnd marker to before k2tog.

First st of Rnd 4 has been worked together with last st of Rnd 3; omit this st at beginning of Rnd 4 only; work as knit st on remaining repeats.

SPINE STITCH

FLAT

(multiple of 4 sts; 2-row repeat)

Row 1 (RS): *LC, RC; repeat from * to end.
Row 2: Purl.
Repeat Rows 1 and 2 for Spine Stitch Flat.

Flat and in the Round

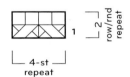

4-st repeat

IN THE ROUND

(multiple of 4 sts; 2-rnd repeat)

Rnd 1: *LC, RC; repeat from * to end.
Rnd 2: Knit.
Repeat Rnds 1 and 2 for Spine Stitch in the Round.

TEXTURED, SLIPPED, AND FANCY

LINEN STITCH

FLAT

(odd number of sts; 2-row repeat)

Row 1 (RS): *K1, slip 1 wyif; repeat from * to last st, k1.
Row 2: P2, *slip 1 wyib, p1; repeat from * to last st, p1.
Repeat Rows 1 and 2 for Linen Stitch Flat.

IN THE ROUND

(odd number of sts; 2-rnd repeat)

Rnd 1: *K1, slip 1 wyif; repeat from * to last st, k1.
Rnd 2: Slip 1 wyif, *k1, slip 1 wyif; repeat from * to end.
Repeat Rnds 1 and 2 for Linen Stitch in the Round.

BAMBOO STITCH

FLAT

(even number of sts; 2-row repeat)

Row 1 (RS): K1, *yo, k2, pass yo over k2; repeat from * to last st, k1.
Row 2: Purl.
Repeat Rows 1 and 2 for Bamboo Stitch Flat.

IN THE ROUND

(even number of sts; 2-rnd repeat)

Rnd 1: *Yo, k2, pass yo over k2; repeat from * to end.
Rnd 2: Knit.
Repeat Rnds 1 and 2 for Bamboo Stitch in the Round.

TEXTURED, SLIPPED, AND FANCY

82

OVERLAPPING LEAVES

OVERLAPPING LEAVES

BOTTOM-UP FLAT

(multiple of 24 sts + 1; 12-row repeat)

Row 1 (RS): *K1, M1-l, skp, k4, k2tog, k3, M1-l, k1, M1-l, k3, skp, k4, k2tog, M1-l; repeat from * to last st, k1.

Row 2 and all WS Rows: Purl.

Row 3: *K1, M1-l, k1, skp, k2, k2tog, k4, M1-l, k1, M1-l, k4, skp, k2, k2tog, k1, M1-l; repeat from * to last st, k1.

Row 5: *K1, M1-l, k2, skp, k2tog, k5, M1-l, k1, M1-l, k5, skp, k2tog, k2, M1-l; repeat from * to last st, k1.

Row 7: *K1, M1-l, k3, skp, k4, k2tog, M1-l, k1, M1-l, skp, k4, k2tog, k3, M1-l; repeat from * to last st, k1.

Row 9: *K1, M1-l, k4, skp, k2, k2tog, [k1, M1-l] twice, k1, skp, k2, k2tog, k4, M1-l; repeat from * to last st, k1.

Row 11: *K1, M1-l, k5, skp, k2tog, k2, M1-l, k1, M1-l, k2, skp, k2tog, k5, M1-l; repeat from * to last st, k1.

Row 12: Purl.

Repeat Rows 1–12 for Overlapping Leaves Bottom-Up Flat.

BOTTOM-UP IN THE ROUND

(multiple of 24 sts; 12-rnd repeat)

Rnd 1: *K1, M1-l, skp, k4, k2tog, k3, M1-l, k1, M1-l, k3, skp, k4, k2tog, M1-l; repeat from * to end.

Rnd 2 and all Even-Numbered Rnds: Knit.

Rnd 3: *K1, M1-l, k1, skp, k2, k2tog, k4, M1-l, k1, M1-l, k4, skp, k2, k2tog, k1, M1-l; repeat from * to end.

Rnd 5: *K1, M1-l, k2, skp, k2tog, k5, M1-l, k1, M1-l, k5, skp, k2tog, k2, M1-l; repeat from * to end.

Rnd 7: *K1, M1-l, k3, skp, k4, k2tog, M1-l, k1, M1-l, skp, k4, k2tog, k3, M1-l; repeat from * to end.

Rnd 9: *K1, M1-l, k4, skp, k2, k2tog, [k1, M1-l] twice, k1, skp, k2, k2tog, k4, M1-l; repeat from * to end.

Rnd 11: *K1, M1-l, k5, skp, k2tog, k2, M1-l, k1, M1-l, k2, skp, k2tog, k5, M1-l; repeat from * to end.

Rnd 12: Knit.

Repeat Rnds 1–12 for Overlapping Leaves Bottom-Up in the Round.

Bottom-Up Flat

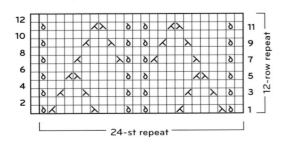

24-st repeat · 12-row repeat

Bottom-Up in the Round

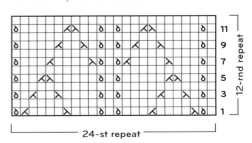

24-st repeat · 12-rnd repeat

TOP-DOWN FLAT

(multiple of 24 sts + 1; 12-row repeat)

Note: Leaves flow in opposite direction than for Overlapping Leaves Bottom-Up Flat.

Row 1 (RS): *K1, M1-l, k5, k2tog, skp, k2, M1-l, k1, M1-l, k2, k2tog, skp, k5, M1-l; repeat from * to last st, k1.

Row 2 and all WS Rows: Purl.

Row 3: *K1, M1-l, k4, k2tog, k2, skp, [k1, M1-l] twice, k1, k2tog, k2, skp, k4, M1-l; repeat from * to last st, k1.

Row 5: *K1, M1-l, k3, k2tog, k4, skp, M1-l, k1, M1-l, k2tog, k4, skp, k3, M1-l; repeat from * to last st, k1.

Row 7: *K1, M1-l, k2, k2tog, skp, k5, M1-l, k1, M1-l, k5, k2tog, skp, k2, M1-l; repeat from * to last st, k1.

Row 9: *K1, M1-l, k1, k2tog, k2, skp, k4, M1-l, k1, M1-l, k4, k2tog, k2, skp, k1, M1-l; repeat from * to last st, k1.

Row 11: *K1, M1-l, k2tog, k4, skp, k3, M1-l, k1, M1-l, k3, k2tog, k4, skp, M1-l; repeat from * to last st, k1.

Row 12: Purl.

Repeat Rows 1–12 for Overlapping Leaves Top-Down Flat.

TOP-DOWN IN THE ROUND

(multiple of 24 sts; 12-rnd repeat)

Note: Leaves flow in opposite direction than for Overlapping Leaves Bottom-Up in the Round.

Rnd 1: *K1, M1-l, k5, k2tog, skp, k2, M1-l, k1, M1-l, k2, k2tog, skp, k5, M1-l; repeat from * to end.

Rnd 2 and all Even-Numbered Rnds: Knit.

Rnd 3: *K1, M1-l, k4, k2tog, k2, skp, [k1, M1-l] twice, k1, k2tog, k2, skp, k4, M1-l; repeat from * to end.

Rnd 5: *K1, M1-l, k3, k2tog, k4, skp, M1-l, k1, M1-l, k2tog, k4, skp, k3, M1-l; repeat from * to end.

Rnd 7: *K1, M1-l, k2, k2tog, skp, k5, M1-l, k1, M1-l, k5, k2tog, skp, k2, M1-l; repeat from * to end.

Rnd 9: *K1, M1-l, k1, k2tog, k2, skp, k4, M1-l, k1, M1-l, k4, k2tog, k2, skp, k1, M1-l; repeat from * to end.

Rnd 11: *K1, M1-l, k2tog, k4, skp, k3, M1-l, k1, M1-l, k3, k2tog, k4, skp, M1-l; repeat from * to end.

Rnd 12: Knit.

Repeat Rnds 1–12 for Overlapping Leaves Top-Down in the Round.

Top-Down Flat

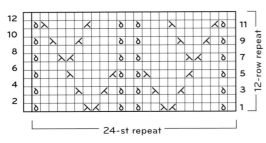

Top-Down in the Round

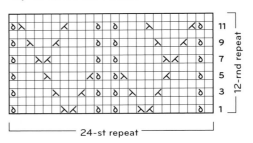

GERMAN HERRINGBONE

BOTTOM-UP FLAT

(multiple of 15 sts + 2; 6-row repeat)

Row 1 (RS): *P2, M1-l, k3, p2, p3tog, p2, k3, M1-l; repeat from * to last 2 sts, p2.
Row 2: K2, *p4, k5, p4, k2; repeat from * to end.
Row 3: *P2, M1-l, k4, p1, p3tog, p1, k4, M1-l; repeat from * to last 2 sts, p2.
Row 4: K2, *p5, k3, p5, k2; repeat from * to end.
Row 5: *P2, M1-l, k5, p3tog, k5, M1-l; repeat from * to last 2 sts, p2.
Row 6: K2, *p6, k1, p6, k2; repeat from * to end.
Repeat Rows 1–6 for German Herringbone Bottom-Up Flat.

BOTTOM-UP IN THE ROUND

(multiple of 15 sts; 6-rnd repeat)

Rnd 1: *P2, M1-l, k3, p2, p3tog, p2, k3, M1-l; repeat from * to end.
Rnd 2: *P2, k4, p5, k4; repeat from * to end.
Rnd 3: *P2, M1-l, k4, p1, p3tog, p1, k4, M1-l; repeat from * to end.
Rnd 4: *P2, k5, p3, k5; repeat from * to end.
Rnd 5: *P2, M1-l, k5, p3tog, k5, M1-l; repeat from * to end.
Rnd 6: *P2, k6, p1, k6; repeat from * to end.
Repeat Rnds 1–6 for German Herringbone Bottom-Up in the Round.

Bottom-Up Flat

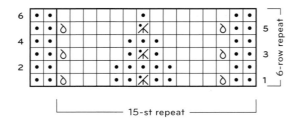

15-st repeat

6-row repeat

Bottom-Up in the Round

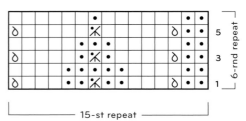

15-st repeat

6-rnd repeat

TOP-DOWN FLAT

(multiple of 15 sts + 2; 6-row repeat)

Note: Pattern begins with a WS row.
Row 1 (WS): K2, *p6, k1, p6, k2; repeat from * to end.
Row 2: *P2, ssk, k4, p1-f/b/f, k4, k2tog; repeat from * to last 2 sts, p2.
Row 3: K2, *p5, k3, p5, k2; repeat from * to end.
Row 4: *P2, ssk, k3, p1, p1-f/b/f, p1, k3, k2tog; repeat from * to last 2 sts, p2.
Row 5: K2, *p4, k5, p4, k2; repeat from * to end.
Row 6: *P2, ssk, k2, p2, p1-f/b/f, p2, k2, k2tog; repeat from * to last 2 sts, p2.
Repeat Rows 1–6 for German Herringbone Top-Down Flat.

TOP-DOWN IN THE ROUND

(multiple of 15 sts; 6-rnd repeat)

Rnd 1: *P2, k6, p1, k6; repeat from * to end.
Rnd 2: *P2, ssk, k4, p1-f/b/f, k4, k2tog; repeat from * to end.
Rnd 3: *P2, k5, p3, k5; repeat from * to end.
Rnd 4: *P2, ssk, k3, p1, p1-f/b/f, p1, k3, k2tog; repeat from * to end.
Rnd 5: *P2, k4, p5, k4; repeat from * to end.
Rnd 6: *P2, ssk, k2, p2, p1-f/b/f, p2, k2, k2tog; repeat from * to end.
Repeat Rnds 1–6 for German Herringbone Top-Down in the Round.

Top-Down Flat

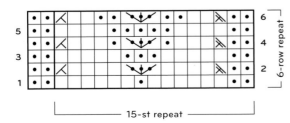

6-row repeat

15-st repeat

Note: Chart begins with a WS row.

Top-Down in the Round

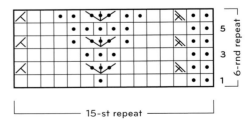

6-rnd repeat

15-st repeat

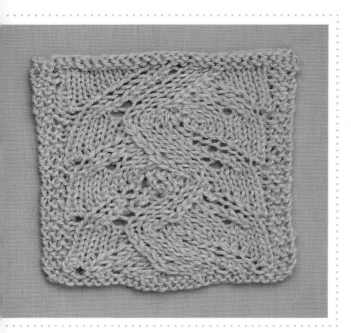

LOTUS
LEAVES

BOTTOM-UP FLAT

(multiple of 22 sts + 1; 20-row repeat)

Row 1 (RS): *P1, yo, k1, ssk, k1, yo, k2, ssk, k5, k2tog, k2, yo, k1, k2tog, k1, yo; repeat from * to last st, p1.

Row 2: K1, *p1, yo, p1, p2tog, p1, yo, p2, p2tog, p3, ssp, p2, yo, p1, ssp, p1, yo, p1, k1; repeat from * to end.

Row 3: *P1, k2, yo, k1, ssk, k1, yo, k2, ssk, k1, k2tog, k2, yo, k1, k2tog, k1, yo, k2; repeat from * to last st, p1.

Row 4: K1, *p3, yo, p1, p2tog, p1, yo, p2, p2sp, p2, yo, p1, ssp, p1, yo, p3, k1; repeat from * to end.

Row 5: *P1, k4, yo, k1, ssk, k1, yo, k2, ssk, k2, k2tog, k1, yo, k4; repeat from * to last st, p1.

Row 6: K1, *p5, yo, p1, p2tog, ssp, p2, yo, p1, ssp, p1, yo, p5, k1; repeat from * to end.

Row 7: *P1, k6, yo, k1, ssk, k1, yo, k2, ssk, k7; repeat from * to last st, p1.

Row 8: K1, *p6, ssp, p2, yo, p1, ssp, p1, yo, p7, k1; repeat from * to end.

Row 9: *P1, k8, yo, k1, ssk, k1, yo, k2, ssk, k5; repeat from * to last st, p1.

Row 10: K1, *p4, ssp, p2, yo, p1, ssp, p1, yo, p9, k1; repeat from * to end.

Rows 11-13: Repeat Rows 1-3.

Row 14: K1, *p3, yo, p1, p2tog, p1, yo, p2, p3tog, p2, yo, p1, ssp, p1, yo, p3, k1; repeat from * to end.

Row 15: *P1, k4, yo, k1, ssk, k2, k2tog, k2, yo, k1, k2tog, k1, yo, k4; repeat from * to last st, p1.

Row 16: K1, *p5, yo, p1, p2tog, p1, yo, p2, p2tog, ssp, p1, yo, p5, k1; repeat from * to end.

Row 17: *P1, k7, k2tog, k2, yo, k1, k2tog, k1, yo, k6; repeat from * to last st, p1.

Row 18: K1, *p7, yo, p1, p2tog, p1, yo, p2, p2tog, p6, k1; repeat from * to end.

Row 19: *P1, k5, k2tog, k2, yo, k1, k2tog, k1, yo, k8; repeat from * to last st, p1.

Row 20: K1, *p9, yo, p1, p2tog, p1, yo, p2, p2tog, p4, k1; repeat from * to end.

Repeat Rows 1-20 for Lotus Leaves Bottom-Up Flat.

Bottom-Up Flat

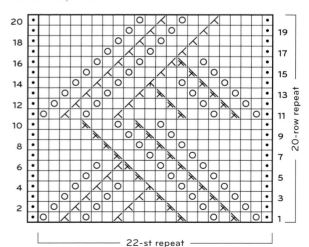

BOTTOM-UP IN THE ROUND

(multiple of 22 sts; 20-rnd repeat)

Rnd 1: *P1, yo, k1, ssk, k1, yo, k2, ssk, k5, k2tog, k2, yo, k1, k2tog, k1, yo; repeat from * to end.
Rnd 2: *P1, k1, yo, k1, ssk, k1, yo, k2, ssk, k3, k2tog, k2, yo, k1, k2tog, k1, yo, k1; repeat from * to end.
Rnd 3: *P1, k2, yo, k1, ssk, k1, yo, k2, ssk, k1, k2tog, k2, yo, k1, k2tog, k1, yo, k2; repeat from * to end.
Rnd 4: *P1, k3, yo, k1, ssk, k1, yo, k2, sk2p, k2, yo, k1, k2tog, k1, yo, k3; repeat from * to end.
Rnd 5: *P1, k4, yo, k1, ssk, k1, yo, k2, ssk, k2, k2tog, k1, yo, k4; repeat from * to end.
Rnd 6: *P1, k5, yo, k1, ssk, k1, yo, k2, ssk, k2tog, k1, yo, k5; repeat from * to end.
Rnd 7: *P1, k6, yo, k1, ssk, k1, yo, k2, ssk, k7; repeat from * to end.
Rnd 8: *P1, k7, yo, k1, ssk, k1, yo, k2, ssk, k6; repeat from * to end.
Rnd 9: *P1, k8, yo, k1, ssk, k1, yo, k2, ssk, k5; repeat from * to end.
Rnd 10: *P1, k9, yo, k1, ssk, k1, yo, k2, ssk, k4; repeat from * to end.
Rnds 11-13: Repeat Rnds 1–3.
Rnd 14: *P1, k3, yo, k1, ssk, k1, yo, k2, k3tog, k2, yo, k1, k2tog, k1, yo, k3; repeat from * to end.
Rnd 15: *P1, k4, yo, k1, ssk, k2, k2tog, k2, yo, k1, k2tog, k1, yo, k4; repeat from * to end.
Rnd 16: *P1, k5, yo, k1, ssk, k2tog, k2, yo, k1, k2tog, k1, yo, k5; repeat from * to end.

Rnd 17: *P1, k7, k2tog, k2, yo, k1, k2tog, k1, yo, k6; repeat from * to end.
Rnd 18: *P1, k6, k2tog, k2, yo, k1, k2tog, k1, yo, k7; repeat from * to end.
Rnd 19: *P1, k5, k2tog, k2, yo, k1, k2tog, k1, yo, k8; repeat from * to end.
Rnd 20: *P1, k4, k2tog, k2, yo, k1, k2tog, k1, yo, k9; repeat from * to end.
Repeat Rnd 1–20 for Lotus Leaves Bottom-Up in the Round.

Bottom-Up in the Round

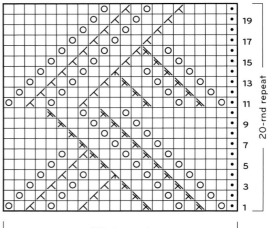

LOTUS LEAVES

(CONTINUED)

TOP-DOWN FLAT

(multiple of 22 sts + 1; 20-row repeat)

Row 1 (RS): *P1, k9, yo, k1, k2tog, k1, yo, k2, k2tog, k4; repeat from * to last st, p1.

Row 2: K1, *p5, p2tog, p2, yo, p1, p2tog, p1, yo, p8, k1; repeat from * to end.

Row 3: *P1, k7, yo, k1, k2tog, k1, yo, k2, k2tog, k6; repeat from * to last st, p1.

Row 4: K1, *p7, p2tog, p2, yo, p1, p2tog, p1, yo, p6, k1; repeat from * to end.

Row 5: *P1, k5, yo, k1, k2tog, k1, yo, k2, k2tog, ssk, k1, yo, k5; repeat from * to last st, p1.

Row 6: K1, *p4, yo, p1, ssp, p2, p2tog, p2, yo, p1, p2tog, p1, yo, p4, k1; repeat from * to end.

Row 7: *P1, k3, yo, k1, k2tog, k1, yo, k2, k3tog, k2, yo, k1, ssk, k1, yo, k3; repeat from * to last st, p1.

Row 8: K1, *p2, yo, p1, ssp, p1, yo, p2, ssp, p1, p2tog, p2, yo, p1, p2tog, p1, yo, p2, k1; repeat from * to end.

Row 9: *P1, k1, yo, k1, k2tog, k1, yo, k2, k2tog, k3, ssk, k2, yo, k1, ssk, k1, yo, k1; repeat from * to last st, p1.

Row 10: K1, *yo, p1, ssp, p1, yo, p2, ssp, p5, p2tog, p2, yo, p1, p2tog, p1, yo, k1; repeat from * to end.

Row 11: *P1, k4, ssk, k2, yo, k1, ssk, k1, yo, k9; repeat from * to last st, p1.

Row 12: K1, *p8, yo, p1, ssp, p1, yo, p2, ssp, p5, k1; repeat from * to end.

Row 13: *P1, k6, ssk, k2, yo, k1, ssk, k1, yo, k7; repeat from * to last st, p1.

Row 14: K1, *p6, yo, p1, ssp, p1, yo, p2, ssp, p7, k1; repeat from * to end.

Row 15: *P1, k5, yo, k1, k2tog, ssk, k2, yo, k1, ssk, k1, yo, k5; repeat from * to last st, p1.

Row 16: K1, *p4, yo, p1, ssp, p1, yo, p2, ssp, p2, p2tog, p1, yo, p4, k1; repeat from * to end.

Row 17: *P1, k3, yo, k1, k2tog, k1, yo, k2, sk2p, k2, yo, k1, ssk, k1, yo, k3; repeat from * to last st, p1.

Row 18: K1, *p2, yo, p1, ssp, p1, yo, p2, ssk, p1, p2tog, p2, yo, p1, p2tog, p1, yo, p2, k1; repeat from * to end.

Row 19: *P1, k1, yo, k1, k2tog, k1, yo, k2, k2tog, k3, ssk, k2, yo, k1, ssk, k1, yo, k1; repeat from * to last st, p1.

Row 20: K1, *yo, p1, ssp, p1, yo, p2, ssp, p5, p2tog, p2, yo, p1, p2tog, p1, yo, k1; repeat from * to end.

Repeat Rows 1–20 for Lotus Leaves Top-Down Flat.

Top-Down Flat

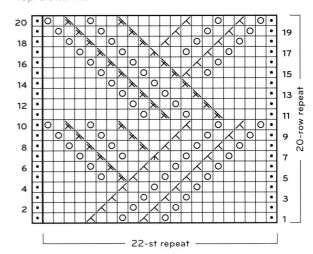

TOP-DOWN IN THE ROUND

(multiple of 22 sts; 20-rnd repeat)

Rnd 1: *P1, k9, yo, k1, k2tog, k1, yo, k2, k2tog, k4; repeat from * to end.
Rnd 2: *P1, k8, yo, k1, k2tog, k1, yo, k2, k2tog, k5; repeat from * to end.
Rnd 3: *P1, k7, yo, k1, k2tog, k1, yo, k2, k2tog, k6; repeat from * to end.
Rnd 4: *P1, k6, yo, k1, k2tog, k1, yo, k2, k2tog, k7; repeat from * to end.
Rnd 5: *P1, k5, yo, k1, k2tog, k1, yo, k2, k2tog, ssk, k1, yo, k5; repeat from * to end.
Rnd 6: *P1, k4, yo, k1, k2tog, k1, yo, k2, k2tog, k2, ssk, k1, yo, k4; repeat from * to end.
Rnd 7: *P1, k3, yo, k1, k2tog, k1, yo, k2, sk2p, k2, yo, k1, ssk, k1, yo, k3; repeat from * to end.
Rnd 8: *P1, k2, yo, k1, k2tog, k1, yo, k2, k2tog, k1, ssk, k2, yo, k1, ssk, k1, yo, k2; repeat from * to end.
Rnd 9: *P1, k1, yo, k1, k2tog, k1, yo, k2, k2tog, k3, ssk, k2, yo, k1, ssk, k1, yo, k1; repeat from * to end.
Rnd 10: *P1, yo, k1, k2tog, k1, yo, k2, k2tog, k5, ssk, k2, yo, k1, ssk, k1, yo; repeat from * to end.
Rnd 11: *P1, k4, ssk, k2, yo, k1, ssk, k1, yo, k9; repeat from * to end.
Rnd 12: *P1, k5, ssk, k2, yo, k1, ssk, k1, yo, k8; repeat from * to end.
Rnd 13: *P1, k6, ssk, k2, yo, k1, ssk, k1, yo, k7; repeat from * to end.
Rnd 14: *P1, k7, ssk, k2, yo, k1, ssk, k1, yo, k6; repeat from * to end.
Rnd 15: *P1, k5, yo, k1, k2tog, ssk, k2, yo, k1, ssk, k1, yo, k5; repeat from * to end.
Rnd 16: *P1, k4, yo, k1, k2tog, k2, ssk, k2, yo, k1, ssk, k1, yo, k4; repeat from * to end.
Rnd 17: *P1, k3, yo, k1, k2tog, k1, yo, k2, sk2p, k2, yo, k1, ssk, k1, yo, k3; repeat from * to end.
Rnd 18: *P1, k2, yo, k1, k2tog, k1, yo, k2, k2tog, k1, ssk, k2, yo, k1, ssk, k1, yo, k2; repeat from * to end.
Rnd 19: *P1, k1, yo, k1, k2tog, k1, yo, k2, k2tog, k3, ssk, k2, yo, k1, ssk, k1, yo, k1; repeat from * to end.
Rnd 20: *P1, yo, k1, k2tog, k1, yo, k2, k2tog, k5, ssk, k2, yo, k1, ssk, k1, yo; repeat from * to end.
Repeat Rnds 1–20 for Lotus Leaves Top-Down in the Round.

Top-Down in the Round

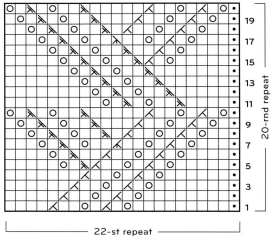

22-st repeat

REVERSE STOCKINETTE ZIGZAG

FLAT

(multiple of 10 sts; 16-row repeat)

Row 1 (RS): *K1, yo, s2kp2, yo, k1, p5; repeat from * to end.

Row 2 and all WS Rows: Knit.

Row 3: P1, *k1, yo, s2kp2, yo, k1, p5; repeat from * to last 9 sts, k1, yo, s2kp2, yo, k1, p4.

Row 5: P2, *k1, yo, s2kp2, yo, k1, p5; repeat from * to last 8 sts, k1, yo, s2kp2, yo, k1, p3.

Row 7: P3, *k1, yo, s2kp2, yo, k1, p5; repeat from * to last 7 sts, k1, yo, s2kp2, yo, k1, p2.

Row 9: P4, *k1, yo, s2kp2, yo, k1, p5; repeat from * to last 6 sts, k1, yo, s2kp2, yo, k1, p1.

Row 11: Repeat Row 7.

Row 13: Repeat Row 5.

Row 15: Repeat Row 3.

Row 16: Knit.

Repeat Rows 1–16 for Reverse Stockinette Zigzag Flat.

IN THE ROUND

(multiple of 10 sts; 16-rnd repeat)

Rnd 1: *K1, yo, s2kp2, yo, k1, p5; repeat from * to end.

Rnd 2 and all Even-Numbered Rnds: Purl.

Rnd 3: *P1, k1, yo, s2kp2, yo, k1, p4; repeat from * to end.

Rnd 5: *P2, k1, yo, s2kp2, yo, k1, p3; repeat from * to end.

Rnd 7: *P3, k1, yo, s2kp2, yo, k1, p2; repeat from * to end.

Rnd 9: *P4, k1, yo, s2kp2, yo, k1, p1; repeat from * to end.

Rnd 11: Repeat Rnd 7.

Rnd 13: Repeat Rnd 5.

Rnd 15: Repeat Rnd 3.

Rnd 16: Purl.

Repeat Rnds 1–16 for Reverse Stockinette Zigzag in the Round.

Flat and in the Round

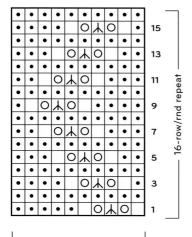

10-st repeat

16-row/rnd repeat

ROLLING WHEAT

BOTTOM-UP FLAT

(multiple of 20 sts; 8-row repeat)

Row 1 (RS): *K5, k2tog, k3, LLI, RLI, k3, skp, k5; repeat from * to end.

Row 2: *P4, ssp, p3, RLI, p2, LLI, p3, p2tog, p4; repeat from * to end.

Row 3: *K3, k2tog, k3, LLI, k4, RLI, k3, skp, k3; repeat from * to end.

Row 4: *P2, ssp, p3, RLI, p6, LLI, p3, p2tog, p2; repeat from * to end.

Row 5: *RLI, k3, skp, k10, k2tog, k3, LLI; repeat from * to end.

Row 6: *P1, LLI, p3, p2tog, p8, ssp, p3, RLI, p1; repeat from * to end.

Row 7: *K2, RLI, k3, skp, k6, k2tog, k3, LLI, k2; repeat from * to end.

Row 8: *P3, LLI, p3, p2tog, p4, ssp, p3, RLI, p3; repeat from * to end.

Repeat Rows 1–8 for Rolling Wheat Bottom-Up Flat.

BOTTOM-UP IN THE ROUND

(multiple of 20 sts; 8-rnd repeat)

Rnd 1: *K5, k2tog, k3, LLI, RLI, k3, skp, k5; repeat from * to end.

Rnd 2: *K4, k2tog, k3, LLI, k2, RLI, k3, skp, k4; repeat from * to end.

Rnd 3: *K3, k2tog, k3, LLI, k4, RLI, k3, skp, k3; repeat from * to end.

Rnd 4: *K2, k2tog, k3, LLI, k6, RLI, k3, skp, k2; repeat from * to end.

Rnd 5: *RLI, k3, skp, k10, k2tog, k3, LLI; repeat from * to end.

Rnd 6: *K1, RLI, k3, skp, k8, k2tog, k3, LLI, k1; repeat from * to end.

Rnd 7: *K2, RLI, k3, skp, k6, k2tog, k3, LLI, k2; repeat from * to end.

Rnd 8: *K3, RLI, k3, skp, k4, k2tog, k3, LLI, k3; repeat from * to end.

Repeat Rnds 1–8 for Rolling Wheat Bottom-Up in the Round.

Bottom-Up Flat and in the Round

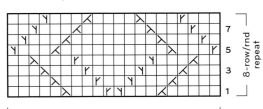

TOP-DOWN FLAT

(multiple of 20 sts; 8-row repeat)

Row 1 (RS): *K3, RLI, k3, k2tog, k4, skp, k3, LLI, k3; repeat from * to end.
Row 2: *P2, LLI, p3, spp, p6, p2tog, p3, RLI, p2; repeat from * to end.
Row 3: *K1, RLI, k3, k2tog, k8, skp, k3, LLI, k1; repeat from * to end.
Row 4: *LLI, p3, spp, p10, p2tog, p3, RLI; repeat from * to end.
Row 5: *K2, skp, k3, LLI, k6, RLI, k3, k2tog, k2; repeat from * to end.
Row 6: *P3, p2tog, p3, RLI, p4, LLI, p3, spp, p3; repeat from * to end.
Row 7: *K4, skp, k3, LLI, k2, RLI, k3, k2tog, k4; repeat from * to end.
Row 8: *P5, p2tog, p3, RLI, LLI, p3, spp, p5; repeat from * to end.
Repeat Rows 1–8 for Rolling Wheat Top-Down Flat.

TOP-DOWN IN THE ROUND

(multiple of 20 sts; 8-rnd repeat)

Rnd 1: *K3, RLI, k3, k2tog, k4, skp, k3, LLI, k3; repeat from * to end.
Rnd 2: *K2, RLI, k3, k2tog, k6, skp, k3, LLI, k2; repeat from * to end.
Rnd 3: *K1, RLI, k3, k2tog, k8, skp, k3, LLI, k1; repeat from * to end.
Rnd 4: *RLI, k3, k2tog, k10, skp, k3, LLI; repeat from * to end.
Rnd 5: *K2, skp, k3, LLI, k6, RLI, k3, k2tog, k2; repeat from * to end.
Rnd 6: *K3, skp, k3, LLI, k4, RLI, k3, k2tog, k3; repeat from * to end.
Rnd 7: *K4, skp, k3, LLI, k2, RLI, k3, k2tog, k4; repeat from * to end.
Rnd 8: *K5, skp, k3, LLI, RLI, k3, k2tog, k5; repeat from * to end.
Repeat Rnds 1–8 for Rolling Wheat Top-Down in the Round.

Top-Down Flat and in the Round

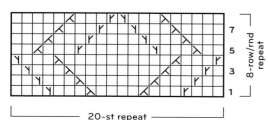

20-st repeat

8-row/rnd repeat

WAVING DIAMONDS

FLAT

(multiple of 10 sts + 2; 24-row repeat)

Row 1 (RS): *P2, M1–r, k1, skp, k5; repeat from * to last 2 sts, p2.

Row 2 and all WS Rows: Purl.

Row 3: *P2, M1–r, k2, skp, k4; repeat from * to last 2 sts, p2.

Row 5: *P2, M1–r, k3, skp, k3; repeat from * to last 2 sts, p2.

Row 7: *P2, M1–r, k4, skp, k2; repeat from * to last 2 sts, p2.

Row 9: *P2, M1–r, k5, skp, k1; repeat from * to last 2 sts, p2.

Row 11: *P2, M1–r, k6, skp; repeat from * to last 2 sts, p2.

Row 13: *P2, k5, k2tog, k1, M1–l; repeat from * to last 2 sts, p2.

Row 15: *P2, K4, k2tog, k2, M1–l; repeat from * to last 2 sts, p2.

Row 17: *P2, K3, k2tog, k3, M1–l; repeat from * to last 2 sts, p2.

Row 19: *P2, K2, k2tog, k4, M1–l; repeat from * to last 2 sts, p2.

Row 21: *P2, k1, k2tog, k5, M1–l; repeat from * to last 2 sts, p2.

Row 23: *P2, k2tog, k6, M1–l; repeat from * to last 2 sts, p2.

Row 24: Purl.

Repeat Rows 1–24 for Waving Diamonds Flat.

Flat

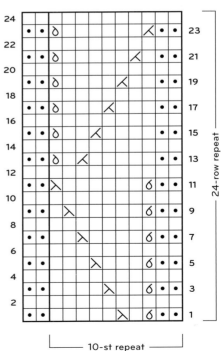

10-st repeat

24-row repeat

TEXTURED, SLIPPED, AND FANCY

IN THE ROUND

(multiple of 10 sts; 24-rnd repeat)

Rnd 1: *P2, M1-r, k1, skp, k5; repeat from * to end.

Rnd 2 and all Even-Numbered Rnds: Knit.

Rnd 3: *P2, M1-r, k2, skp, k4; repeat from * to end.

Rnd 5: *P2, M1-r, k3, skp, k3; repeat from * to end.

Rnd 7: *P2, M1-r, k4, skp, k2; repeat from * to end.

Rnd 9: *P2, M1-r, k5, skp, k1; repeat from * to end.

Rnd 11: *P2, M1-r, k6, skp; repeat from * to end.

Rnd 13: *P2, k5, k2tog, k1, M1-l; repeat from * to end.

Rnd 15: *P2, k4, k2tog, k2, M1-l; repeat from * to end.

Rnd 17: *P2, k3, k2tog, k3, M1-l; repeat from * to end.

Rnd 19: *P2, k2, k2tog, k4, M1-l; repeat from * to end.

Rnd 21: *P2, k1, k2tog, k5, M1-l; repeat from * to end.

Rnd 23: *P2, k2tog, k6, M1-l; repeat from * to end.

Rnd 24: Knit.

Repeat Rnds 1–24 for Waving Diamonds in the Round.

In the Round

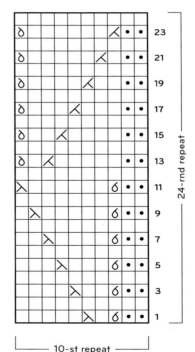

10-st repeat

24-rnd repeat

WOVEN LADDERS BED SOCKS

These socks feature the in-the-round version of the Woven Ladders stitch pattern on page 71. The slipped stitches create a pretty waffle pattern on the socks' surface, and the thick fabric created by the stitch pattern makes them nice and cozy (I imagine wearing them while reading in bed). If you want to add durability, carry along a strand of reinforcement thread while working the heels and toes. Oh, and make sure that your tension is even; otherwise your "waffles" won't be that waffle-y.

STITCH PATTERNS

1x1 Rib in the Round
(even number of sts; 1-rnd repeat)

All Rnds: *K1, p1; repeat from * to end.

Woven Ladders in the Round
(see page 71 for chart)
(multiple of 8 sts; 8-rnd repeat)

Rnds 1-3: *Slip 3 wyif, k5; repeat from * to end.

Rnd 4: Knit.

Rnds 5-7: *K4, slip 3 wyif, k1; repeat from * to end.

Rnd 8: Knit.

Repeat Rnds 1-8 for Woven Ladders in the Round.

LEG

Cast on 32 (48, 64) sts. Divide sts among 3 needles [8-8-16 (12-12-24, 16-16-32)]. Join for working in the rnd, being careful not to twist sts; pm for beginning of rnd. Begin 1x1 Rib; work even until piece measures 1½" (4 cm) from the beginning. Change to Woven Ladders in the Round; work even

until piece measures approximately 4 (5, 6)" [10 (12.5, 15) cm] from the beginning, ending with Rnd 8 of pattern.

HEEL FLAP

Row 1 (WS): Working back and forth on 16 (24, 32) sts on third needle only, slip 1, purl to end, turn.

Row 2: *Slip 1, k1; repeat from * to end.

Repeat Rows 1 and 2 six (10, 14) times, then Repeat Row 1 once.

TURN HEEL

Row 1 (RS): K10 (14, 18), ssk, k1, turn.

Row 2: Slip 1, p5, p2tog, p1, turn.

Row 3: Slip 1, knit to 1 st before gap, ssk (the 2 sts on either side of gap), k1, turn.

Row 4: Slip 1, purl to 1 st before gap (the 2 sts on either side of gap), p2tog, p1, turn.

Repeat Rows 3 and 4 one (3, 5) time(s), omitting final k1 and p1 sts in last repeat of Rows 3 and 4—10 (14, 18) sts remain.

SIZES

Child's (Women's Medium, Women's Large)

FINISHED MEASUREMENTS

Approximately 4 ½ (6 ¾, 9 ¼)" [11.5 (17, 23.5) cm] Foot circumference

Approximately 6 (10, 11)" [15 (25.5, 28) cm] Foot length from back of Heel

Approximately 6 (8, 10)" [15 (20.5, 25.5) cm] Leg length to base of Heel

YARN

Blue Sky Alpacas Sport Weight (100% baby alpaca; 110 yards / 50 grams): 1 (3, 3) hank(s) #548 Aquamarine

NEEDLES

One set of five double-pointed needles (dpn) size US 3 (3.25 mm)

Change needle size if necessary to obtain correct gauge.

NOTIONS

Stitch marker

GAUGE

28 sts and 32 rnds = 4" (10 cm) in Woven Ladders

TEXTURED, SLIPPED, AND FANCY

GUSSET

Note: Needles will be renumbered on the next row.

Next Row (RS): *Needle 1:* Knit across Heel Flap sts, pick up and knit 8 (12, 16) sts along left side of Heel Flap; *Needles 2 and 3:* Work Woven Ladders; *Needle 4:* Using an empty needle, pick up and knit 8 (12, 16) sts along right side of Heel Flap, k5 (7, 9) from Needle 1—42 (62, 82) sts [13-8-8-13 (19-12-12-19, 25-16-16-25)]. Join for working in the rnd; pm for new beginning of rnd.

Decrease Rnd: *Needle 1:* Knit to last 3 sts, k2tog, k1; *Needles 2 and 3:* Work in Woven Ladders as established; *Needle 4:* K1, ssk, knit to end—40 (60, 80) sts remain. Work even for 1 rnd.

Repeat Decrease Rnd every other rnd 4 (6, 8) times—32 (48, 64) sts remain [8 (12, 16) sts each needle].

FOOT

Work even in patterns as established until piece measures 5 (8¼, 8¾)" [12.5 (21, 22) cm], or to 1 (1¾, 2¼)" [2.5 (4.5, 5.5) cm] less than desired length from back of Heel.

TOE

Decrease Rnd: *Needle 1:* Knit to last 3 sts, ssk, k1; *Needle 2:* K1, k2tog, knit to end. *Needles 3 and 4:* Repeat Needles 1 and 2—28 (44, 60) sts remain. Knit 1 rnd.

Repeat Decrease Rnd every other rnd 3 (6, 6) times, then every rnd 0 (0, 4) times—16 (20, 20) sts remain. Knit to end of Needle 1.

FINISHING

Break yarn, leaving an 18" tail. Transfer sts from Needle 1 to Needle 4, and sts from Needle 3 to Needle 2. Using Kitchener st (see Special Techniques, page 282), graft Toe sts.

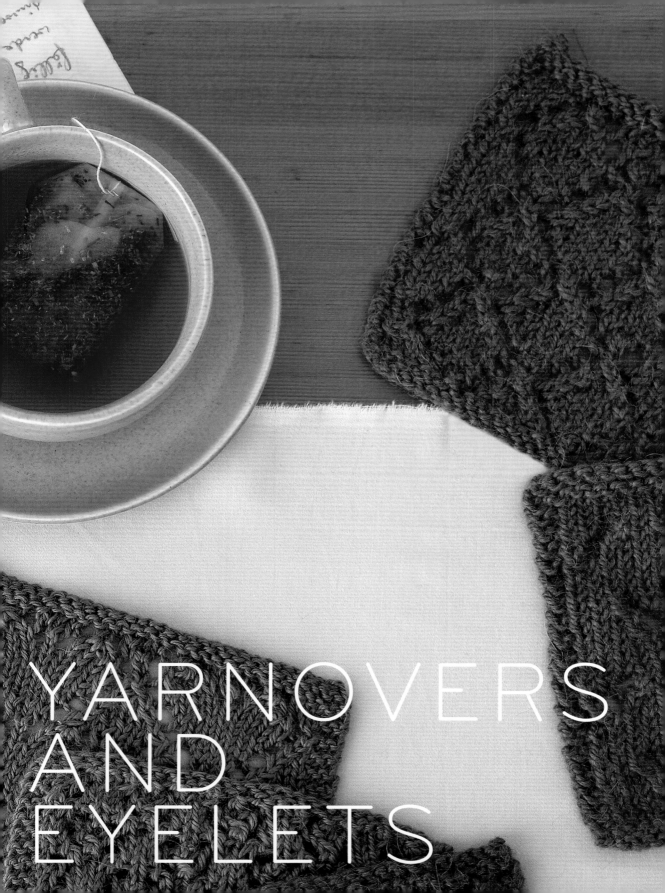

YARNOVERS
AND
EYELETS

Yarnovers and eyelets are both created by bringing the yarn over your needle to make intentional "holes" in the fabric, giving it a lovely, open feel. It's especially lovely, in my opinion, when the holes line up to create shapes like hearts and diamonds.

Yarnover and eyelet patterns are often whimsical and work great for smaller garments like boleros, scarves, or children's clothing, and in panels on sweaters or cardigans. When you are creating intentional holes, you'll want to think about their placement. Would you consider using an eyelet stitch pattern for a close-fitting cap? Or would your hair stick out of the holes? Another example is a pullover. Unless it is a garment that would be worn over another garment, you might want to rethink using lots of eyelets on your sweater, or be mindful about where the holes appear.

EYELET ROWS

FLAT

(odd number of sts; 4-row repeat)

Row 1 (RS): Knit.
Rows 2 and 3: Knit.
Row 4: K1, *yo, skp; repeat from * to end.
Repeat Rows 1–4 for Eyelet Rows Flat.

IN THE ROUND

(even number of sts; 4-rnd repeat)

Rnd 1: Knit.
Rnd 2: Purl.
Rnd 3: Knit.
Rnd 4: *Yo, spp; repeat from * to end.
Repeat Rnds 1–4 for Eyelet Rows in the Round.

SNOWDROP EYELETS

FLAT

(multiple of 5 sts + 2; 6-row repeat)

Row 1 (RS): *P2, k3; repeat from * to last 2 sts, p2.
Row 2 and all WS Rows: K2, *p3, k2; repeat from * to end.
Row 3: Repeat Row 1.
Row 5: *P2, yo, sk2p, yo; repeat from * to last 2 sts, p2.
Row 6: Repeat Row 2.
Repeat Rows 1–6 for Snowdrop Eyelets Flat.

IN THE ROUND

(multiple of 5 sts; 6-rnd repeat)

Rnds 1-4: *P1, k3, p1; repeat from * to end.
Rnd 5: *P1, yo, sk2p, yo, p1; repeat from * to end.
Rnd 6: Repeat Rnd 1.
Repeat Rnds 1–6 for Snowdrop Eyelets in the Round.

Flat

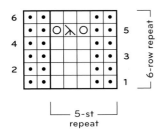

In the Round

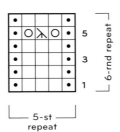

SNOWFLAKE EYELETS

FLAT

(multiple of 6 sts + 1; 12-row repeat)

Note: Two sts are increased per repeat on Rows 3 and 9; original st count is restored on Rows 5 and 11.

Row 1 (RS): *K1, yo, skp, k1, k2tog, yo; repeat from * to last st, k1.

Row 2 and all WS Rows: Purl.

Row 3: K2, yo, *k3, yo; repeat from * to last 2 sts, k2.

Row 5: K2tog, yo, *skp, k1, k2tog, yo, sk2p, yo; repeat from * to last 7 sts, skp, k1, k2tog, yo, skp.

Row 7: *K1, k2tog, yo, k1, yo, skp; repeat from * to last st, k1.

Row 9: Repeat Row 3.

Row 11: *K1, k2tog, yo, sk2p, yo, skp; repeat from * to last st, k1.

Row 12: Purl.

Repeat Rows 1–12 for Snowflake Eyelets Flat.

IN THE ROUND

(multiple of 6 sts; 12-rnd repeat)

Note: Two sts are increased per repeat on Rnds 3 and 9; original st count is restored on Rnds 5 and 11.

Rnd 1: *Skp, k1, k2tog, yo, k1, yo; repeat from * to end.

Rnd 2 and all Even-Numbered Rnds: Knit.

Rnd 3: *K3, yo; repeat from * to end.

Rnd 5: *Skp, k1, k2tog, yo, sk2p, yo; repeat from * to end.

Rnd 7: *Yo, k1, yo, skp, k1, k2tog; repeat from * to end.

Rnd 9: Repeat Rnd 3.

Rnd 11: *Yo, sk2p, yo, skp, k1, k2tog; repeat from * to end.

Rnd 12: Knit.

Repeat Rnds 1–12 for Snowflake Eyelets in the Round.

Flat

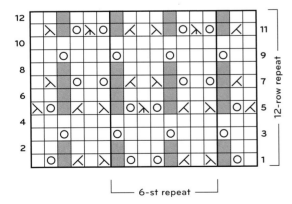

In the Round

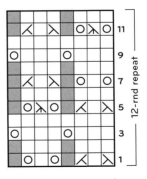

6-st repeat

12-row repeat

6-st repeat

12-rnd repeat

ROMAN STRIPE

FLAT (REVERSIBLE)

(even number of sts; 7-row repeat)

Note: Since this pattern has an odd number of rows, you will work Row 1 on a RS row the first time, then on a WS row the next time, continuing to alternate in this manner. If you prefer, you may make this pattern have a RS and a WS by omitting Row 7. One st is increased per repeat on Row 1; original st count is restored on Row 2.

Row 1: K1, *yo, k1; repeat from * to last st, k1.

Row 2: K1, purl to last st, k1.

Row 3: K1, *k2tog; repeat from * to last st, k1.

Rows 4 and 5: K1, *yo, k2tog; repeat from * to last st, k1.

Rows 6 and 7: Knit.

Repeat Rows 1–7 for Roman Stripe Flat.

IN THE ROUND (REVERSIBLE)

(even number of sts; 14-rnd repeat)

Note: If you work the flat version on Rows 1–6 only, omitting Row 7, you may work Rnds 1–6 only of the in-the-Round version to match. One st is increased per repeat on Rnds 1 and 8; original st count is restored on Rnds 2 and 9.

Rnd 1: *Yo, k1; repeat from * to end.

Rnd 2: Knit.

Rnd 3: *K2tog; repeat from * to end.

Rnd 4: *P2tog, yo; repeat from * to end.

Rnd 5: *Yo, k2tog; repeat from * to end.

Rnd 6: Purl.

Rnd 7: Knit.

Rnd 8: *P1, yo; repeat from * to end.

Rnd 9: Purl.

Rnd 10: *P2tog; repeat from * to end.

Rnd 11: *Yo, k2tog; repeat from * to end.

Rnd 12: *P2tog, yo; repeat from * to end.

Rnd 13: Knit.

Rnd 14: Purl.

Repeat Rnds 1–4 for Roman Stripe in the Round.

WHEAT EYELETS

FLAT

(multiple of 10 sts + 1; 16-row repeat)

Rows 1, 3, 5, and 7 (RS): *K1, yo, k2, skp, k1, k2tog, k2, yo; repeat from * to last st, k1.
Row 2 and all WS Rows: Purl.
Rows 9, 11, 13, and 15: *K1, k2tog, k2, yo, k1, yo, k2, skp; repeat from * to last st, k1.
Row 16: Purl.
Repeat Rows 1–16 for Wheat Eyelets Flat.

IN THE ROUND

(multiple of 10 sts; 16-rnd repeat)

Rnds 1, 3, 5, and 7: *K1, yo, k2, skp, k1, k2tog, k2, yo; repeat from * to end.
Rnd 2 and all Even-Numbered Rnds: Knit.
Rnds 9, 11, 13, and 15: *K1, k2tog, k2, yo, k1, yo, k2, skp; repeat from * to end.
Rnd 16: Knit.
Repeat Rnds 1–16 for Wheat Eyelets in the Round.

Flat

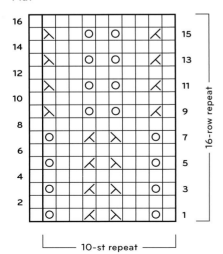

In the Round

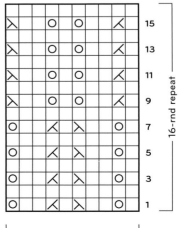

EYELET CRESCENTS

FLAT

(multiple of 10 sts + 1; 12-row repeat)

Row 1 (RS): *P1, yo, k3, skp, k4; repeat from * to last st, p1.

Row and all WS Rows: K1, *p9, k1; repeat from * to end.

Row 3: *P1, k1, yo, k3, skp, k3; repeat from * to last st, p1.

Row 5: *P1, k2, yo, k3, skp, k2; repeat from * to last st, p1.

Row 7: *P1, k3, yo, k3, skp, k1; repeat from * to last st, p1.

Row 9: *P1, k4, yo, k3, skp; repeat from * to last st, p1.

Row 11: Knit.

Row 12: Purl.

Repeat Rows 1–12 for Eyelet Crescents Flat.

IN THE ROUND

(multiple of 10 sts; 12-rnd repeat)

Rnd 1: *P1, yo, k3, skp, k4; repeat from * to end.

Rnd 2 and all Even-Numbered Rnds: *P1, k9; repeat from * to end.

Rnd 3: *P1, k1, yo, k3, skp, k3; repeat from * to end.

Rnd 5: *P1, k2, yo, k3, skp, k2; repeat from * to end.

Rnd 7: *P1, k3, yo, k3, skp, k1; repeat from * to end.

Rnd 9: *P1, k4, yo, k3, skp; repeat from * to end.

Rnds 11 and 12: Knit.

Repeat Rnds 1–12 for Eyelet Crescents in the Round.

Flat

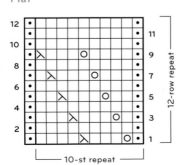

In the Round

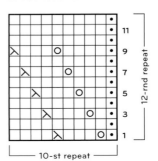

WANDERING LEAVES

WANDERING LEAVES

BOTTOM-UP FLAT

(multiple of 15 sts; 16-row repeat)

Row 1 (RS): *P1, k9, k3tog, yo, k1, yo, p1; repeat from * to end.

Row 2 and all WS Rows: *K1, p13, k1; repeat from * to end.

Row 3: *P1, k7, k3tog, [k1, yo] twice, k1, p1; repeat from * to end.

Row 5: *P1, k5, k3tog, k2, yo, k1, yo, k2, p1; repeat from * to end.

Row 7: *P1, k3, k3tog, k3, yo, k1, yo, k3, p1; repeat from * to end.

Row 9: *P1, yo, k1, yo, sk2p, k9, p1; repeat from * to end.

Row 11: *P1, [k1, yo] twice, k1, sk2p, k7, p1; repeat from * to end.

Row 13: *P1, k2, yo, k1, yo, k2, sk2p, k5, p1; repeat from * to end.

Row 15: *P1, k3, yo, k1, yo, k3, sk2p, k3, p1; repeat from * to end.

Row 16: Repeat Row 2.

Repeat Rows 1–16 for Wandering Leaves Bottom-Up Flat.

BOTTOM-UP IN THE ROUND

(multiple of 15 sts; 16-rnd repeat)

Rnd 1: *P1, k9, k3tog, yo, k1, yo, p1; repeat from * to end.

Rnd 2 and all Even-Numbered Rnds: *P1, k13, p1; repeat from * to end.

Rnd 3: *P1, k7, k3tog, [k1, yo] twice, k1, p1; repeat from * to end.

Rnd 5: *P1, k5, k3tog, k2, yo, k1, yo, k2, p1; repeat from * to end.

Rnd 7: *P1, k3, k3tog, k3, yo, k1, yo, k3, p1; repeat from * to end.

Rnd 9: *P1, yo, k1, yo, sk2p, k9, p1; repeat from * to end.

Rnd 11: *P1, [k1, yo] twice, k1, sk2p, k7, p1; repeat from * to end.

Rnd 13: *P1, k2, yo, k1, yo, k2, sk2p, k5, p1; repeat from * to end.

Rnd 15: *P1, k3, yo, k1, yo, k3, sk2p, k3, p1; repeat from * to end.

Rnd 16: Repeat Rnd 2.

Repeat Rnds 1–16 for Wandering Leaves Bottom-Up in the Round.

Bottom-Up Flat and in the Round

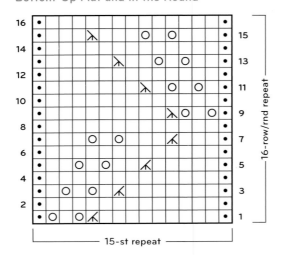

15-st repeat

16-row/rnd repeat

TOP-DOWN FLAT

(multiple of 15 sts; 16-row repeat)

Row 1 (RS): *P1, k3, sk2p, k3, yo, k1, yo, k3, p1; repeat from * to end.

Row 2 and all WS Rows: *K1, p13, k1; repeat from * to end.

Row 3: *P1, k5, sk2p, k2, yo, k1, yo, k2, p1; repeat from * to end.

Row 5: *P1, k7, sk2p, [k1, yo] twice, k1, p1; repeat from, * to end.

Row 7: *P1, k9, sk2p, yo, k1, yo, p1; repeat from * to end.

Row 9: *P1, k3, yo, k1, yo, k3, k3tog, k3, p1; repeat from * to end.

Row 11: *P1, k2, yo, k1, yo, k2, k3tog, k5, p1; repeat from * to end.

Row 13: *P1, [k1, yo] twice, k1, k3tog, k7, p1; repeat from * to end.

Row 15: *P1, yo, k1, yo, k3tog, k9, p1; repeat from * to end.

Row 16: Repeat Row 2.
Repeat Rows 1–16 for Wandering Leaves Top-Down Flat.

TOP-DOWN IN THE ROUND

(multiple of 15 sts; 16-rnd repeat)

Rnd 1 (RS): *P1, k3, sk2p, k3, yo, k1, yo, p1; repeat from * to end.

Rnd 2 and all Even-Numbered Rnds: *P1, k13, p1; repeat from * to end.

Rnd 3: *P1, k5, sk2p, k2, yo, k1, yo, k2, p1; repeat from * to end.

Rnd 5: *P1, k7, sk2p, [k1, yo] twice, k1, p1; repeat from, * to end.

Rnd 7: *P1, k9, sk2p, yo, k1, yo, p1; repeat from * to end.

Rnd 9: *P1, k3, yo, k1, yo, k3, k3tog, k3, p1; repeat from * to end.

Rnd 11: *P1, k2, yo, k1, yo, k2, k3tog, k5, p1; repeat from * to end.

Rnd 13: *P1, [k1, yo] twice, k1, k3tog, k7, p1; repeat from * to end.

Rnd 15: *P1, yo, k1, yo, k3tog, k9, p1; repeat from * to end.

Rnd 16: Repeat Rnd 2.
Repeat Rnds 1–16 for Wandering Leaves Top-Down in the Round.

Top-Down Flat and in the Round

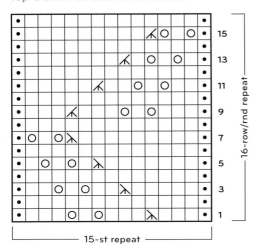

15-st repeat

16-row/rnd repeat

CASCADING GARTER FANS

FLAT

(multiple of 15 sts; 12-row repeat)

Row 1 (RS): *K5, p2tog, yo, p1, yo, spp, k5; repeat from * to end.
Row 2: *P7, k1, p7; repeat from * to end.
Row 3: *K4, p2tog, [p1, yo] twice, p1, spp, k4; repeat from * to end.
Row 4: Repeat Row 2.
Row 5: *K3, p2tog, p2, yo, p1, yo, p2, spp, k3; repeat from * to end.
Row 6: Repeat Row 2.
Row 7: *K2, p2tog, p3, yo, p1, yo, p3, spp, k2; repeat from * to end.
Row 8: Repeat Row 2.
Row 9: *K1, p2tog, p4, yo, p1, yo, p4, spp, k1; repeat from * to end.
Row 10: Repeat Row 2.
Row 11: *P2tog, p5, yo, p1, yo, p5, spp; repeat from * to end.
Row 12: Purl.
Repeat Rows 1–12 for Cascading Garter Fans Flat.

IN THE ROUND

(multiple of 15 sts; 12-rnd repeat)

Rnd 1: *K5, p2tog, yo, p1, yo, spp, k5; repeat from * to end.
Rnd 2: *K7, p1, k7; repeat from * to end.
Rnd 3: *K4, p2tog, [p1, yo] twice, p1, spp, k4; repeat from * to end.
Rnd 4: Repeat Rnd 2.
Rnd 5: *K3, p2tog, p2, yo, p1, yo, p2, spp, k3; repeat from * to end.
Rnd 8: Repeat Rnd 2.
Rnd 7: *K2, p2tog, p3, yo, p1, yo, p3, spp, k2; repeat from * to end.
Rnd 8: Repeat Rnd 2.
Rnd 9: *K1, p2tog, p4, yo, p1, yo, p4, spp, k1; repeat from * to end.
Rnd 10: Repeat Rnd 2.
Rnd 11: *P2tog, p5, yo, p1, yo, p5, spp; repeat from * to end.
Rnd 12: Purl.
Repeat Rnds 1–12 for Cascading Garter Fans in the Round.

Flat and in the Round

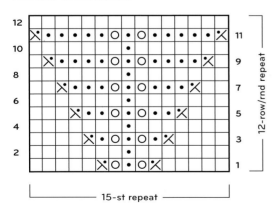

12-row/rnd repeat

15-st repeat

EYELET SQUARES

FLAT

(multiple of 16 sts + 1; 16-row repeat)

Row 1 (RS): K1, *k8, [yo, skp] 4 times; repeat from * to end.
Row 2 and all WS Rows: Purl.
Rows 3, 5, and 7: Repeat Row 1.
Rows 9, 11, 13, and 15: K1, *[yo, skp] 4 times, k8; repeat from * to end.
Row 16: Purl.
Repeat Rows 1–16 for Eyelet Squares Flat.

IN THE ROUND

(multiple of 16 sts; 16-rnd repeat)

Rnd 1: *K8, [yo, skp] 4 times; repeat from * to end.
Rnd 2 and all Even-Numbered Rnds: Knit.
Rnds 3, 5, and 7: Repeat Rnd 1.
Rnds 9, 11, 13, and 15: *[Yo, skp] 4 times, k8; repeat from * to end.
Rnd 16: Knit.
Repeat Rnds 1–16 for Eyelet Squares in the Round.

Flat

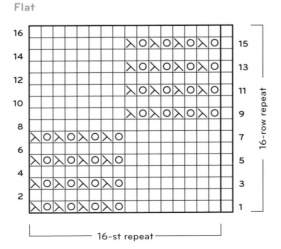

In the Round

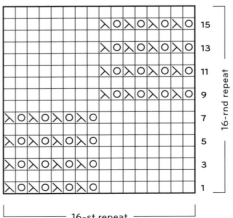

ZIGZAG EYELETS

FLAT

(multiple of 9 sts; 20-row repeat)

Row 1 (RS): *Yo, skp, k7; repeat from * to end.
Row 2 and all WS Rows: *K3, p6; repeat from * to end.
Row 3: *K1, yo, skp, k6; repeat from * to end.
Row 5: *K2, yo, skp, k5; repeat from * to end.
Row 7: *K3, yo, skp, k4; repeat from * to end.
Row 9: *K4, yo, skp, k3; repeat from * to end.
Row 11: *K4, k2tog, yo, k3; repeat from * to end.
Row 13: *K3, k2tog, yo, k4; repeat from * to end.
Row 15: *K2, k2tog, yo, k5; repeat from * to end.
Row 17: *K1, k2tog, yo, k6; repeat from * to end.
Row 19: *K2tog, yo, k7; repeat from * to end.
Row 20: Repeat Row 2.
Repeat Rows 1–20 for Zigzag Eyelets Flat.

Flat and in the Round

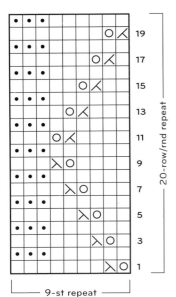

IN THE ROUND

(multiple of 9 sts; 20-rnd repeat)

Rnd 1 (RS): *Yo, skp, k7; repeat from * to end.
Rnd 2 and all Even-Numbered Rnds: *K6, p3; repeat from * to end.
Rnd 3: *K1, yo, skp, k6; repeat from * to end.
Rnd 5: *K2, yo, skp, k5; repeat from * to end.
Rnd 7: *K3, yo, skp, k4; repeat from * to end.
Rnd 9: *K4, yo, skp, k3; repeat from * to end.
Rnd 11: *K4, k2tog, yo, k3; repeat from * to end.
Rnd 13: *K3, k2tog, yo, k4; repeat from * to end.
Rnd 15: *K2, k2tog, yo, k5; repeat from * to end.
Rnd 17: *K1, k2tog, yo, k6; repeat from * to end.
Rnd 19: *K2tog, yo, k7; repeat from * to end.
Rnd 20: Repeat Rnd 2.
Repeat Rnds 1–20 for Zigzag Eyelets in the Round.

SYCAMORE EYELETS

BOTTOM-UP FLAT

(multiple of 6 sts + 3; 16-row repeat)

Row 1 (RS): Knit.
Row 2 and all WS Rows: Purl.
Row 3: Knit.
Row 5: *K4, yo, skp; repeat from * to last 3 sts, k3.
Row 7: K1, *k1, k2tog, yo, k1, yo, skp; repeat from * to last 2 sts, k2.
Rows 9 and 11: Knit.
Row 13: K1, *yo, skp, k4; repeat from * to last 2 sts, yo, skp.
Row 15: K1, *k1, yo, skp, k1, k2tog, yo; repeat from * to last 2 sts, k2.
Row 16: Purl.
Repeat Rows 1–16 for Sycamore Eyelets Bottom-Up Flat.

BOTTOM-UP IN THE ROUND

(multiple of 6 sts; 16-rnd repeat)

Rnds 1-4: Knit.
Rnd 5: *K3, yo, skp, k1; repeat from * to end.
Rnd 6: Knit.
Rnd 7: *K1, k2tog, yo, k1, yo, skp; repeat from * to end.
Rnds 8-12: Knit.
Rnd 13: *Yo, skp, k4; repeat from * to end.
Rnd 14: Knit.
Rnd 15: *K1, yo, skp, k1, k2tog, yo; repeat from * to end.
Rnd 16: Knit.
Repeat Rnds 1–16 for Sycamore Eyelets Bottom-Up in the Round.

Bottom-up Flat

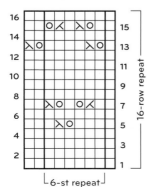

Bottom-up in the Round

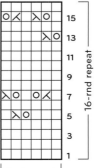

TOP-DOWN FLAT

(multiple of 6 sts + 3; 16-row repeat)

Row 1 (RS): Knit.
Row 2 and all WS Rows: Purl.
Row 3: Knit.
Row 5: K1, *k1, yo, k2tog, k1, ssk, yo; repeat from * to last 2 sts, k2.
Row 7: *Ssk, yo, k4; repeat from * to last 3 sts, ssk, yo, k1.
Rows 9 and 11: Knit.
Row 13: K1, *k1, ssk, yo, k1, yo, k2tog; repeat from * to last 2 sts, k2.
Row 15: K3, *ssk, yo, k4; repeat from * to end.
Row 16: Purl.
Repeat Rows 1–16 for Sycamore Eyelets Top-Down Flat.

TOP-DOWN IN THE ROUND

(multiple of 6 sts; 16-rnd repeat)

Rnds 1-4: Knit.
Rnd 5: *Yo, k2tog, k1, ssk, yo, k1; repeat from * to end.
Rnd 6: Knit.
Rnd 7: *K4, ssk, yo; repeat from * to end.
Rnds 8-12: Knit.
Rnd 13: *Ssk, yo, k1, yo, k2tog, k1; repeat from * to end.
Rnd 14: Knit.
Rnd 15: *K1, ssk, yo, k3; repeat from * to end.
Rnd 16: Knit.
Repeat Rnds 1–16 for Sycamore Eyelets Top-Down in the Round.

Top-Down Flat

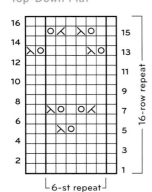

Top-Down in the Round

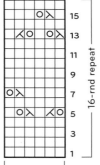

ROSETTE EYELETS

FLAT

(multiple of 10 sts + 1; 12-row repeat)

Row 1 (RS): K1, *yo, k2tog, [k1, p1] twice, k1, ssk, yo, k1; repeat from * to end.
Row 2: *P4, k1, p1, k1, p3; repeat from * to last st, p1.
Row 3: K1, *k1, yo, k2tog, p1, k1, p1, ssk, yo, k2; repeat from * to end.
Row 4: Repeat Row 2.
Row 5: Ssk, *yo, k2, p1, k1, p1, k2, yo, s2kp2; repeat from * to last 9 sts, yo, k2, p1, k1, p1, k2, yo, k2tog.
Row 6: *P1, k1, p2, k1; repeat from * to last st, p1.
Row 7: K1, *p1, k1, ssk, yo, k1, yo, k2tog, k1, p1, k1; repeat from * to end.
Row 8: *P1, k1, p7, k1; repeat from * to last st, p1.
Row 9: K1, *p1, ssk, yo, k3, yo, k2tog, p1, k1; repeat from * to end.
Row 10: Repeat Row 8.
Row 11: K1, *p1, k2, yo, s2kp2, yo, k2, p1, k1; repeat from * to end.
Row 12: Repeat Row 8.
Repeat Rows 1–12 for Rosette Eyelets Flat.

IN THE ROUND

(multiple of 10 sts; 12-rnd repeat)

Rnd 1: *K1, yo, k2tog, [k1, p1] twice, k1, ssk, yo; repeat from * to end.
Rnd 2: *K4, p1, k1, p1, k3; repeat from * to end.
Rnd 3: *K2, yo, k2tog, p1, k1, p1, ssk, yo, k1; repeat from * to end.
Rnd 4: *K4, p1, k1, p1, k3; repeat from * to last 10 sts, k4, p1, k1, p1, k2; reposition marker to before last st.
Rnd 5: *S2kp2, yo, k2, p1, k1, p1, k2, yo; repeat from * to end.
Rnd 6: *K1, p1, k2, p1, k1, p1, k2, p1; repeat from * to end.
Rnd 7: *K1, p1, k1, ssk, yo, k1, yo, k2tog, k1, p1; repeat from * to end.
Rnd 8: *K1, p1, k7, p1; repeat from * to end.
Rnd 9: *K1, p1, ssk, yo, k3, yo, k2tog, p1; repeat from * to end.
Rnd 10: Repeat Rnd 8.
Rnd 11: *K1, p1, k2, yo, s2kp2, yo, k2, p1; repeat from * to end.
Rnd 12: Repeat Rnd 8.
Repeat Rnds 1–12 for Rosette Eyelets in the Round.

Flat

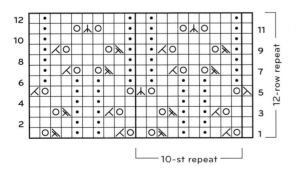

10-st repeat

12-row repeat

In the Round

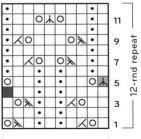

10-st repeat

12-rnd repeat

On final repeat of Rnd 4 only, end repeat 1 st before beginning-of-rnd marker; reposition beginning-of-rnd marker to before final st of rnd.

On first repeat of Rnd 5 only, work s2kp2 on what was last st of Rnd 4 and first 2 sts of Rnd 5; beginning-of-rnd marker should be before this s2kp2.

HERRINGBONE EYELETS

FLAT

(multiple of 9 sts + 3; 8-row repeat)

Row 1 (RS): K2tog, yo, *k7, k2tog, yo; repeat from * to last st, k1.
Row 2 and all WS Rows: Purl.
Row 3: K2, *yo, ssk, k4, k2tog, yo, k1; repeat from * to last st, k1.
Row 5: K2, *k1, yo, ssk, k2, k2tog, yo, k2; repeat from * to last st, k1.
Row 7: K2, *k2, yo, ssk, k2tog, yo, k3; repeat from * to last st, k1.
Row 8: Purl.
Repeat Rows 1–8 for Herringbone Eyelets Flat.

IN THE ROUND

(multiple of 9 sts; 8-rnd repeat)

Rnd 1 (RS): *K7, k2tog, yo; repeat from * to end.
Rnd 2 and all Even-Numbered Rnds: Knit.
Rnd 3: *Yo, ssk, k4, k2tog, yo, k1; repeat from * to end.
Rnd 5: *K1, yo, ssk, k2, k2tog, yo, k2; repeat from * to end.
Rnd 7: *K2, yo, ssk, k2tog, yo, k3; repeat from * to end.
Rnd 8: Purl.
Repeat Rnds 1–8 for Herringbone Eyelets in the Round.

Flat

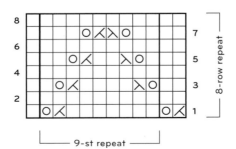

In the Round

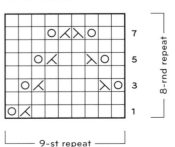

EYELET
POLKA DOTS

FLAT

(multiple of 8 sts; 12-row repeat)

Row 1 (RS): Knit.
Row 2: Purl.
Row 3: *K4, skp, [yo] twice, k2tog; repeat from * to end.
Row 4: *P1, [k1, p1] into double yo, p5; repeat from * to end.
Rows 5-8: Repeat Rows 1 and 2.
Row 9: *Skp, [yo] twice, k2tog, k4; repeat from * to end.
Row 10: *P5, [k1, p1] into double yo, p1; repeat from * to end.
Rows 11 and 12: Repeat Rows 1 and 2.
Repeat Rows 1–12 for Eyelet Polka Dots Flat.

IN THE ROUND

(multiple of 8 sts; 12-rnd repeat)

Rnds 1 and 2: Knit.
Rnd 3: *K4, skp, [yo] twice, k2tog; repeat from * to end.
Rnd 4: *K5, [k1, p1] into double yo, k1; repeat from * to end.
Rnds 5-8: Knit.
Rnd 9: *Skp, [yo] twice, k2tog, k4; repeat from * to end.
Rnd 10: *K1, [k1, p1] into double yo, k5; repeat from * to end.
Rnds 11 and 12: Knit.
Repeat Rnds 1–12 for Eyelet Polka Dots in the Round.

Flat and in the Round

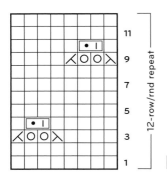

[K1, p1] into double yo.

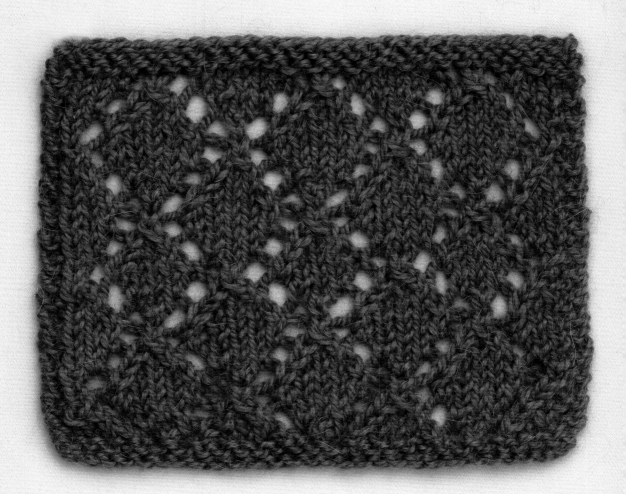

DIAMOND EYELETS

FLAT

(multiple of 8 sts + 1; 12-row repeat)

Row 1 (RS): *K2, k2tog, yo, k1, yo, k2tog, k1; repeat from * to last st, k1.
Row 2 and all WS Rows: Purl.
Row 3: *K1, k2tog, yo, k3, yo, k2tog; repeat from * to last st, k1.
Row 5: K2tog, yo, *k5, yo, sk2p, yo; repeat from * to last 7 sts, k5, yo, k2tog.
Row 7: *K1, yo, k2tog, k3, k2tog, yo; repeat from * to last st, k1.
Row 9: *K2, yo, k2tog, k1, k2tog, yo, k1; repeat from * to last st, k1.
Row 11: K3, *yo, sk2p, yo, k5; repeat from * to last 6 sts, yo, sk2p, yo, k3.
Row 12: Purl.
Repeat Rows 1–12 for Diamond Eyelets Flat.

IN THE ROUND

(multiple of 8 sts; 12-rnd repeat)

Rnd 1: *K2, k2tog, yo, k1, yo, k2tog, k1; repeat from * to end.
Rnd 2: Knit.
Rnd 3: *K1, k2tog, yo, k3, yo, k2tog; repeat from * to end.
Rnd 4: Knit to last st, reposition beginning-of-rnd marker to before last st.
Rnd 5: *Sk2p, yo, k5, yo; repeat from * to end.
Rnd 6: Knit.
Rnd 7: *K1, yo, k2tog, k3, k2tog, yo; repeat from * to end.
Rnd 8: Knit.
Rnd 9: *K2, yo, k2tog, k1, k2tog, yo, k1; repeat from * to end.
Rnd 10: Knit.
Rnd 11: *K3, yo, sk2p, yo, k2; repeat from * to end.
Rnd 12: Knit.
Repeat Rnds 1–12 for Diamond Eyelets in the Round.

Flat

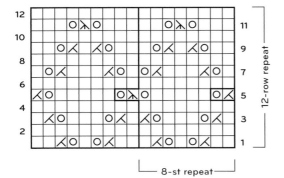

In the Round

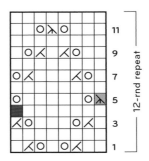

On Rnd 4, end 1 st before beginning-of-rnd marker; reposition beginning-of-rnd marker to before final st of rnd.

On first repeat of Rnd 5 only, work sk2p on what was last st of Rnd 4 and first 2 sts of Rnd 5; beginning-of-rnd marker should be before this sk2p.

LOZENGES

FLAT

(multiple of 10 sts + 3; 16-row repeat)

Row 1 (RS): K2, *yo, skp, k5, k2tog, yo, k1; repeat from * to last st, k1.
Row 2 and all WS Rows: Purl.
Row 3: K2, *k1, yo, skp, k3, k2tog, yo, k2; repeat from * to last st, k1.
Row 5: K2, *k2, yo, skp, k1, k2tog, yo, k3; repeat from * to last st, k1.
Row 7: K2, *k3, yo, sk2p, yo, k4; repeat from * to last st, k1.

Row 9: K2, *k2, k2tog, yo, k1, yo, skp, k3; repeat from * to last st, k1.
Row 11: K2, *k1, k2tog, yo, k3, yo, skp, k2; repeat from * to last st, k1.
Row 13: K2, *k2tog, yo, k5, yo, skp, k1; repeat from * to last st, k1.
Row 15: K1, k2tog, *yo, k7, yo, sk2p; repeat from * to last 10 sts, yo, k7, yo, skp, k1.
Row 16: Purl.
Repeat Rows 1–16 for Lozenges Flat.

Flat

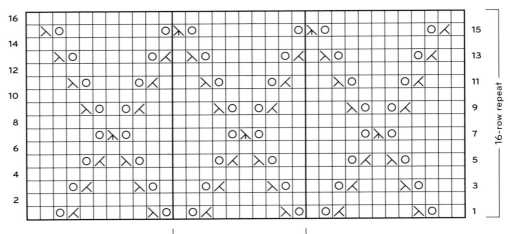

IN THE ROUND

(multiple of 10 sts; 16-rnd repeat)

Rnd 1: *K1, yo, skp, k5, k2tog, yo; repeat from * to end.

Rnd 2: Knit.

Rnd 3: *K2, yo, skp, k3, k2tog, yo, k1; repeat from * to end.

Rnd 4: Knit.

Rnd 5: *K3, yo, skp, k1, k2tog, yo, k2; repeat from * to end.

Rnd 6: Knit.

Rnd 7: *K4, yo, sk2p, yo, k3; repeat from * to end.

Rnd 8: Knit.

Rnd 9: *K3, k2tog, yo, k1, yo, skp, k2; repeat from * to end.

Rnd 10: Knit.

Rnd 11: *K2, k2tog, yo, k3, yo, skp, k1; repeat from * to end.

Rnd 12: Knit.

Rnd 13: *K1, k2tog, yo, k5, yo, skp; repeat from * to end.

Rnd 14: Knit to last st, reposition beginning-of-rnd marker to before last st.

Rnd 15: *Sk2p, yo, k7, yo; repeat from * to end.

Rnd 16: Knit.

Repeat Rnds 1–16 for Lozenges in the Round.

In the Round

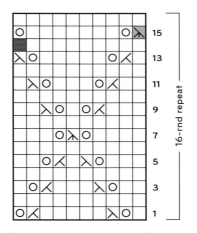

On Rnd 14, end 1 st before beginning-of-rnd marker; reposition beginning-of-rnd marker to before final st of rnd.

On first repeat of Rnd 15 only, work sk2p on what was last st of Rnd 14 and first 2 sts of Rnd 5; beginning-of-rnd marker should be before this sk2p.

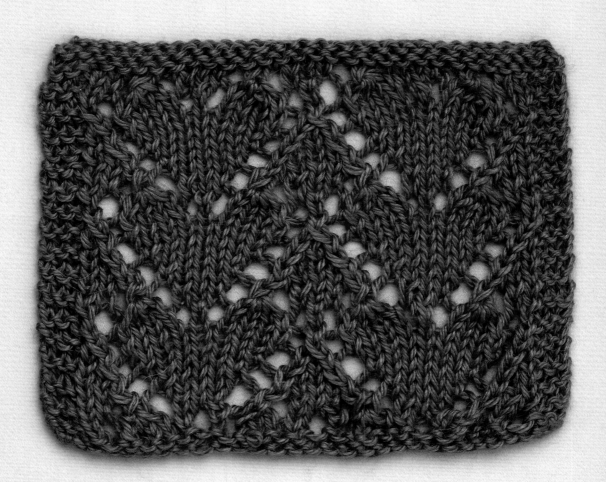

HEARTS AND DIAMONDS

Note: This pattern does not have a top-down version; if you want a top-down heart pattern, work Hearts Top-Down instead (page 130).

FLAT

(multiple of 12 sts + 1; 10-row repeat)

Note: Two sts are increased per repeat on Row 1; original st count will be restored on Row 3.

Row 1 (RS): K1, *yo, k2tog, k3, yo, k1, yo, k3, skp, yo, k1; repeat from * to end.

Row 2 and all WS Rows: Purl.

Row 3: K1, *k1, yo, k4tog, yo, k3; repeat from * to last 6 sts, yo, k4tog, yo, k2.

Row 5: K1, *k1, k2tog, yo, k5, yo, skp, k2; repeat from * to end.

Row 7: K1, *k2tog, yo, k7, yo, skp, k1; repeat from * to end.

Row 9: K2tog, yo, *k9, yo, sk2p, yo; repeat from * to last 11 sts, k9, yo, skp.

Row 10: Purl.

Repeat Rows 1–10 for Hearts and Diamonds Flat.

IN THE ROUND

(multiple of 14 sts; 10-rnd repeat)

Note: Two sts are increased per repeat on Rnd 1; original st count will be restored on Rnd 3.

Rnd 1: *K1, yo, k2tog, k3, yo, k1, yo, k3, skp, yo; repeat from * to end.

Rnd 2: Knit.

Rnd 3: *K2, yo, k4tog, yo, k3, yo, k4tog, yo, k1; repeat from * to end.

Rnd 4: Knit.

Rnd 5: *K2, k2tog, yo, k5, yo, skp, k1; repeat from * to end.

Rnd 6: Knit.

Rnd 7: *K1, k2tog, yo, k7, yo, skp; repeat from * to end.

Rnd 8: Knit to last st, reposition beginning-of-rnd marker to before last st.

Rnd 9: *Sk2p, yo, k9, yo; repeat from * to end.

Rnd 10: Knit.

Repeat Rnds 1–10 for Hearts and Diamonds in the Round.

Flat

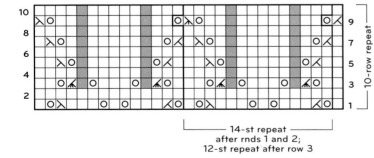

— 14-st repeat —
after rnds 1 and 2;
12-st repeat after row 3

In the Round

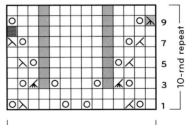

— 14-st repeat —
after rnds 1 and 2;
12-st repeat after rnd 3

■ On Rnd 8, end 1 st before beginning-of-rnd marker; reposition beginning-of-rnd marker to before final st of rnd.

▨ On first repeat of Rnd 9 only, work sk2p on last st of Rnd 8 and first 2 sts of Rnd 9; beginning-of-rnd marker should be before first sk2p of rnd.

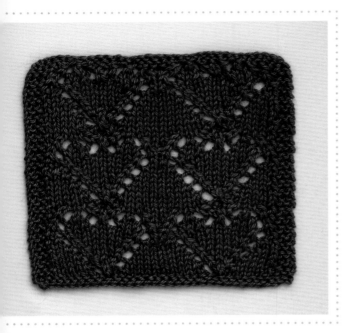

HEARTS

BOTTOM-UP FLAT

(multiple of 13 sts; 16-row repeat)

Row 1 (RS): *K5, k2tog, yo, k6; repeat from * to end.

Row 2 and all WS Rows: Purl.

Row 3: *K5, yo, s2kp2, yo, k5; repeat from * to end.

Row 5: *K4, yo, k2tog, k1, ssk, yo, k4; repeat from * to end.

Row 7: *K3, yo, k2tog, k3, ssk, yo, k3; repeat from * to end.

Row 9: *K2; yo, k2tog, k5, ssk, yo, k2; repeat from * to end.

Row 11: *K1, yo, k2tog, k7, ssk, yo, k1; repeat from * to end.

Row 13: *Ssk, yo, k3, yo, s2kp2, yo, k3, yo, k2tog; repeat from * to end.

Row 15: *K1, ssk, yo, k1, yo, k2tog, k1, ssk, yo, k1, yo, k2tog, k1; repeat from * to end.

Row 16: Purl.

Repeat Rows 1–16 for Hearts Bottom-Up Flat.

BOTTOM-UP IN THE ROUND

(multiple of 13 sts; 16-rnd repeat)

Rnd 1 (RS): *K5, k2tog, yo, k6; repeat from * to end.

Rnd 2 and all Even-Numbered Rnds: Knit.

Rnd 3: *K5, yo, s2kp2, yo, k5; repeat from * to end.

Rnd 5: *K4, yo, k2tog, k1, ssk, yo, k4; repeat from * to end.

Rnd 7: *K3, yo, k2tog, k3, ssk, yo, k3; repeat from * to end.

Rnd 9: *K2; yo, k2tog, k5, ssk, yo, k2; repeat from * to end.

Rnd 11: *K1, yo, k2tog, k7, ssk, yo, k1; repeat from * to end.

Rnd 13: *Ssk, yo, k3, yo, s2kp2, yo, k3, yo, k2tog; repeat from * to end.

Rnd 15: *K1, ssk, yo, k1, yo, k2tog, k1, ssk, yo, k1, yo, k2tog, k1; repeat from * to end.

Rnd 16: Knit.

Repeat Rnds 1–16 for Hearts Bottom-Up in the Round.

Bottom-Up Flat and in the Round

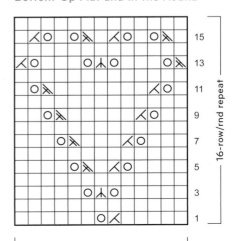

13-st repeat

16-row/rnd repeat

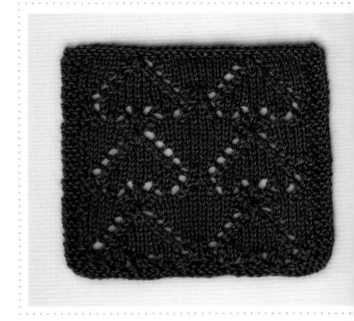

TOP-DOWN FLAT

(multiple of 13 sts; 16-row repeat)

Row 1 (RS): *[K1, k2tog, yo, k1, yo, ssk] twice, k1; repeat from * to end.
Row 2 and all WS Rows: Purl.
Row 3: *K2tog, yo, k3, yo, s2kp2, yo, k3, yo, ssk; repeat from * to end.
Row 5: *K1, yo, ssk, k7, k2tog, yo, k1; repeat from * to end.
Row 7: *K2, yo, ssk, k5, k2tog, yo, k2; repeat from * to end.
Row 9: *K3, yo, ssk, k3, k2tog, yo, k3; repeat from * to end.
Row 11: *K4, yo, ssk, k1, k2tog, yo, k4; repeat from * to end.
Row 13: *K5, yo, s2kp2, yo, k5; repeat from * to end.
Row 15: *K6, yo, k2tog, k5; repeat from * to end.
Row 16: Purl.
Repeat Rows 1–16 for Hearts Top-Down Flat.

Top-Down Flat and in the Round

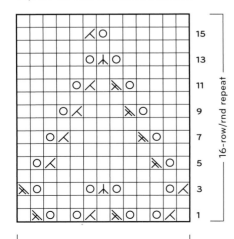

TOP-DOWN IN THE ROUND

(multiple of 13 sts; 16-rnd repeat)

Rnd 1 (RS): *[K1, k2tog, yo, k1, yo, ssk] twice, k1; repeat from * to end.
Rnd 2 and all Even-Numbered Rnds: Knit.
Rnd 3: *K2tog, yo, k3, yo, s2kp2, yo, k3, yo, ssk; repeat from * to end.
Rnd 5: *K1, yo, ssk, k7, k2tog, yo, k1; repeat from * to end.
Rnd 7: *K2, yo, ssk, k5, k2tog, yo, k2; repeat from * to end.
Rnd 9: *K3, yo, ssk, k3, k2tog, yo, k3; repeat from * to end.
Rnd 11: *K4, yo, ssk, k1, k2tog, yo, k4; repeat from * to end.
Rnd 13: *K5, yo, s2kp2, yo, k5; repeat from * to end.
Rnd 15: *K6, yo, k2tog, k5; repeat from * to end.
Rnd 16: Purl.
Repeat Rnds 1–16 for Hearts Top-Down in the Round.

HOURGLASS EYELETS

FLAT

(multiple of 6 sts + 1; 8-row repeat)

Row 1 (RS): *P1, k5; repeat from * to last st, p1.
Row 2: K1, *p5, k1; repeat from * to end.
Row 3: *K1, yo, ssk, p1, k2tog, yo; repeat from * to last st, k1.
Row 4: P1, *p2, k1, p3; repeat from * to end.
Row 5: *K3, p1, k2; repeat from * to last st, k1.
Row 6: Repeat Row 4.
Row 7: *P1, k2tog, yo, k1, yo, ssk; repeat from * to last st, p1.
Row 8: Repeat Row 2.
Repeat Rows 1–8 for Hourglass Eyelets Flat.

IN THE ROUND

(multiple of 6 sts; 8-rnd repeat)

Rnds 1 and 2: *K5, p1; repeat from * to end.
Rnd 3: *Yo, ssk, p1, k2tog, yo, k1; repeat from * to end.
Rnds 4-6: *K2, p1, k3; repeat from * to end.
Rnd 7: *K2tog, yo, k1, yo, ssk, p1; repeat from * to end.
Rnd 8: Repeat Rnd 1.
Repeat Rnds 1–8 for Hourglass Eyelets in the Round.

Flat

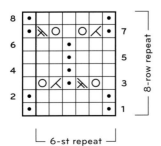

In the Round

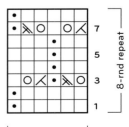

ALTERNATING LEAF STITCH

ALTERNATING LEAF STITCH

BOTTOM-UP FLAT

(multiple of 9 sts + 3; 12-row repeat)

Row 1 (RS): Knit.
Row 2: Purl.
Row 3: K3, *k2tog, k1, yo, k6; repeat from * to end.
Row 4: P1, *p6, yo, p1, p2tog; repeat from * to last 2 sts, p2.
Row 5: K1, *k2tog, k1, yo, k6; repeat from * to last 2 sts, k2.
Row 6: P3, *p6, yo, p1, p2tog; repeat from * to end.
Rows 7 and 8: Repeat Rows 1 and 2.
Row 9: *K6, yo, k1, ssk; repeat from * to last 3 sts, k3.
Row 10: P2, *ssp, p1, yo, p6; repeat from * to last st, p1.
Row 11: K2, *k6, yo, k1, ssk; repeat from * to last st, k1.
Row 12: *Ssp, p1, yo, p6; repeat from * to last 3 sts, p3.
Repeat Rows 1–12 for Alternating Leaf Stitch Bottom-Up Flat.

BOTTOM-UP IN THE ROUND

(multiple of 9 sts; 12-rnd repeat)

Rnds 1 and 2: Knit.
Rnd 3: *K6, k2tog, k1, yo; repeat from * to end.
Rnd 4: *K5, k2tog, k1, yo, k1; repeat from * to end.
Rnd 5: *K4, k2tog, k1, yo, k2; repeat from * to end.
Rnd 6: *K3, k2tog, k1, yo, k3; repeat from * to end.
Rnds 7 and 8: Knit.
Rnd 9: *Yo, k1, ssk, k6; repeat from * to end.
Rnd 10: *K1, yo, k1, ssk, k5; repeat from * to end.
Rnd 11: *K2, yo, k1, ssk, k4; repeat from * to end.
Rnd 12: *K3, yo, k1, ssk, k3; repeat from * to end.
Repeat Rnds 1–12 for Alternating Leaf Stitch Bottom-Up in the Round.

Bottom-Up Flat

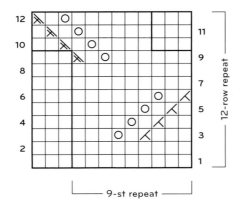

Bottom-Up in the Round

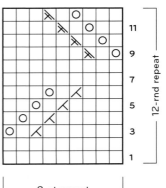

TOP-DOWN FLAT

(multiple of 9 sts + 3; 12-row repeat)

Row 1 (RS): Knit.
Row 2: Purl.
Row 3: *Ssk, k1, yo, k6; repeat from * to last 3 sts, k3.
Row 4: P2, *p6, yo, p1, ssp; repeat from * to last st, p1.
Row 5: K2, *ssk, k1, yo, k6; repeat from * to last st, p1.
Row 6: *P6, yo, p1, ssp; repeat from * to last 3 sts, p3.
Rows 7 and 8: Repeat Rows 1 and 2.
Row 9: K3, *k6, yo, k1, k2tog; repeat from * to end.
Row 10: P1, *p2tog, p1, yo, p6; repeat from * to last 2 sts, p2.
Row 11: K1, *k6, yo, k1, k2tog; repeat from * to last 2 sts, k2.
Row 12: P3, *p2tog, p1, yo, p6; repeat from * to end.
Repeat Rows 1–12 for Alternating Leaf Stitch Top-Down Flat.

TOP-DOWN IN THE ROUND

(multiple of 9 sts; 12-rnd repeat)

Rnds 1 and 2: Knit.
Rnd 3: *K3, ssk, k1, yo, k3; repeat from * to end.
Rnd 4: *K4, ssk, k1, yo, k2; repeat from * to end.
Rnd 5: *K5, ssk, k1, yo, k1; repeat from * to end.
Rnd 6: *K6, ssk, k1, yo; repeat from * to end.
Rnds 7 and 8: Knit.
Rnd 9: *K3, yo, k1, k2tog, k3; repeat from * to end.
Rnd 10: *K2, yo, k1, k2tog, k4; repeat from * to end.
Rnd 11: *K1, yo, k1, k2tog, k5; repeat from * to end.
Rnd 12: *Yo, k1, k2tog, k6; repeat from * to end.
Repeat Rnds 1–12 for Alternating Leaf Stitch Top-Down in the Round.

Top-Down Flat

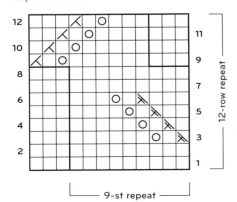

Top-Down in the Round

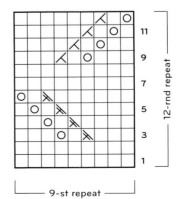

POLKA DOT BOLERO

One of my favorite motifs is the polka dot. It's just so happy-looking. If you want, you can easily substitute other eyelet patterns from this chapter—or even other stitch patterns from other chapters—just make sure that the multiple of stitches is either two, four, or eight.

STITCH PATTERNS

Eyelet Polka Dots Flat
(multiple of 8 sts; 12-row repeat)

Row 1 (RS): *K4, skp, [yo] twice, k2tog; repeat from * to end.

Row 2: *P1, [k1, p1] into double yo, p5; repeat from * to end.

Row 3: Knit.

Row 4: Purl.

Rows 5 and 6: Repeat Rows 3 and 4.

Row 7: *Skp, [yo] twice, k2tog, k4; repeat from * to end.

Row 8: *P5, [k1, p1] into double yo, p1; repeat from * to end.

Row 9: Knit.

Row 10: Purl.

Rows 11 and 12: Repeat Rows 9 and 10.

Repeat Rows 1–12 for Eyelet Polka Dots Flat.

1x1 Rib
(even number of sts; 1-row repeat)

Row 1: Slip 1, k1, *p1, k1; repeat from * to end.

Row 2: Slip 1, knit the knit sts and purl the purl sts as they face you.

Repeat Row 2 for 1x1 Rib.

NOTE

When working Yoke and neck shaping in Eyelet Polka Dots Flat, work all increased sts in St st until you have enough increased sts on either side to be able to work the entire phrase "skp, [yo] twice, k2tog" when working Row 1 or 7; do not work only a portion of the phrase. You may wish to use removable markers to mark the original sts of the pattern on Row 3 of Yoke shaping, then shift the markers as necessary to mark new full pattern repeats as you increase sts.

YOKE

Using larger circ needle, CO 1 st for Left Front, pm, 8 sts for Left Sleeve, pm, 40 (40, 48, 48, 56, 64, 72) sts for Back, pm, 8 sts for Right Sleeve, pm, 1 st for Right Front—58 (58, 66, 66, 74, 82, 90) sts.

Shape Yoke and Neck

Row 1 (RS): K1–f/b, sm, k1–f/b, [work to 1 st before marker, k1–f/b, sm, k1–f/b] 3 times—66 (66, 74, 74, 82, 90, 98) sts.

Row 2: Purl.

Row 3: K1–f/b, [k1–f/b, sm, k1–f/b, work Eyelet Polka Dots Flat to 1 st before next marker] 3 times, k1–f/b, sm, [k1–f/b] twice—76 (76, 84, 84, 92, 100, 108) sts.

FINISHED MEASUREMENTS

32 (34 ½, 37 ½, 42 ½, 48, 50 ½, 56)" [81.5 (87.5, 95.5, 108, 122, 128.5, 142) cm] bust, wrapped

YARN

Blue Sky Alpacas Melange (100% baby alpaca; 110 yards / 50 grams): 4 (5, 5, 6, 7, 8, 8) hanks #809 Toasted Almond

NEEDLES

One 29" (70 cm) long or longer circular (circ) needle size US 3 (3.25 mm)

One set of five double-pointed needles (dpns) size US 3 (3.25 mm)

One pair straight needles size US 2 (2.5 mm)

Change needle size if necessary to obtain correct gauge.

NOTIONS

Stitch markers; removable markers (optional); waste yarn

GAUGE

24 sts and 28 rows = 4" (10 cm) in Eyelet Polka Dot, using larger needles

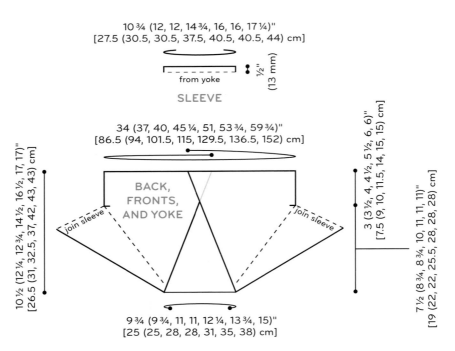

10 ¾ (12, 12, 14 ¾, 16, 16, 17 ¼)"
[27.5 (30.5, 30.5, 37.5, 40.5, 40.5, 44) cm]

from yoke

½" (13 mm)

SLEEVE

34 (37, 40, 45 ¼, 51, 53 ¾, 59 ¾)"
[86.5 (94, 101.5, 115, 129.5, 136.5, 152) cm]

BACK, FRONTS, AND YOKE

10 ½ (12 ¼, 12 ¾, 14 ½, 16 ½, 17, 17)"
[26.5 (31, 32.5, 37, 42, 43, 43) cm]

join sleeve

join sleeve

3 (3 ½, 4, 4 ½, 5 ½, 6, 6)"
[7.5 (9, 10, 11.5, 14, 15, 15) cm]

7 ½ (8 ¾, 8 ¾, 10, 11, 11, 11)"
[19 (22, 22, 25.5, 28, 28, 28) cm]

9 ¾ (9 ¾, 11, 11, 12 ¼, 13 ¾, 15)"
[25 (25, 28, 28, 31, 35, 38) cm]

Note: Piece is worked from the top down.

Row 4: Purl.

Row 5: Continuing in patterns as established, and working increased sts as per NOTE, [work to 1 st before marker, k1-f/b, sm, k1-f/b] 4 times, work to end—84 (84, 92, 92, 100, 108, 116) sts.

Row 6: Purl.

Row 7: K1-f/b, [work to 1 st before marker, k1-f/b, sm, k1-f/b] 4 times, work to last st, k1-f/b—94 (94, 102, 102, 110, 118, 126) sts.

Row 8: Purl.

Note: Eyelet Polka Dots Flat will begin on the Fronts while Yoke and neck shaping are worked at the same time; please read entire section through before beginning.

Repeat Rows 5–8 five times. AT THE SAME TIME, beginning on Row 15, and continuing

Yoke and neck shaping as established, begin Eyelet Polka Dots Flat on Fronts from Charts. Continue to work shaping and st patterns as established, working increased sts into pattern as per NOTE, until you have completed Row 28 of Chart—184 (184, 192, 192, 200, 208, 216) sts [22 sts each Front, 36 sts each Sleeve, 68 (68, 76, 76, 84, 92, 100) sts for Back].

Next Row: Continuing to work Eyelet Polka Dots Flat as established, increase 8 Yoke sts on RS rows every other row 10 (14, 14, 18, 22, 22, 22) times as established on Row 5 and, AT THE SAME TIME, increase 1 st at each neck edge every 4 rows 2 (7, 4, 9, 11, 10, 4) times, then every other row 7 (1, 7, 1, 0, 3, 15) time(s)—282 (312, 326, 356, 398, 410, 430) sts [41 (44, 47, 50, 55, 57, 63) sts each Front, 56 (64, 64, 72, 80, 80, 80) sts each Sleeve, 88 (96, 104, 112, 128, 136, 144) sts for Back]. Purl 1 row.

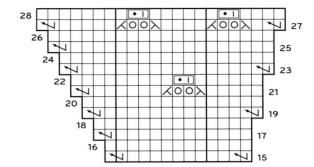

Right Front

Left Front

BODY

Next Row (RS): Working Eyelet Polka Dots Flat across all sts, work across Left Front, transfer next 56 (64, 64, 72, 80, 80, 80) sts to waste yarn for Left Sleeve, removing markers, CO 8 (8, 8, 16, 16, 16, 24) sts for underarm, work across 88 (96, 104, 112, 128, 136, 144) sts of Back, transfer next 56 (64, 64, 72, 80, 80, 80) sts to waste yarn for Right Sleeve, removing markers, CO 8 (8, 8, 16, 16, 16, 24) sts for underarm, work to end—186 (200, 214, 244, 270, 282, 318) sts. Purl 1 row.

Continuing in pattern as established, increase 1 st at each neck edge every 4 rows 0 (0, 0, 1, 1, 0, 0) time(s), then every other row 9 (11, 13, 13, 17, 20, 20) times, ending with a WS row—204 (222, 240, 272, 306, 322, 358) sts. BO all sts.

SLEEVES

Transfer Sleeve sts from waste yarn to dpns. With RS facing, join yarn at underarm; work to end, pick up and knit 4 (4, 4, 8, 8, 8, 12) sts from sts CO for underarm, pm for beginning of rnd, pick up and knit 4 (4, 4, 8, 8, 8, 12) sts from sts CO for underarm—64 (72, 72, 88, 96, 96, 104) sts. Join for working in the rnd. Knit 3 rnds. BO all sts.

TIE

Using smaller needles, CO 8 sts. Begin 1x1 Rib; work even until piece measures 85 (87, 89, 90, 94, 96, 97)" [216 (221, 226, 228.5, 239, 244, 246.5) cm] from the beginning. BO all sts in pattern.

FINISHING

Neckband

With RS facing, using larger circ needle, and beginning at lower Right Front edge, pick up and knit approximately 2 sts for every 3 rows and 1 st for every CO st around neck opening. Begin St st; work even for 3 rows. BO all sts.

Block as desired.

Place marker 14 (14, 14, 14, 16, 16, 16)" [35.5 (35.5, 35.5, 35.5, 40.5, 40.5, 40.5) cm] in from one end of Tie. Sew side edge of Tie, beginning with marker at lower right Front corner, to BO edge of Body, easing Tie as necessary; the long free length of the Tie will wrap around your back to tie at the right Front corner.

CABLES

Cables are classic and totally versatile, and they are almost always worked on a background of purl stitches, which gives the fabric a nice, embossed effect. If you don't want the wrong side of a cable to show, make sure you use them for projects where the wrong side won't be visible (like hats or socks). You can use cables for an allover pattern on a sweater or just use a combination of them for a centered cable panel, much like the Royal Cable Vest pattern on page 172.

With a little patience, some note taking, and a few calculations, it's fun to combine your favorite cable stitches and come up with a pattern of your own. When planning your masterpiece, keep in mind that cables tend to pull the fabric together, so swatching and measuring is an absolute necessity! If you don't think you're quite ready to design an entire sweater from the get-go, you might simply take a favorite sweater pattern that you have on hand and insert a panel of your own design. Usually, a panel will run down the center front of a garment and be flanked by an area of Reverse Stockinette stitch so the cables stand out. If you do this, look for one main cable and perhaps another with a smaller multiple of stitches to run along both sides. Add Reverse Stockinette between the cables and count the number of stitches you need in total. If you are centering the cable panel, simply follow the directions in Example #3 on page 16.

FOUR-STITCH CABLE

FLAT

(panel of 4 sts worked on a background of Rev St st; 4-row repeat)

Row 1 (RS): K4.
Row 2: P4.
Row 3: C4B (for right cross) or C4F (for left cross).
Row 4: P4.
Repeat Rows 1–4 for Four-Stitch Cable Flat.

IN THE ROUND

(panel of 4 sts worked on a background of Rev St st; 4-rnd repeat)

Rnds 1 and 2: K4.
Rnd 3: C4B (for right cross) or C4F (for left cross).
Rnd 4: K4.
Repeat Rnds 1–4 for Four-Stitch Cable in the Round.

Flat and in the Round

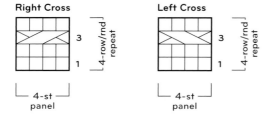

SIX-STITCH CABLE

FLAT

(panel of 6 sts worked on a background of Rev St st; 6-row repeat)

Row 1 (RS): K6.
Row 2: P6.
Rows 3 and 4: Repeat Rows 1 and 2.
Row 5: C6B (for right cross) or C6F (for left cross).
Row 6: P6.
Repeat Rows 1-6 for Six-Stitch Cable Flat.

IN THE ROUND

(panel of 6 sts worked on a background of Rev St st; 6-rnd repeat)

Rnds 1-4: K6.
Rnd 5: C6B (for right cross) or C6F (for left cross).
Rnd 6: K6.
Repeat Rnds 1-6 for Six-Stitch Cable in the Round.

Flat and in the Round

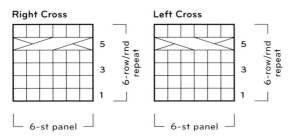

PICOT EYELET CABLE

IN THE ROUND

(panel of 6 sts worked on a background of Rev St st; 18-rnd repeat)

Rnd 1: K1, k2tog, [yo] twice, ssk, k1.
Rnd 2: K2, [k1, p1] into double yo, k2.
Rnds 3 and 4: K6.
Rnd 5: Slip next 4 sts to cn, hold to front, k2, slip last 2 sts from cn back to left-hand needle, k2, k2 from cn.
Rnd 6: K6.
Rnds 7-18: Repeat Rnds 1–4.
Repeat Rnds 1–18 for Picot Eyelet Cable in the Round.

FLAT

(panel of 6 sts worked on a background of Rev St st; 18-row repeat)

Row 1 (RS): K1, k2tog, [yo] twice, ssk, k1.
Row 2: P2, [k1, p1] into double yo, p2.
Row 3: K6.
Row 4: P6.
Row 5: Slip next 4 sts to cn, hold to front, k2, slip last 2 sts from cn back to left-hand needle, k2, k2 from cn.
Row 6: P6.
Rows 7-18: Repeat Rows 1–4.
Repeat Rows 1–18 for Picot Eyelet Cable Flat.

Flat and in the Round

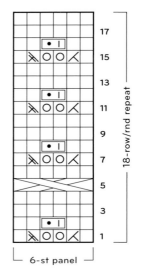

[• I] [K1, p1] into double yo.

BIG AND LITTLE CABLES

FLAT

(panel of 8 sts worked on a background of
Rev St st; 18-row repeat)

Row 1 (RS): K3, p2, k3.
Row 2 and all WS Rows: Knit the knit sts and
purl the purl sts as they face you.
Rows 3, 5, and 7: Repeat Row 2.
Row 9: C8F.
Rows 11 and 13: K8.
Row 15: Slip 4 sts to cn, hold to front, k3, p1,
[p1, k3] from cn.
Rows 17 and 18: Repeat Row 2.
Repeat Rows 1–18 for Big and Little Cables Flat.

IN THE ROUND

(panel of 8 sts worked on a background of
Rev St st; 18-rnd repeat)

Rnd 1-8: K3, p2, k3.
Rnd 9: C8F.
Rnds 10-14: K8.
Rnd 15: Slip 4 sts to cn, hold to front, k3, p1,
[p1, k3] from cn.
Rnds 17-18: Repeat Rnd 1.
Repeat Rnds 1–18 for Big and Little Cables
in the Round.

Flat and in the Round

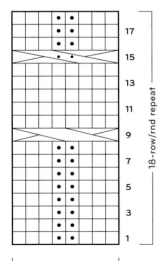

8-st panel

Slip 4 sts to cn, hold to front,
k3, p1, [p1, k3] from cn.

HONEYCOMB

FLAT

(multiple of 6 sts; 10-row repeat)

Row 1 (RS): *P2, k2, p2; repeat from * to end.
Row 2 and all WS Rows: Knit the knit sts and purl the purl sts as they face you.
Row 3: Repeat Row 2.
Row 5: *1/2 RC-p, 1/2 LC-p; repeat from * to end.
Row 7: Repeat Row 2.
Row 9: *1/2 LC-p, 1/2 RC-p; repeat from * to end.
Row 10: Repeat Row 2.
Repeat Rows 1–10 for Honeycomb Flat.

IN THE ROUND

(multiple of 6 sts; 10-rnd repeat)

Rnds 1-4: *P2, k2, p2; repeat from * to end.
Rnd 5: *1/2 RC-p, 1/2 LC-p; repeat from * to end.
Rnds 6-8: *K1, p4, k1; repeat from * to end.
Rnd 9: *1/2 LC-p, 1/2 RC-p; repeat from * to end.
Rnd 10: Repeat Rnd 1.
Repeat Rnds 1–10 for Honeycomb in the Round.

Flat and in the Round

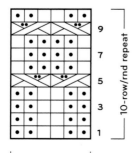

6-st repeat

10-row/rnd repeat

SAND PATTERN

FLAT

(multiple of 12 sts; 8-row repeat)

Row 1 (RS): Knit.
Row 2 and all WS Rows: Purl.
Row 3: *C6F, k6; repeat from * to end.
Row 5: Knit.
Row 7: *K6, C6B; repeat from * to end.
Row 8: Purl.
Repeat Rows 1–8 for Sand Pattern Flat.

IN THE ROUND

(multiple of 12 sts; 8-rnd repeat)

Rnds 1 and 2: Knit.
Rnd 3: *C6F, k6; repeat from * to end.
Rnds 4–6: Knit.
Rnd 7: *K6, C6B; repeat from * to end.
Rnd 8: Knit.
Repeat Rnds 1–8 for Sand Pattern in the Round.

Flat and in the Round

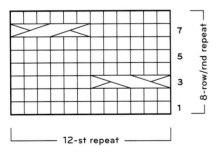

CABLES

LOBSTER CLAW CABLES

BOTTOM-UP FLAT

(panel of 8 sts worked on a background of Rev St st; 8-row repeat)

Note: Pattern begins with a WS row.
Row 1 (WS): K8.
Row 2: K1, p6, k1.
Row 3: P2, k4, p2.
Row 4: K2, p4, k2.
Rows 5 and 6: Repeat Rows 3 and 4.
Row 7: Repeat Row 3.
Row 8: Slip 2 sts to cn, hold to front, p2, yo, ssk from cn, slip 2 sts to cn, hold to back, k2tog, yo, p2 from cn.
Repeat Rows 1–8 for Lobster Claw Cables Bottom–Up Flat.

BOTTOM-UP IN THE ROUND

(panel of 8 sts worked on a background of Rev St st; 8-rnd repeat)

Rnd 1: P8.
Rnd 2: K1, p6, k1.
Rnds 3-7: K2, p4, k2.
Rnd 8: Slip 2 sts to cn, hold to front, p2, yo, ssk from cn, slip 2 sts to cn, hold to back, k2tog, yo, p2 from cn.
Repeat Rnds 1–8 for Lobster Claw Cables Bottom–Up in the Round.

Bottom-Up Flat and in the Round

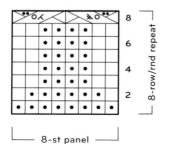

Slip 2 sts to cn, hold to back, k2tog, yo, p2 from cn.

Slip 2 sts to cn, hold to front, p2, yo, ssk from cn.

Note: Chart for Bottom-Up Flat pattern begins with a WS row.

TOP-DOWN FLAT

(panel of 8 sts worked on a background of
Rev St st; 8-row repeat)

Row 1 (RS): Slip 2 sts to cn, hold to back,
k2tog, yo, p2 from cn, slip 2 sts to cn, hold to
front, p2, yo, ssk from cn.
Row 2: P2, k4, p2.
Row 3: K2, p4, k2.
Rows 4 and 5: Repeat Rows 2 and 3.
Row 6: Repeat Row 2.
Row 7: K1, p6, k1.
Row 8: K8.
Repeat Rows 1–8 for Lobster Claw Cables
Top-Down Flat.

TOP-DOWN IN THE ROUND

(panel of 8 worked on a background of Rev St
st; 8-rnd repeat)

Rnd 1: Slip 2 sts to cn, hold to back, k2tog, yo,
p2 from cn, slip 2 sts to cn, hold to front, p2, yo,
ssk from cn.
Rnds 2-6: K2, p4, k2.
Rnd 7: K1, p6, k1.
Rnd 8: P8.
Repeat Rnds 1–8 for Lobster Claw Cables
Top-Down in the Round.

Top-Down Flat and in the Round

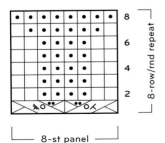

8-st panel

LACY CABLES

FLAT

(multiple of 11 sts + 7; 32-row repeat)

Row 1 (RS): K1, *yo, ssk, k1, k2tog, yo, k6; repeat from * to last 6 sts, yo, ssk, k1, k2tog, yo, k1.
Row 2 and all WS Rows: Purl.
Row 3: K2, *yo, sk2p, yo, k1, C6B, k1; repeat from * to last 5 sts, yo, sk2p, yo, k2.
Row 5: Repeat Row 1.
Row 7: K2, *yo, sk2p, yo, k8; repeat from * to last 5 sts, yo, sk2p, yo, k2.
Row 9: Repeat Row 1.
Row 11: K2, *yo, sk2p, yo, k1, C6F, k1; repeat from * to last 5 sts, yo, sk2p, yo, k2.
Rows 13-19: Repeat Rows 5–11.
Rows 31-25: Repeat Rows 5–9.
Rows 27-32: Repeat Rows 3–8.
Repeat Rows 1–32 for Lacy Cables Flat.

IN THE ROUND

(multiple of 11 sts; 32-rnd repeat)

Rnd 1: *Yo, ssk, k1, k2tog, yo, k6; repeat from * to end.
Rnd 2 and all Even-Numbered Rnds: Knit.
Rnd 3: *K1, yo, sk2p, yo, k1, C6B; repeat from * to end.
Rnd 5: Repeat Rnd 1.
Rnd 7: *K1, yo, sk2p, yo, k7; repeat from * to end.
Rnd 9: Repeat Rnd 1.
Rnd 11: *K1, yo, sk2p, yo, k1, C6F; repeat from * to end.
Rnds 13-19: Repeat Rnds 5–11.
Rnds 31-25: Repeat Rnds 5–9.
Rnds 27-32: Repeat Rnds 3–8.
Repeat Rnds 1–32 for Lacy Cables in the Round.

Flat

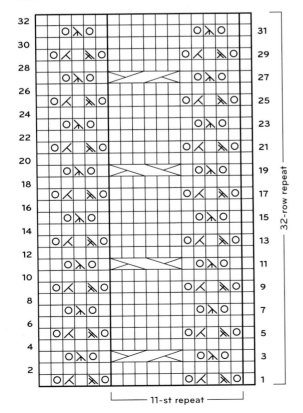

In the Round

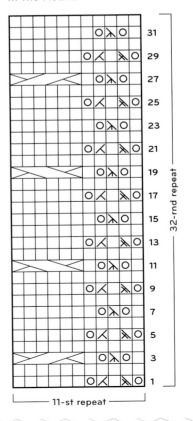

STAIRCASE CABLES

FLAT

(panel of 9 sts worked on a background of Rev St st; 4-row repeat)

Row 1 (RS): K4, k1-tbl, C4B.
Row 2: P4, p1-tbl, p4.
Row 3: C4F, k1-tbl, k4.
Row 4: Repeat Row 2.
Repeat Rows 1–4 for Staircase Cables Flat.

IN THE ROUND

(panel of 9 sts worked on a background of Rev St st; 4-rnd repeat)

Rnd 1: K4, k1-tbl, C4B.
Rnd 2: K4, k1-tbl, k4.
Rnd 3: C4F, k1-tbl, k4.
Rnd 4: Repeat Rnd 2.
Repeat Rnds 1–4 for Staircase Cables in the Round.

Flat and in the Round

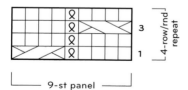

Note: To convert this pattern for working top-down, simply work C4B instead of C4F, and C4F instead of C4B.

HUGS AND KISSES CABLES

FLAT

(panel of 8 sts worked on a background of
Rev St st; 16-row repeat)

Row 1 (RS): K8.
Row 2: P8.
Row 3: C4B, C4F.
Row 4: P8.
Rows 5-8: Repeat Rows 1–4.
Row 9: K8.
Row 10: P8.
Row 11: C4F, C4B.
Row 12: P8.
Rows 13-16: Repeat Rows 9–12.
Repeat Rows 1–16 for Hugs and Kisses Cables Flat.

IN THE ROUND

(panel of 8 sts worked on a background of
Rev St st; 16-rnd repeat)

Rnds 1 and 2: K8.
Rnd 3: C4B, C4F.
Rnd 4: K8.
Rnds 5-8: Repeat Rnds 1–4.
Rnds 9 and 10: K8.
Rnd 11: C4F, C4B.
Rnd 12: K8.
Rnds 13-16: Repeat Rnds 9–12.
Repeat Rnds 1–16 for Hugs and Kisses Cables
in the Round.

Flat and in the Round

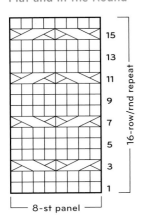

ELONGATED CABLES

FLAT

(panel of 12 sts worked on a background of Rev St st; 16-row repeat)

Row 1 (RS): K4, p1, k2, p1, k4.
Row 2 and all WS rows: Knit the knit sts and purl the purl sts as they face you.
Row 3: Repeat Row 2.
Rows 5, 7, and 9: K4, p1, RC, p1, k4.
Rows 11 and 13: Repeat Row 2.
Row 15: C4F, p1, k2, p1, C4F.
Row 16: Repeat Row 2.
Repeat Rows 1–16 for Elongated Cables Flat.

IN THE ROUND

(panel of 12 sts worked on a background of Rev St st; 16-rnd repeat)

Rnds 1-4: K4, p1, k2, p1, k4.
Rnd 5: K4, p1, RC, p1, k4.
Rnd 6: Repeat Rnd 1.
Rnds 7-10: Repeat Rnds 5 and 6.
Rnds 11-14: Repeat Rnd 1.
Rnd 15: C4F, p1, k2, p1, C4F.
Rnd 16: Repeat Rnd 1.
Repeat Rnds 1–16 for Elongated Cables in the Round.

Flat and in the Round

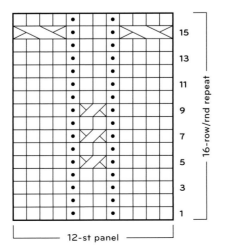

CABLES

OPULENT CABLES

FLAT

(panel of 13 sts worked on a background of Rev St st; 20-row repeat)

Row 1 (RS): K6, p1, k6.
Row 2: P6, k1, p6.
Rows 3-12: Repeat Rows 1 and 2.
Row 13: Slip 6 sts to cn, hold to front, k6, p1, k6 from cn.
Row 14: Repeat Row 2.
Rows 15-18: Repeat Rows 1 and 2.
Row 19: Repeat Row 13.
Row 20: Repeat Row 2.
Repeat Rows 1–20 for Opulent Cables Flat.

IN THE ROUND

(panel of 13 sts worked on a background of Rev St st; 20-rnd repeat)

Rnds 1-12: K6, p1, k6.
Rnd 13: Slip 6 sts to cn, hold to front, k6, p1, k6 from cn.
Rnds 14-18: Repeat Rnd 1.
Rnd 19: Repeat Rnd 13.
Rnd 20: Repeat Rnd 1.
Repeat Rnds 1–20 for Opulent Cables in the Round.

Flat and in the Round

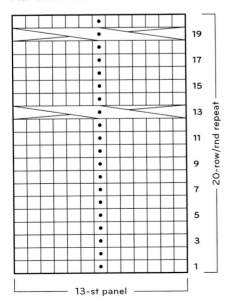

Slip 6 sts to cn, hold to front,
p1, k6 from cn.

WOVEN CABLE

FLAT

(panel of 18 sts worked on a background of Rev St st; 8-row repeat)

Row 1 (RS): K18.
Row 2 and all WS Rows: P18.
Row 3: [C6B] 3 times.
Row 5: K18.
Row 7: K3, [C6F] twice, k3.
Row 8: P18.
Repeat Rows 1–8 for Woven Cable Flat.

IN THE ROUND

(panel of 18 sts worked on a background of Rev St st; 8-rnd repeat)

Rnds 1 and 2: K18.
Rnd 3: [C6B] 3 times.
Rnds 4-6: K18.
Rnd 7: K3, [C6F] twice, k3.
Rnd 8: K18.
Repeat Rnds 1–8 for Woven Cable in the Round.

Flat and in the Round

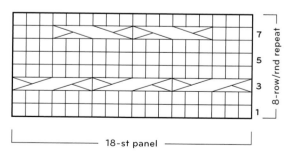

8-row/rnd repeat

18-st panel

WINDING CABLES

FLAT

(panel of 6 sts worked on a background of
Rev St st; 16-row repeat)

Row 1 (RS): K6.
Row 2 and all WS Rows: P6.
Row 3: K6.
Row 5: C6F.
Rows 7, 9, and 11: K6.
Row 13: C6B.
Row 15: K6.
Row 16: P6.
Repeat Rows 1-16 for Winding Cables Flat.

IN THE ROUND

(panel of 6 sts worked on a background of
Rev St st; 16-rnd repeat)

Rnds 1-4: K6.
Rnd 5: C6F.
Rnds 6-12: K6.
Rnd 13: C6B.
Rnds 14-16: K6.
Repeat Rnds 1-16 for Winding Cables in the
Round.

Flat and in the Round

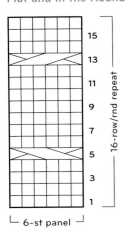

6-st panel

16-row/rnd repeat

STAGHORN CABLE

BOTTOM-UP FLAT

(panel of 16 sts worked on a background of
Rev St st; 6-row repeat)

Note: Pattern begins with a WS row.
Row 1 (WS): P16.
Row 2: K4, C4B, C4F, k4.
Row 3: P16.
Row 4: K2, C4B, k4, C4F, k2.
Row 5: P16.
Row 6: C4B, k8, C4F.
Repeat Rows 1–6 for Staghorn Cable Bottom-Up Flat.

BOTTOM-UP IN THE ROUND

(panel of 16 sts worked on a background of
Rev St st; 6-rnd repeat)

Rnd 1: K16.
Rnd 2: K4, C4B, C4F, k4.
Rnd 3: K16.
Rnd 4: K2, C4B, k4, C4F, k2.
Rnd 5: K16.
Rnd 6: C4B, k8, C4F.
Repeat Rnds 1–6 for Staghorn Cable Bottom-Up in the Round.

TOP-DOWN FLAT

(panel of 16 sts worked on a background of
Rev St st; 6-row repeat)

Note: Pattern begins with a WS row.
Row 1 (WS): P16.
Row 2: C4F, k8, C4B.
Row 3: P16.
Row 4: K2, C4F, k4, C4B, k2.
Row 5 P16.
Row 6: K4, C4F, C4B, k4.
Repeat Rows 1–6 for Staghorn Cable Top-Down Flat.

TOP-DOWN IN THE ROUND

(panel of 16 sts worked on a background of
Rev St st; 6-rnd repeat)

Rnd 1: K16.
Rnd 2: C4F, k8, C4B.
Rnd 3: K16.
Rnd 4: K2, C4F, k4, C4B, k2.
Rnd 5: K16.
Rnd 6: K4, C4F, C4B, k4.
Repeat Rnds 1–6 for Staghorn Cable Top-Down in the Round.

Bottom-Up Flat and in the Round

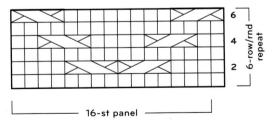

16-st panel

6-row/rnd repeat

Note: Chart for Flat pattern begins with a WS row.

Top-Down Flat and in the Round

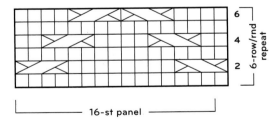

16-st panel

6-row/rnd repeat

Note: Chart for Flat pattern begins with a WS row.

WILD OATS

FLAT

(multiple of 4 sts + 1; 8-row repeat)

Row 1 (RS): *K2, slip 1, k1; repeat from * to last st, k1.
Row 2: P1, *p1, slip 1, p2; repeat from * to end.
Row 3: *1/2 RC, k1; repeat from * to last st, k1.
Row 4: Purl.
Rows 5 and 6: Repeat Rows 1 and 2.
Row 7: K1, *k1, 1/2 LC; repeat from * to end.
Row 8: Purl.
Repeat Rows 1–8 for Wild Oats Flat.

IN THE ROUND

(multiple of 4 sts; 8-rnd repeat)

Rnds 1 and 2: *K2, slip 1, k1; repeat from * to end.
Rnd 3: *1/2 RC, k1; repeat from * to end.
Rnd 4: Knit.
Rnds 5 and 6: Repeat Rnd 1.
Rnd 7: K1, *k1, 1/2 LC; repeat from * to end.
Note: On final repeat, work 1/2 LC on last 2 sts of Rnd 7 and first st of Rnd 8; reposition beginning-of-rnd marker to before last st of 1/2 LC.
Rnd 8: Knit.
Repeat Rnds 1–8 for Wild Oats in the Round.

Flat

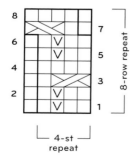

In the Round

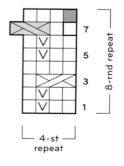

 On last repeat of 1/2 LC on Rnd 7, work 1/2 LC on last 2 sts of Rnd 7 and first st of Rnd 8; reposition beginning-of-rnd marker to before last st of 1/2 LC.

On first repeat of Rnd 8, omit this st; it was worked with last 2 sts of Rnd 7. Work as knit st on subsequent repeats.

ROUNDED HONEYCOMB

FLAT

(panel of 8 sts worked on a background of
Rev St st; 8-row repeat)

Row 1 (RS): K8.
Row 2 and all WS Rows: P8.
Row 3: C4F, C4B.
Row 5: K8.
Row 7: C4B, C4F.
Row 8: P8.
Repeat Rows 1–8 for Rounded Honeycomb Flat.

IN THE ROUND

(panel of 8 sts worked on a background of
Rev St st; 8-rnd repeat)

Rnds 1 and 2: K8.
Rnd 3: C4F, C4B.
Rnds 4-6: K8.
Rnd 7: C4B, C4F.
Rnd 8: K8.
Repeat Rnds 1–8 for Rounded Honeycomb
in the Round.

Flat and in the Round

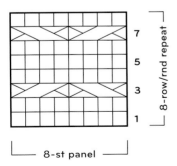

8-row/rnd repeat

8-st panel

SCARAB CHECKS

FLAT

(multiple of 12 sts + 2; 20-row repeat)

Row 1 (RS): K1, *k3, p6, k3; repeat from * to last st, k1.

Row 2: Knit the knit sts and purl the purl sts as they face you.

Row 3: K1, *k2, 1/3 LC-p, 1/3 RC-p, k2; repeat from * to last st, k1.

Row 4: Repeat Row 2.

Row 5: K1, *k1, 1/3 LC-p, k2, 1/3 RC-p, k1; repeat from * to last st, k1.

Row 6: Repeat Row 2.

Row 7: K1, *1/3 LC-p, k4, 1/3 RC-p; repeat from * to last st, k1.

Row 8: K1, *k3, p6, k3; repeat from * to last st, k1.

Rows 9-12: Repeat Row 2.

Row 13: K1, *1/3 RC-p, k4, 1/3 LC-p; repeat from * to last st, k1.

Row 14: Repeat Row 2.

Row 15: K1, *k1, 1/3 RC-p, k2, 1/3 LC-p, k1; repeat from * to last st, k1.

Row 16: Repeat Row 2.

Row 17: K1, *k2, 1/3 RC-p, 1/3 LC-p, k2; repeat from * to last st, k1.

Row 18: Repeat Row 2.

Rows 19 and 20: Repeat Rows 1 and 2.
Repeat Rows 1-20 for Scarab Checks Flat.

Flat

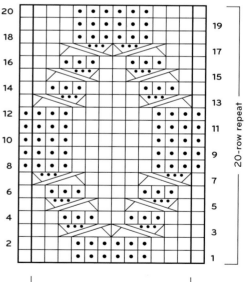

IN THE ROUND

(multiple of 12 sts; 20-rnd repeat)

Rnd 1: *K3, p6, k3; repeat from * to end.

Rnd 2: Knit the knit sts and purl the purl sts as they face you.

Rnd 3: *K2, 1/3 LC–p, 1/3 RC–p, k2; repeat from * to end.

Rnd 4: Repeat Rnd 2.

Rnd 5: *K1, 1/3 LC–p, k2, 1/3 RC–p, k1; repeat from * to end.

Rnd 6: Repeat Rnd 2.

Rnd 7: *1/3 LC–p, k4, 1/3 RC–p; repeat from * to end.

Rnds 8-12: Repeat Rnd 2.

Rnd 13: *1/3 RC–p, k4, 1/3 LC–p; repeat from * to end.

Rnd 14: Repeat Rnd 2.

Rnd 15: *K1, 1/3 RC–p, k2, 1/3 LC–p, k1; repeat from * to end.

Rnd 16: Repeat Rnd 2.

Rnd 17: *K2, 1/3 RC–p, 1/3 LC–p, k2; repeat from * to end.

Rnds 18-20: Repeat Rnd 1.

Repeat Rnds 1–20 for Scarab Checks in the Round.

In the Round

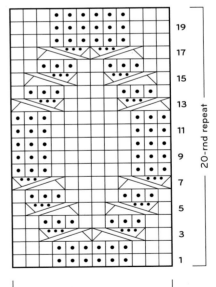

TILTED CABLE LADDERS

FLAT

(panel of 11 sts worked on a background of Rev St st; 24-row repeat)

Note: Pattern begins with a WS row.
Row 1 (WS): P5, k1, p5.
Row 2: K1, [yo, k2tog] twice, p1, k5.
Row 3: P4, k2, p5.
Row 4: K1, [yo, k2tog] twice, p2, k4.
Row 5: Repeat Row 3.
Row 6: K1, [yo, k2tog] twice, p2, C4B.
Rows 7-10: Repeat Rows 3-6.
Rows 11 and 12: Repeat Rows 3 and 4.
Row 13: Repeat Row 1.
Row 14: K5, p1, [ssk, yo] twice, k1.
Row 15: P5, k2, p4.
Row 16: K4, p2, [ssk, yo] twice, k1.
Row 17: Repeat Row 15.
Row 18: C4F, p2, [ssk, yo] twice, k1.
Rows 19-22: Repeat Rows 15-18.
Rows 23 and 24: Repeat Rows 15 and 16.
Repeat Rows 1-24 for Tilted Cable Ladders Flat.

IN THE ROUND

(panel of 11 sts worked on a background of Rev St st; 24-rnd repeat)

Rnd 1: K5, p1, k5.
Rnd 2: K1, [yo, k2tog] twice, p1, k5.
Rnd 3: K5, p2, k4.
Rnd 4: K1, [yo, k2tog] twice, p2, k4.
Rnd 5: Repeat Rnd 3.
Rnd 6: K1, [yo, k2tog] twice, p2, C4B.
Rnds 7-10: Repeat Rnds 3-6.
Rnds 11 and 12: Repeat Rnds 3 and 4.
Rnd 13: Repeat Rnd 1.
Rnd 14: K5, p1, [ssk, yo] twice, k1.
Rnd 15: K4, p2, k5.
Rnd 16: K4, p2, [ssk, yo] twice, k1.
Rnd 17: Repeat Rnd 15.
Rnd 18: C4F, p2, [ssk, yo] twice, k1.
Rnds 19-22: Repeat Rnds 15-18.
Rnds 23 and 24: Repeat Rnds 15 and 16.
Repeat Rnds 1-24 for Tilted Cable Ladders in the Round.

Flat and in the Round

Note: Chart for Flat pattern begins with a WS row.

11-st panel

24-row/rnd repeat

BRAID CABLE

FLAT

(panel of 9 sts worked on a background of Rev St st; 8-row repeat)

Note: Pattern begins with a WS row.
Row 1 (WS): K1, p4, k2, p2.
Row 2: 2/1 LC-p, 2/1 RC-p, 2/1 LC-p.
Row 3 and all Following WS Rows: Knit the knit sts and purl the purl sts as they face you.
Row 4: P1, C4B, p2, k2.
Row 6: 2/1 RC-p, 2/1 LC-p, 2/1 RC-p.
Row 8: K2, p2, C4F, p1.
Repeat Rows 1–8 for Braid Cable Flat.

IN THE ROUND

(panel of 9 sts worked on a background of Rev St st; 8-rnd repeat)

Rnd 1: K2, p2, k4, p1.
Rnd 2: 2/1 LC-p, 2/1 RC-p, 2/1 LC-p.
Rnd 3 and all Following Odd-Numbered Rnds: Knit the knit sts and purl the purl sts as they face you.
Rnd 4: P1, C4B, p2, k2.
Rnd 6: 2/1 RC-p, 2/1 LC-p, 2/1 RC-p.
Rnd 8: K2, p2, C4F, p1.
Repeat Rnds 1–8 for Braid Cable in the Round.

Flat and in the Round

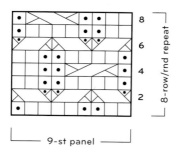

9-st panel

8-row/rnd repeat

Note: Chart for Flat pattern begins with a WS row.

RIBBED CABLE

FLAT

(panel of 7 sts worked on a background of Rev St st; 16-row repeat)

Rows 1 (RS): K1-tbl, [p1-tbl, k1-tbl] 3 times.
Row 2 and all WS Rows: P1-tbl, [k1-tbl, p1-tbl] 3 times.
Rows 3 and 5: Repeat Row 1.
Row 7: Slip 4 sts to cn, hold to front, k1, p1, k1, slip last st from cn to left-hand needle, p1, [k1, p1, k1] from cn.
Row 9, 11, 13 and 15: Repeat Row 1.
Row 16: Repeat Row 2.
Repeat Rows 1–16 for Ribbed Cable Flat.

IN THE ROUND

(panel of 7 sts worked on a background of Rev St st; 16-rnd repeat)

Rnds 1-6: K1-tbl, [p1-tbl, k1-tbl] 3 times.
Rnd 7: Slip 4 sts to cn, hold to front, k1, p1, k1, slip last st from cn to left-hand needle, p1, [k1, p1, k1] from cn.
Rnds 8-16: Repeat Rnd 1.
Repeat Rnds 1–16 for Ribbed Cable in the Round.

Flat and in the Round

16-row/rnd repeat

Slip 4 sts to cn, hold to front, k1, p1, k1, slip last st from cn to left-hand needle, p1, [k1, p1, k1] from cn.

7-st panel

DIAMOND AND MOSS CABLE

FLAT

(panel of 13 sts worked on a background of Rev St st; 22-row repeat)

Note: Pattern begins with a WS row.
Row 1 (WS): K5, p1, k1, p1, k5.
Row 2: P5, slip 2 sts to cn, hold to front, k1-tbl, slip last st from cn back to left-hand needle, p1, k1-tbl from cn, p5.
Row 3: Repeat Row 1.
Row 4: P4, 1/1 RT-p, k1, 1/1 LT-p, p4.
Row 5 and all Following WS Rows: Knit the knit sts and purl the purl sts as they face you.
Row 6: P3, 1/1 RT-p, k1, p1, k1, 1/1 LT-p, p3.
Row 8: P2, 1/1 RT-p, [k1, p1] twice, k1, 1/1 LT-p, p2.

Row 10: P1, 1/1 RT-p, [k1, p1] 3 times, k1, 1/1 LT-p, p1.
Row 12: 1/1 RT-p, [k1, p1] 4 times, k1, 1/1 LT-p.
Row 14: 1/1 LT-p, [p1, k1] 4 times, p1, 1/1 RT-p.
Row 16: P1, 1/1 LT-p, [p1, k1] 3 times, p1, 1/1 RT-p, p1.
Row 18: P2, 1/1 LT-p, [p1, k1] twice, p1, 1/1 RT-p, p2.
Row 20: P3, 1/1 LT-p, p1, k1, p1, 1/1 RT-p, p3.
Row 22: P4, 1/1 LT-p, p1, 1/1 RT-p, p4.
Repeat Rows 1-22 for Diamond and Moss Cable Flat.

Flat and in the Round

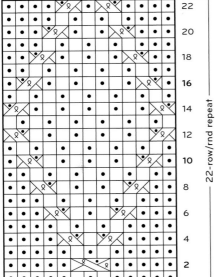

22
20
18
16
14
12
10
8
6
4
2

22-row/rnd repeat

— 13-st panel —

Note: Chart for Flat pattern begins with a WS row.

 Slip 2 sts to cn, hold to front, k1-tbl, slip last st from cn back to left-hand needle, p1, k1-tbl from cn.

1/1 RT-p

1/1 LT-p

IN THE ROUND

(panel of 13 sts worked on a background of Rev St st; 22-rnd repeat)

Rnd 1: P5, k1, p1, k1, p5.
Rnd 2: P5, slip 2 sts to cn, hold to front, k1-tbl, slip last st from cn back to left-hand needle, p1, k1-tbl from cn, p5.
Rnd 3: Repeat Rnd 1.
Rnd 4: P4, 1/1 RT-p, k1, 1/1 LT-p, p4.
Rnd 5 and all Following Odd-Numbered Rnds: Knit the knit sts and purl the purl sts as they face you.
Rnd 6: P3, 1/1 RT-p, k1, p1, k1, 1/1 LT-p, p3.
Rnd 8: P2, 1/1 RT-p, [k1, p1] twice, k1, 1/1 LT-p, p2.
Rnd 10: P1, 1/1 RT-p, [k1, p1] 3 times, k1, 1/1 LT-p, p1.
Rnd 12: 1/1 RT-p, [k1, p1] 4 times, k1, 1/1 LT-p.
Rnd 14: 1/1 LT-p, [p1, k1] 4 times, p1, 1/1 RT-p.
Rnd 16: P1, 1/1 LT-p, [p1, k1] 3 times, p1, 1/1 RT-p, p1.
Rnd 18: P2, 1/1 LT-p, [p1, k1] twice, p1, 1/1 RT-p, p2.
Rnd 20: P3, 1/1 LT-p, p1, k1, p1, 1/1 RT-p, p3.
Rnd 22: P4, 1/1 LT-p, p1, 1/1 RT-p, p4.
Repeat Rnds 1–22 for Diamond and Moss Cable in the Round.

ALTERNATING BROKEN RIBS

FLAT

(multiple of 10 sts + 4; 16-row repeat)

Row 1 (RS): *K4, p2, k2, p2; repeat from * to last 4 sts, k4.

Rows 2, 3, and all WS rows: Knit the knit sts and purl the purl sts as they face you.

Row 5: *C4B, p2, k2, p2; repeat from * to last 4 sts, C4B.

Row 7: Repeat Row 2.

Row 9 and 11: *P1, k2, p2, k4, p1; repeat from * to last 4 sts, p1, k2, p1.

Row 13: *P1, k2, p2, C4F, p1; repeat from * to last 4 sts, p1, k2, p1.

Rows 15 and 16: Repeat Rows 9 and 10.

Repeat Rows 1-16 for Alternating Broken Ribs Flat.

IN THE ROUND

(multiple of 10 sts; 16-rnd repeat)

Rnds 1-4: *K4, p2, k2, p2; repeat from * to end.

Rnd 5: *C4B, p2, k2, p2; repeat from * to end.

Rnds 6-8: Repeat Rnd 1.

Rnds 9-12: *P1, k2, p2, k4, p1; repeat from * to end.

Rnd 13: *P1, k2, p2, C4F, p1; repeat from * to end.

Rnds 14-16: Repeat Rnd 9.

Repeat Rnds 1-16 for Alternating Broken Ribs in the Round.

Flat

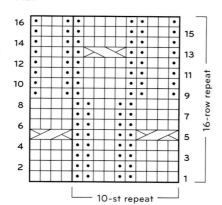

In the Round

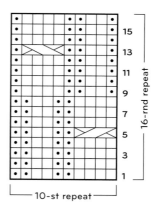

CABLES

ASYMMETRIC CABLES

FLAT

(panel of 6 sts worked on a background of
Rev St st; 12-row repeat)

Note: Pattern begins with a WS row.
Row 1 and all WS Rows (WS): P6.
Row 2: K2, C4F.
Row 4: K6.
Row 6: Repeat Row 2.
Row 8: C4B, k2.
Row 10: K6.
Row 12: Repeat Row 8.
Repeat Rows 1–12 for Asymmetric Cables Flat.

IN THE ROUND

(panel of 6 sts worked on a background of
Rev St st; 12-rnd repeat)

Rnd 1: K6.
Rnd 2: K2, C4F.
Rnds 3–5: K6.
Rnd 6: Repeat Rnd 2.
Rnd 7: K6.
Rnd 8: C4B, k2.
Rnds 9–11: K6.
Rnd 12: Repeat Rnd 8.
Repeat Rnds 1–12 for Asymmetric Cables
in the Round.

Flat and in the Round

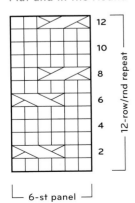

6-st panel

12-row/rnd repeat

Note: Chart for Flat pattern begins with a WS row.

ROYAL CABLE VEST

Even though you switch from working flat to in the round in this top-down vest, your cables will still flow perfectly. If you want to experiment, try switching out other cables from this chapter to make your own personal statement. Just create a swatch first, following the "flat" instructions for your chosen cables, and combine them to your liking to see how the cables look together.

STITCH PATTERNS

Four-Stitch Left Cable Flat
(see page 142 for chart)
(panel of 4 sts; 4-row repeat)

Rows 1 and 3 (WS): P4.

Row 2: K4.

Row 4: C4F.

Repeat Rows 1–4 for Four-Stitch Left Cable Flat.

Four-Stitch Right Cable Flat
(see page 142 for chart)
(panel of 4 sts; 4-row repeat)

Rows 1 and 3 (WS): P4.

Row 2: K4.

Row 4: C4B.

Repeat Rows 1–4 for Four-Stitch Right Cable Flat.

Four-Stitch Left Cable in the Round
(see page 142 for chart)
(panel of 4 sts; 4-row repeat)

Rnds 1-3: K4.

Rnd 4: C4F.

Repeat Rnds 1–4 for Four-Stitch Left Cable in the Round.

Four-Stitch Right Cable in the Round
(see page 142 for chart)
(panel of 4 sts; 4-row repeat)

Rnds 1-3: K4.

Rnd 4: C4B.

Repeat Rnds 1–4 for Four-Stitch Right Cable in the Round.

Big and Little Cables in the Round
(panel of 12 sts; 18-rnd repeat)

Rnd 1: C8F.

Rnds 2-6: K8.

Rnd 7: Slip 4 sts to cn, hold to front, k3, p1, [p1, k3] from cn.

Rnds 8-18: K3, p2, k3.

Repeat Rnds 1–18 for Big and Little Cables in the Round.

Twisted Rib
(even number of sts; 1-rnd repeat)

All Rnds: *P1-tbl, k1-tbl; repeat from * to end, end p1-tbl if an odd number of sts.

NOTES

The Vest is worked from the top down. The Back is worked first to the end of the armholes, then sts

SIZES
X-Small (Small, Medium, Large, 1X-Large, 2X-Large, 3X-Large)

FINISHED MEASUREMENTS
To fit bust sizes 30 (32, 34, 38, 42, 46, 50)" [76 (81.5, 86.5, 96.5, 106.5, 117, 127) cm]

YARN
Blue Sky Alpacas Royal (100% alpaca; 288 yards / 100 grams): 3 (3, 4, 4, 4, 5, 5) hanks #707 Patina

NEEDLES
One 29" (70 cm) long or longer circular (circ) needle size US 3 (3.25 mm)

One 24" (60 cm) long or longer circular needle size US 2 (2.75 mm)

One 16" (40 cm) long or longer circular needle size US 2 (2.75 mm)

One pair double-pointed needles (dpn) size US 3 (3.25 mm)

Change needle size if necessary to obtain correct gauge.

NOTIONS
Waste yarn; stitch markers in 2 colors; cable needle (cn)

GAUGE
26 sts and 36 rows = 4" (10 cm) in Stockinette stitch (St st), using larger needles

for the Front shoulders are picked up from the Back CO edge, and the Front is worked to the end of the armholes, with neck shaping worked as you go.

BACK

Using larger circ needle, CO 68 (72, 74, 78, 82, 96, 96) sts. Begin St st, beginning with a purl row; work even for 5" (12.5 cm), ending with a WS row.

Shape Armholes (RS): Increase 1 st each side this row, then every other row 4 (7, 7, 9, 10, 11, 11) times, as follows: K1, M1-r, knit to last st, M1-l, k1—78 (88, 90, 98, 104, 120, 120) sts. Purl 1 row.

Next Row (RS): Using Backward Loop CO (see Special Techniques, page 282), CO 2 sts at beginning and end of every RS row 3 (2, 3, 3, 4, 3, 5) times—90 (96, 102, 110, 120, 132, 140) sts. Purl 1 row. Transfer sts to waste yarn for Body. Place markers 14 (16, 16, 18, 22, 26, 26) sts in from each side on original CO row.

FRONT

With RS facing, using larger circ needle, beginning at right armhole edge of Back and working to right neck edge marker, pick up and knit 14 (16, 16, 18, 22, 26, 26) sts from Back CO edge. Join a second ball of yarn; beginning at left neck edge marker, pick up and knit 14 (16, 16, 18, 22, 26, 26) sts from marker to armhole edge.

Row 1 (WS): Working both sides at the same time, on left Front, p1 (3, 3, 5, 9, 13, 13), pm (color A), k1-tbl, p1-tbl, k1-tbl, p4, k2, p4; on right Front, p4, k2, p4, k1-tbl, p1-tbl, k1-tbl, pm (color A), p1 (3, 3, 5, 9, 13, 13).

Row 2: On right Front, knit to marker, work 3 sts in Twisted Rib as established, work Four-Stitch Left Cable Flat, p2, k4; on left Front, k4, p2, work Four-Stitch Right Cable Flat, work 3 sts in Twisted Rib as established, knit to end.

Row 3: Work even in patterns as established.

Note: Neck and armhole shaping will be worked at the same time; neck shaping will not be completed until after pieces are joined. Please read entire section through before beginning.

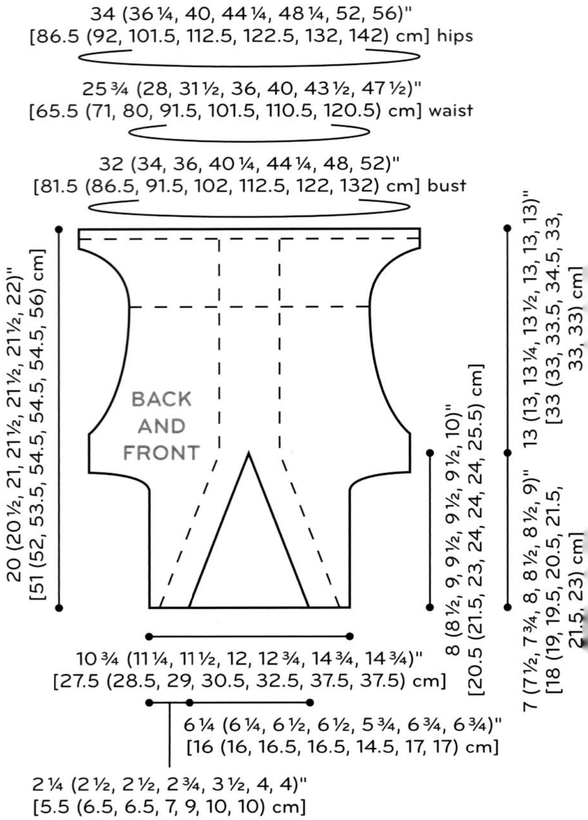

34 (36¼, 40, 44¼, 48¼, 52, 56)"
[86.5 (92, 101.5, 112.5, 122.5, 132, 142) cm] hips

25¾ (28, 31½, 36, 40, 43½, 47½)"
[65.5 (71, 80, 91.5, 101.5, 110.5, 120.5) cm] waist

32 (34, 36, 40¼, 44¼, 48, 52)"
[81.5 (86.5, 91.5, 102, 112.5, 122, 132) cm] bust

BACK AND FRONT

20 (20½, 21, 21½, 21½, 21½, 22)"
[51 (52, 53.5, 54.5, 54.5, 54.5, 56) cm]

13 (13, 13½, 13, 13, 13, 13)"
[33 (33, 33.5, 34.5, 33, 33, 33) cm]

8 (8½, 9, 9½, 9½, 9½, 10)"
[20.5 (21.5, 23, 24, 24, 24, 25.5) cm]

7 (7½, 7¾, 8, 8½, 8½, 9)"
[18 (19.5, 20.5, 21.5, 21.5, 23) cm]

10¾ (11¼, 11½, 12, 12¾, 14¾, 14¾)"
[27.5 (28.5, 29, 30.5, 32.5, 37.5, 37.5) cm]

6¼ (6¼, 6½, 6½, 5¾, 6¾, 6¾)"
[16 (16, 16.5, 16.5, 14.5, 17, 17) cm]

2¼ (2½, 2½, 2¾, 3½, 4, 4)"
[5.5 (6.5, 6.5, 7, 9, 10, 10) cm]

Shape Neck and Armholes (RS): Increase 1 st at each neck edge this row, every 4 rows 14 (15, 18, 18, 21, 18, 22) times, then every other row 8 (8, 4, 6, 0, 6, 1) time(s), as follows: On right Front, work to marker, M1-l, sm, work to end; on left Front, work to marker, sm, M1-r, work to end. AT THE SAME TIME, when piece measures same as for Back to beginning of armholes, shape armholes as for Back, ending with a WS row. When armhole shaping is complete, break yarn for right Front.

BODY

Join Back and Fronts (RS): With RS facing, transfer Back sts, then Right Front sts to left-hand end of circ needle. Your sts should now be in the following order, from right to left, with RS facing; Left Front, Back, Right Front. Using yarn attached to Left Front, and continuing neck shaping, work across Left Front, CO 7 (7, 8, 10, 12, 12, 15) sts for underarm, pm (color B) for side, CO 7 (7, 8, 10, 12, 12, 15) sts for underarm, work across Back, CO 7 (7, 8, 10, 12, 12, 15) sts for underarm, pm (color B) for side, CO 7 (7, 8, 10, 12, 12, 15) sts for underarm, then work across Right Front. Continue as established until neck shaping is complete, ending with a WS row—214 (228, 240, 268, 294, 318, 344) sts. Break yarn.

Join Fronts (RS): With RS facing, transfer 55 (59, 61, 69, 75, 81, 87) left Front sts to left-hand end of needle, so that sts are now in the following order, with RS facing: Back, right Front, left Front. Rejoin yarn to Back sts. Work across Back, right Front, then left Front. Join for working in the rnd; left side marker is now beginning-of-rnd marker. Work even for 2 rnds.

Next Rnd: Work to first A marker, p1–tbl, k1–tbl, p1–tbl, work Four-Stitch Left Cable in the Round, beginning with rnd following last row worked in Four-Stitch Left Cable Flat, p2, work Big and Little Cables in the Round over center 8 sts, p2, work Four-Stitch Right Cable in the Round, beginning with rnd following last rnd worked in Four-Stitch Right Cable Flat, p1–tbl, k1–tbl, p1–tbl, work to end. Work even in patterns as established until piece measures 2 1/4 (2 1/4, 4 3/4, 4 3/4, 4 1/4, 4 3/4, 4 1/4)" [5.5 (5.5, 12, 12, 11, 12, 11) cm] from underarm, ending with a WS row.

Shape Waist: Decrease 4 sts this rnd, every 6 rnds 7 (7, 2, 4, 4, 0, 4) times, then every 5 rnds 2 (2, 4, 2, 2, 6, 2) times, as follows: [K1, k2tog, work to 3 sts before B marker, ssk, k1, sm] twice—174 (188, 212, 240, 266, 290, 316) sts remain. Work even for approximately 4 rnds, ending with a non-cable rnd of Big and Little Cables.

Next Rnd: Purl all sts.

Next Rnd: Knit to first A marker, work patterns as before purl rnd to next A marker, knit to end. Work even for 2 rnds.

Next Rnd: Knit to first A marker, work 9 sts, work Rnd 8 of Big and Little Cables, work to end. *Note:* From this point forward, repeat Rnd 8 of Big and Little Cables across center 8 sts on every rnd.

Shape Hips: Continuing to work patterns as established, increase 6 sts this rnd, then every 3 rnds 8 times, as follows: K1, M1-l, work to 1 st before B marker, M1-r, k1, sm, k1, M1-l, work to A marker, k1, sm, work to next A marker, sm, M1-l, work to last st, M1-r, k1—228 (242, 266, 294, 320, 344, 370) sts. Work even for 5 rnds.

Next Rnd: Work Twisted Rib to 12 sts after first A marker, [p1-tbl] twice, k1-tbl, work Twisted Rib to end. Work even for 4 rnds. BO all sts in pattern, but working all sts through front loop rather than back loop.

FINISHING

Neckband

With RS facing, using smaller 24" (60 cm) circ needle, and beginning at center Back neck, pick up and knit an odd number of sts to base of Front neck shaping, pm, 1 st at center, then an even number of sts to center Back neck. Join for working in the rnd; pm for beginning of rnd. Begin Twisted Rib; work even for 1 rnd.

Next Rnd: Work to 2 sts before marker, ssk, sm, k1-tbl, k2tog, work to end. Work even for 1 rnd.

Next Rnd: Work to 2 sts before marker, s2kp2, removing marker, work to end. Work even for 1 rnd. BO all sts as for Body.

Armhole Edging

With RS facing, using smaller 16" (40 cm) circ needle, and beginning at center underarm, pick up and knit an even number of sts around armhole. Join for working in the rnd; pm for beginning of rnd. Begin Twisted Rib; work even for 5 rnds. BO all sts as for Body.

I-Cord Waist Trim

Using larger dpns, work Applied I-Cord along purl ridge at waist, beginning at left side, as follows: CO 2 sts. *Transfer needle with sts to left hand, sliding sts to opposite end of needle, bring yarn around behind work to right-hand end of needle; wyib, insert tip of left-hand needle into first purl bump at waist from the bottom up; k2tog (first I-Cord st and picked-up st), k1; repeat from * around entire waist. BO all sts. Sew CO and BO edges together.

Block as desired.

LACE

New knitters tend to think that creating lace is a difficult thing, but you know what? It really isn't. Lace is simply comprised of yarnovers paired with decreases. If you tend to lose your place when working lace patterns, place markers between every lace repeat. If you get lost or your stitch count is off, just inspect the last repeat you completed. If you find a mistake, you only have to rip back one small section of stitches.

Unless they are Garter-Stitch based, lace patterns will have a right side and a wrong side. But when worked in fine yarns, most lace looks nice on both sides, making stoles and scarves ideal canvases for lace. Also keep in mind the size of the lace motif. If you're knitting small items like socks, you may want to stick with daintier motifs. But for a larger garment like a pullover, it will take a lot of needle wrangling to cover that much ground with a small motif. If you do want to use a small-scale pattern on a large garment, it might help to incorporate lace panels rather than working an allover pattern, like in the Checkerboard Mesh Pullover on page 214.

If you want the lace pattern to be visible and distinct, it's important to select solid or semi-solid yarns. There are times, however, when subtly variegated yarns will show off the lace pattern—especially if you're using large needles and the lace pattern is nice and loose. Of course, no one is going to come knock on your door if you use variegated yarn, but just know that if you do, your carefully wrought lacework might not be visible.

CHECKERBOARD MESH

FLAT

(multiple of 10 sts + 4; 20-row repeat)

Row 1 (RS): K4, *yo, ssk, k1, [k2tog, yo] twice, k3; repeat from * to end.
Row 2 and all WS Rows: Purl.
Row 3: *K3, [yo, ssk] twice, k1, k2tog, yo; repeat from * to last 4 sts, k4.
Row 5: K2, *[yo, ssk] 3 times, k4; repeat from * to last 2 sts, yo, ssk.
Row 7: K1, *[yo, ssk] 4 times, k2; repeat from * to last 3 sts, yo, ssk, k1.
Row 9: Repeat Row 5.
Row 11: Repeat Row 3.
Row 13: Repeat Row 1.
Row 15: K2tog, yo, *k4, [k2tog, yo] 3 times; repeat from * to last 2 sts, k2.
Row 17: K1, k2tog, yo, *k2, [k2tog, yo] 4 times; repeat from * to last st, k1.
Row 19: Repeat Row 15.
Row 20: Purl.
Repeat Rows 1–20 for Checkerboard Mesh Flat.

IN THE ROUND

(multiple of 10 sts; 20-rnd repeat)

Rnd 1: *Yo, ssk, k1, [k2tog, yo] twice, k3; repeat from * to end.
Rnd 2 and all Even-Numbered Rnds: Knit.
Rnd 3: *Ssk, yo, ssk, k1, k2tog, yo, k3, yo; repeat from * to end.
Rnd 5: *[Yo, ssk] twice, k4, yo, ssk; repeat from * to end.
Rnd 7: *Ssk, [yo, ssk] twice, k2, yo, ssk, yo; repeat from * to end.
Rnd 9: Repeat Rnd 5.
Rnd 11: Repeat Rnd 3.
Rnd 13: Repeat Rnd 1.
Rnd 15: *K2, [k2tog, yo] 3 times, k2; repeat from * to end.
Rnd 17: *K1, [k2tog, yo] 4 times, k1; repeat from * to end.
Rnd 19: Repeat Rnd 15.
Rnd 20: Knit.
Repeat Rnds 1–20 for Checkerboard Mesh in the Round.

Flat

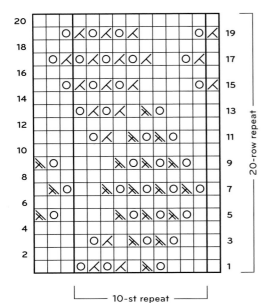

In the Round

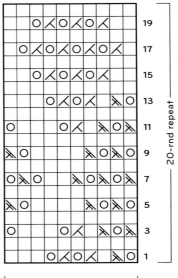

ORIEL LACE

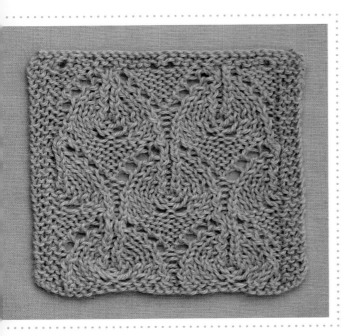

BOTTOM-UP FLAT

(multiple of 12 sts + 1; 28-row repeat)

Row 1 (RS): *P1, ssk, k3, yo, p1, yo, k3, k2tog; repeat from * to last st, p1.

Row 2: K1, *p5, k1; repeat from * to end.

Rows 3-6: Repeat Rows 1 and 2.

Row 7: *P1, yo, k3, k2tog, p1, ssk, k3, yo; repeat from * to last st, p1.

Row 8: Repeat Row 2.

Row 9: *P2, yo, k2, k2tog, p1, ssk, k2, yo, p1; repeat from * to last st, p1.

Row 10: K1, *[k1, p4] twice, k2; repeat from * to end.

Row 11: *P3, yo, k1, k2tog, p1, ssk, k1, yo, p2; repeat from * to last st, p1.

Row 12: K1, *k2, p3, k1, p3, k3; repeat from * to end.

Row 13: *P4, yo, k2tog, p1, ssk, yo, p3; repeat from * to last st, p1.

Row 14: K1, *k3, p2, k1, p2, k4; repeat from * to end.

Row 15: Repeat Row 7.

Rows 16: Repeat Row 2.

Rows 17-20: Repeat Rows 15 and 16.

Rows 21 and 22: Repeat Rows 1 and 2.

Row 23: *P1, ssk, k2, yo, p3, yo, k2, k2tog; repeat from * to last st, p1.

Row 24: K1, *p4, k3, p4, k1; repeat from * to end.

Row 25: *P1, ssk, k1, yo, p5, yo, k1, k2tog; repeat from * to last st, p1.

Row 26: K1, *p3, k5, p3, k1; repeat from * to end.

Row 27: *P1, ssk, yo, p7, yo, k2tog; repeat from * to last st, p1.

Row 28: K1, *p2, k7, p2, k1; repeat from * to end.

Repeat Rows 1–28 for Oriel Lace Bottom-Up Flat.

Bottom-Up Flat

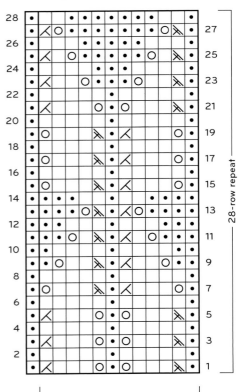

BOTTOM-UP IN THE ROUND

(multiple of 12 sts; 28-rnd repeat)

Rnd 1: *Ssk, k3, yo, p1, yo, k3, k2tog, p1; repeat from * to end.

Rnd 2: *K5, p1; repeat from * to end.

Rnds 3-6: Repeat Rnds 1 and 2.

Rnd 7: *Yo, k3, k2tog, p1, ssk, k3, yo, p1; repeat from * to end.

Rnd 8: Repeat Rnd 2.

Rnd 9: *P1, yo, k2, k2tog, p1, ssk, k2, yo, p2; repeat from * to end.

Rnd 10: *[P1, k4] twice, p2; repeat from * to end.

Rnd 11: *P2, yo, k1, k2tog, p1, ssk, k1, yo, p3; repeat from * to end.

Rnd 12: *P2, k3, p1, k3, p3; repeat from * to end.

Rnd 13: *P3, yo, k2tog, p1, ssk, yo, p4; repeat from * to end.

Rnd 14: *P3, k2, p1, k2, p4; repeat from * to end.

Rnd 15: Repeat Rnd 7.

Rnd 16: Repeat Rnd 2.

Rnds 17-20: Repeat Rnds 15 and 16.

Rnds 21 and 22: Repeat Rnds 1 and 2.

Rnd 23: *Ssk, k2, yo, p3, yo, k2, k2tog, p1; repeat from * to end.

Rnd 24: *K4, p3, k4, p1; repeat from * to end.

Rnd 25: *Ssk, k1, yo, p5, yo, k1, k2tog, p1; repeat from * to end.

Rnd 26: *K3, p5, k3, p1; repeat from * to end.

Rnd 27: *Ssk, yo, p7, yo, k2tog, p1; repeat from * to end.

Rnd 28: *K2, p7, k2, p1; repeat from * to end.

Repeat Rnds 1-28 for Oriel Lace Bottom-Up in the Round.

Bottom-Up in the Round

28-rnd repeat

12-st repeat

ORIEL LACE

(CONTINUED)

TOP-DOWN FLAT

(multiple of 12 sts + 1; 28-row repeat)

Row 1 (RS): *P1, k2tog, yo, p7, yo, ssk; repeat from * to last st, p1.

Row 2: K1, *p3, k5, p3, k1; repeat from * to end.

Row 3: *P1, k2tog, k1, yo, p5, yo, k1, ssk; repeat from * to last st, p1.

Row 4: K1, *p4, k3, p4, k1; repeat from * to end.

Row 5: *P1, k2tog, k2, yo, p3, yo, k2, ssk; repeat from * to last st, p1.

Row 6: K1, *p5, k1; repeat from * to end.

Row 7: *P1, k2tog, k3, yo, p1, yo, k3, ssk; repeat from * to last st, p1.

Row 8: Repeat Row 6.

Row 9: *P1, yo, k3, ssk, p1, k2tog, k3, yo; repeat from * to last st, p1.

Rows 10-13: Repeat Rows 8 and 9.

Row 14: K1, *k3, p2, k1, p2, k4; repeat from * to end.

Row 15: *P4, yo, ssk, p1, k2tog, yo, p3; repeat from * to last st, p1.

Row 16: K1, *k2, p3, k1, p3, k3; repeat from * to end.

Row 17: *P3, yo, k1, ssk, p1, k2tog, k1, yo, p2; repeat from * to last st, p1.

Row 18: K1, *[k1, p4] twice, k2; repeat from * to end.

Row 19: *P2, yo, k2, ssk, p1, k2tog, k2, yo, p1; repeat from * to last st, p1.

Row 20: Repeat Row 6.

Row 21: Repeat Row 9.

Rows 22-27: Repeat Rows 6 and 7.

Row 28: K1, *p2, k7, p2, k1; repeat from * to end.

Repeat Rows 1-28 for Oriel Lace Top-Down Flat.

Top-Down Flat

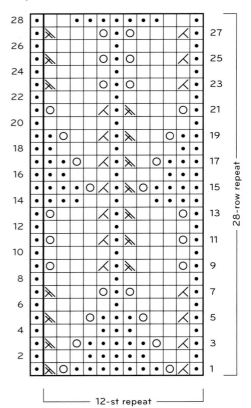

12-st repeat

TOP-DOWN IN THE ROUND

(multiple of 12 sts; 28-rnd repeat)

Rnd 1: *P1, k2tog, yo, p7, yo, ssk; repeat from * to end.

Rnd 2: *P1, k3, p5, k3; repeat from * to end.

Rnd 3: *P1, k2tog, k1, yo, p5, yo, k1, ssk; repeat from * to end.

Rnd 4: *P1, k4, p3, k4; repeat from * to end.

Rnd 5: *P1, k2tog, k2, yo, p3, yo, k2, ssk; repeat from * to end.

Rnd 6: *P1, k5; repeat from * to end.

Rnd 7: *P1, k2tog, k3, yo, p1, yo, k3, ssk; repeat from * to end.

Rnd 8: Repeat Rnd 6.

Rnd 9: *P1, yo, k3, ssk, p1, k2tog, k3, yo; repeat from * to end.

Rnds 10-13: Repeat Rnds 8 and 9.

Rnd 14: *P4, k2, p1, k2, p3; repeat from * to end.

Rnd 15: *P4, yo, ssk, p1, k2tog, yo, p3; repeat from * to end.

Rnd 16: *P3, k3, p1, k3, p2; repeat from * to end.

Rnd 17: *P3, yo, k1, ssk, p1, k2tog, k1, yo, k2; repeat from * to end.

Rnd 18: *P2, [k4, p1] twice; repeat from * to end.

Rnd 19: *P2, yo, k2, ssk, p1, k2tog, k2, yo, p1; repeat from * to end.

Rnd 20: Repeat Rnd 6.

Rnd 21: Repeat Rnd 9.

Rnds 22-27: Repeat Rnds 6 and 7.

Rnd 28: *P1, k2, p7, k2; repeat from * to end.
Repeat Rnds 1-28 for Oriel Lace Top-Down in the Round.

Top-Down in the Round

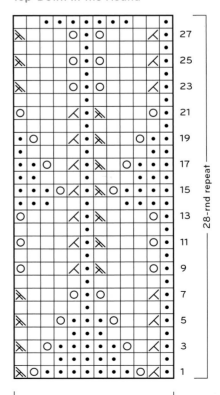

28-rnd repeat

12-st repeat

LACE

183

MADEIRA VANDYKE LACE

FLAT

(multiple of 8 sts + 4; 14-row repeat)

Row 1 (RS): K2, *k6, k2tog, yo; repeat from * to last 2 sts, k2.
Row 2: P2, *p1, yo, p2tog, p5; repeat from * to last 2 sts, p2.
Row 3: K2, *k4, k2tog, yo, k2; repeat from * to last 2 sts, k2.
Row 4: P2, *p3, yo, p3tog, p3; repeat from * to last 2 sts, p2.
Row 5: K2, *k2, k2tog, yo, k4; repeat from * to last 2 sts, k2.
Row 6: P2, *p5, yo, p2tog, p1; repeat from * to last 2 sts, p2.
Row 7: K2, *k2tog, yo, k6; repeat from * to last 2 sts, k2.
Row 8: P2, *p6, ssp, yo; repeat from * to last 2 sts, p2.
Row 9: K2, *k1, yo, ssk, k5; repeat from * to last 2 sts, k2.
Row 10: P2, *p4, ssp, yo, p2; repeat from * to last 2 sts, p2.
Row 11: K2, *k3, yo, ssk, k3; repeat from * to last 2 sts, k2.
Row 12: P2, *p2, ssp, yo, p4; repeat from * to last 2 sts, p2.
Row 13: K2, *k5, yo, ssk, k1; repeat from * to last 2 sts, k2.
Row 14: P2, *ssp, yo, p6; repeat from * to last 2 sts, p2.
Repeat Rows 1-14 for Madeira Vandyke Lace Flat.

IN THE ROUND

(multiple of 8 sts; 14-rnd repeat)

Rnd 1: *K6, k2tog, yo; repeat from * to end.
Rnd 2: *K5, k2tog, yo, k1; repeat from * to end.
Rnd 3: *K4, k2tog, yo, k2; repeat from * to end.
Rnd 4: *K3, k2tog, yo, k3; repeat from * to end.
Rnd 5: *K2, k2tog, yo, k4; repeat from * to end.
Rnd 6: *K1, k2tog, yo, k5; repeat from * to end.
Rnd 7: *K2tog, yo, k6; repeat from * to end.
Rnd 8: *Yo, ssk, k6; repeat from * to end.
Rnd 9: *K1, yo, ssk, k5; repeat from * to end.
Rnd 10: *K2, yo, ssk, k4; repeat from * to end.
Rnd 11: *K3, yo, ssk, k3; repeat from * to end.
Rnd 12: *K4, yo, ssk, k2; repeat from * to end.
Rnd 13: *K5, yo, ssk, k1; repeat from * to end.
Rnd 14: *K6, yo, ssk; repeat from * to end.
Repeat Rnds 1-14 for Madeira Vandyke Lace in the Round.

Flat

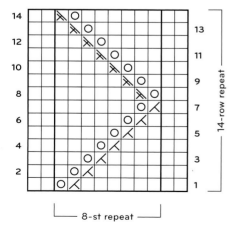

8-st repeat

In the Round

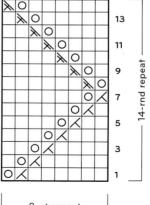

8-st repeat

CAT'S EYES LACE

FLAT (REVERSIBLE)

(multiple of 4 sts; 4-row repeat)

Note: You will increase 2 sts per repeat on Rows 1 and 3; original st count is restored on Rows 2 and 4.

Row 1 (RS): K4, *[yo] twice, k4; repeat from * to end.

Row 2: P2, *p2tog, [p1, k1] into double yo, p2tog; repeat from * to last 2 sts, p2.

Row 3: K2, yo, *k4, [yo] twice; repeat from * to last 6 sts, k4, yo, k2.

Row 4: P3, *[p2tog] twice, [p1, k1] into double yo; repeat from * to last 7 sts, [p2tog] twice, p3.

Repeat Rows 1–4 for Cat's Eyes Lace Flat.

IN THE ROUND (REVERSIBLE)

(multiple of 4 sts; 4-rnd repeat)

Note: You will increase 2 sts per repeat on Rnds 1 and 3; original st count is restored on Rnds 2 and 4.

Rnd 1: *[Yo] twice, k4; repeat from * to end.

Rnd 2: *[P1, k1] into double yo, [k2tog] twice; repeat from * to end.

Rnd 3: K3, *[yo] twice, k4; repeat from * to last st, [yo] twice, k1.

Rnd 4: Remove marker, slip 1, pm for new beginning of rnd, *k2tog, [p1, k1] into double yo, k2tog; repeat from * to end.

Note: Beginning of rnd will shift 1 st to the left each time Rnd 4 is worked.

Repeat Rnds 1–4 for Cat's Eyes Lace in the Round.

Flat

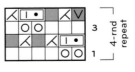

4-st repeat
4-row repeat

In the Round

4-st repeat
4-rnd repeat

| I • | P1, k1 into double yo.

 On first repeat of Rnd 4 only, remove beginning-of-rnd marker, slip 1, pm for new beginning-of-rnd; on following repeats, omit this st. **Note:** Beginning of rnd will shift 1 st to the left each time Rnd 4 is worked.

SLIP STITCH LACE

FLAT

(multiple of 4 sts + 1; 4-row repeat)

Note: You will increase 1 st per repeat on Row 2; original st count is restored on Row 3.

Row 1 (RS): Knit.

Row 2: *P4, yo; repeat from * to last st, p1.

Row 3: K1, *drop yo from Row 2, yo, slip 1, k3, psso; repeat from * to end.

Row 4: Purl.

Repeat Rows 1–4 for Slip Stitch Lace Flat.

IN THE ROUND

(multiple of 4 sts; 4-rnd repeat)

Rnd 1: Knit.

Rnd 2: *Yo, k4; repeat from * to end.

Rnd 3: *Drop yo from Rnd 2, yo, slip 1, k3, psso; repeat from * to end.

Rnd 4: Knit.

Repeat Rnds 1–4 for Slip Stitch Lace in the Round.

EASY LACE

FLAT

(multiple of 6 sts + 1; 8-row repeat)

Row 1 (RS): K1, *yo, skp, k1, k2tog, yo, k1; repeat from * to end.
Row 2 and all WS Rows: Purl.
Row 3: K2, *yo, sk2p, yo, k3; repeat from * to last 5 sts, yo, sk2p, yo, k2.
Row 5: K1, *k2tog, yo, k1, yo, skp, k1; repeat from * to end.
Row 7: K2tog, *yo, k3, yo, sk2p; repeat from * to last 5 sts, yo, k3, yo, skp.
Row 8: Purl.
Repeat Rows 1–8 for Easy Lace Flat.

Flat

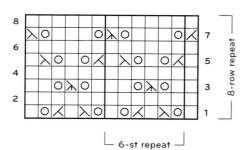

IN THE ROUND

(multiple of 6 sts; 8-rnd repeat)

Rnd 1: *K1, yo, skp, k1, k2tog, yo; repeat from * to end.
Rnd 2: Knit.
Rnd 3: *K2, yo, sk2p, yo, k1; repeat from * to end.
Rnd 4: Knit.
Rnd 5: *K1, k2tog, yo, k1, yo, skp; repeat from * to end.
Rnd 6: Knit to last st, reposition beginning-of-rnd marker to before last st.
Rnd 7: *Sk2p, yo, k3, yo; repeat from * to end.
Rnd 8: Knit.
Repeat Rnds 1–8 for Easy Lace in the Round.

In the Round

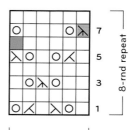

On Rnd 6 only, end rnd 1 st before beginning-of-rnd marker; reposition beginning-of-rnd marker to before final st of rnd.

On first repeat of Rnd 7 only, work sk2p on what was last st of Rnd 6 and first 2 sts of Rnd 7; beginning-of-rnd marker should be before this sk2p.

TILTED BLOCKS

FLAT (REVERSIBLE)

(multiple of 16 sts + 1; 16-row repeat)

Row 1 (RS): *[Ssk, yo] 4 times, k8; repeat from * to last st, k1.
Row 2: *K9, p7; repeat from * to last st, k1.
Rows 3-8: Repeat Rows 1 and 2.
Row 9: K1, *k8, [yo, k2tog] 4 times; repeat from * to end.
Row 10: K1, *p7, k9; repeat from * to end.
Rows 11-16: Repeat Rows 9 and 10.
Repeat Rows 1-16 for Tilted Blocks Flat.

IN THE ROUND

(multiple of 16 sts; 16-rnd repeat)

Rnd 1: *K7, [ssk, yo] 4 times, k1; repeat from * to end.
Rnd 2: *P8, k7, p1; repeat from * to end.
Rnds 3-8: Repeat Rnds 1 and 2.
Rnd 9: *[Yo, k2tog] 4 times, k8; repeat from * to end.
Rnd 10: *K8, p8; repeat from * to end.
Rnds 11-16: Repeat Rnds 9 and 10.
Repeat Rnds 1-16 for Tilted Blocks in the Round.

Flat

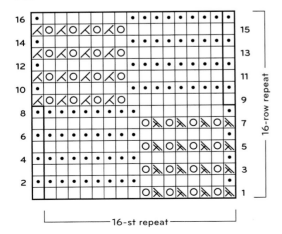

In the Round

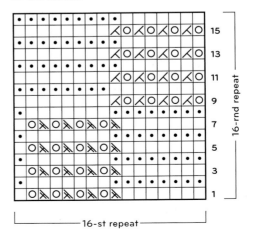

JAPANESE FEATHER

FLAT

(multiple of 11 sts + 1; 28-row repeat)

Note: Pattern begins with a WS row.
Row 1 and all WS Rows (RS): K1, *p10, k1; repeat from * to end.
Rows 2 and 4: *P1, k10; repeat from * to last st, p1.
Row 6: *P1, k1, [yo, k1] 3 times, [ssk] 3 times; repeat from * to last st, p1.
Row 8: *P1, k2, [yo, k1] twice, yo, [ssk] 3 times; repeat from * to last st, p1.
Rows 10 and 12: Repeat Rows 6 and 8.
Row 14: Repeat Row 6.
Rows 16 and 18: Repeat Row 2.
Row 20: *P1, [k2tog] 3 times, [k1, yo] 3 times, k1; repeat from * to last st, p1.
Row 22: *P1, [k2tog] 3 times, [yo, k1] twice, yo, k2; repeat from * to last st, p1.
Rows 24 and 26: Repeat Rows 20 and 22.
Row 28: Repeat Row 20.
Repeat Rows 1–28 for Japanese Feather Flat.

IN THE ROUND

(multiple of 11 sts; 28-rnd repeat)

Rnds 1-5 and all Odd-Numbered Rnds: *P1, k10; repeat from * to end.
Rnd 6: *P1, k1, [yo, k1] 3 times, [ssk] 3 times; repeat from * to end.
Rnd 8: *P1, k2, [yo, k1] twice, yo, [ssk] 3 times; repeat from * to end.
Rnds 10 and 12: Repeat Rnds 6 and 8.
Rnd 14: Repeat Rnd 6.
Rnds 16 and 18: Repeat Rnd 1.
Rnd 20: *P1, [ssk] 3 times, [k1, yo] 3 times, k1; repeat from * to end.
Rnd 22: *P1, [k2tog] 3 times, [yo, k1] twice, yo, k2; repeat from * to end.
Rnds 24 and 26: Repeat Rnds 20 and 22.
Rnd 28: Repeat Rnd 20.
Repeat Rnds 1–28 for Japanese Feather in the Round.

Flat

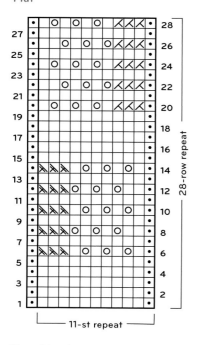

In the Round

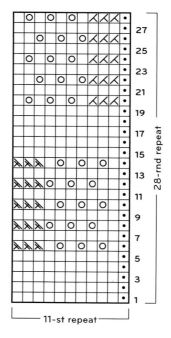

Note: Chart begins with a WS row.

HORSESHOE LACE

FLAT

(multiple of 10 sts + 1; 8-row repeat)

Row 1 (RS): *K1, yo, k3, sk2p, k3, yo; repeat from * to last st, k1.

Rnd 2 and all WS Rows: Purl.

Row 3: *K2, yo, k2, sk2p, k2, yo, k1; repeat from * to last st, k1.

Row 5: *K3, yo, k1, sk2p, k1, yo, k2; repeat from * to last st, k1.

Row 7: *K4, yo, sk2p, yo, k3; repeat from * to last st, k1.

Row 8: Purl.

Repeat Rows 1–8 for Horseshoe Lace Flat.

IN THE ROUND

(multiple of 10 sts; 8-rnd repeat)

Rnd 1: *Yo, k3, sk2p, k3, yo, k1; repeat from * to end.

Rnd 2 and all Even-Numbered Rnds: Knit.

Rnd 3: *K1, yo, k2, sk2p, k2, yo, k2; repeat from * to end.

Rnd 5: *K2, yo, k1, sk2p, k1, yo, k3; repeat from * to end.

Rnd 7: *K3, yo, sk2p, yo, k4; repeat from * to end.

Rnd 8: Knit.

Repeat Rnds 1–8 for Horseshoe Lace in the Round.

Flat

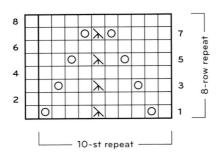

In the Round

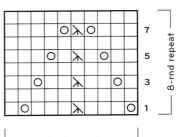

MILANESE LACE

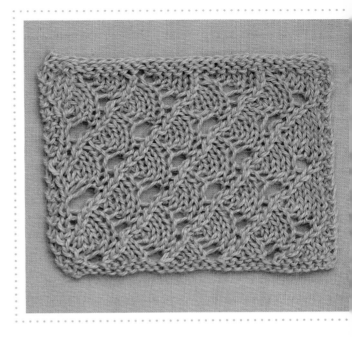

FLAT

(multiple of 6 sts + 2; 10-row repeat)

Row 1 (RS): K1, *k4, k2tog, yo; repeat from * to last st, k1.

Row 2: P1, *yo, p1, p2tog, p3; repeat from * to last st, p1.

Row 3: K1, *k2, k2tog, k2, yo; repeat from * to last st, k1.

Row 4: P1, *yo, p3, p2tog, p1; repeat from * to last st, p1.

Row 5: K1, *k2tog, k4, yo; repeat from * to last st, k1.

Row 6: P2, *p4, yo, p2tog; repeat from * to end.

Row 7: K1, *k1, yo, k3, k2tog; repeat from * to last st, k1.

Row 8: P1, *p2tog, p2, yo, p2; repeat from * to last st, p1.

Row 9: K1, *k3, yo, k1, k2tog; repeat from * to last st, k1.

Row 10: P1, *p2tog, yo, p4; repeat from * to last st, p1.

Repeat Rows 1–10 for Milanese Lace Flat.

IN THE ROUND

(multiple of 6 sts; 10-rnd repeat)

Rnd 1: *K4, k2tog, yo; repeat from * to end.

Rnd 2: *K3, k2tog, k1, yo; repeat from * to end.

Rnd 3: *K2, k2tog, k2, yo; repeat from * to end.

Rnd 4: *K1, k2tog, k3, yo; repeat from * to end.

Rnd 5: *K2tog, k4, yo; repeat from * to end.

Rnd 6: Remove beginning-of-rnd marker, slip 1, pm for new beginning of rnd, *yo, k4, k2tog; repeat from * to end. **Note:** Beginning of rnd will shift 1 st to the left each time Rnd 6 is worked.

Rnd 7: *K1, yo, k3, k2tog; repeat from * to end.

Rnd 8: *K2, yo, k2, k2tog; repeat from * to end.

Rnd 9: *K3, yo, k1, k2tog; repeat from * to end.

Rnd 10: *K4, yo, k2tog; repeat from * to end.

Repeat Rnds 1–10 for Milanese Lace in the Round.

Flat

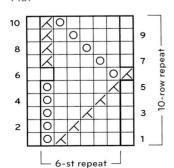

⌐ 6-st repeat ⌐

In the Round

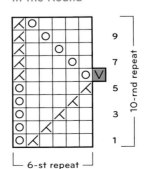

⌐ 6-st repeat ⌐

On first repeat of Rnd 6 only, remove beginning-of-rnd marker, slip 1, pm for new beginning-of-rnd. **Note:** Beginning of rnd will shift 1 st to the left each time Rnd 6 is worked.

LACE

CHEVRON LACE

FLAT

(multiple of 12 sts + 1; 14-row repeat)

Row 1: K4, *k2tog, yo, k1, yo, skp, k7; repeat from * to last 9 sts, k2tog, yo, k1, yo, skp, k4.
Row 2 and all WS Rows: Purl.
Row 3: K3, *k2tog, yo, k3, yo, skp, k5; repeat from * to last 10 sts, k2tog, yo, k3, yo, skp, k3.
Row 5: K2, *[k2tog, yo] twice, k1, [yo, skp] twice, k3; repeat from * to last 11 sts, [k2tog, yo] twice, k1, [yo, skp] twice, k2.
Row 7: K1, *[k2tog, yo] twice, k3, [yo, skp] twice, k1; repeat from * to end.
Row 9: [K2tog, yo] twice, *k5, yo, skp, yo, sk2p, yo, k2tog, yo; repeat from * to last 9 sts, k5, [yo, skp] twice.
Row 11: K1, *k2tog, yo, k1, yo, skp, k1; repeat from * to end.
Row 13: K2tog, yo, *k3, yo, sk2p, yo; repeat from * to last 5 sts, k3, yo, skp.
Row 14: Purl.
Repeat Rows 1–14 for Chevron Lace Flat.

IN THE ROUND

(multiple of 12 sts; 14-rnd repeat)

Rnd 1: *K4, k2tog, yo, k1, yo, skp, k3; repeat from * to end.
Rnd 2: Knit.
Rnd 3: *K3, k2tog, yo, k3, yo, skp, k2; repeat from * to end.
Rnd 4: Knit.
Rnd 5: *K2, [k2tog, yo] twice, k1, [yo, skp] twice, k1; repeat from * to end.
Rnd 6: Knit.
Rnd 7: *K1, [k2tog, yo] twice, k3, [yo, skp] twice; repeat from * to end.
Rnd 8: Knit to last st, reposition beginning-of-rnd marker to before last st.
Rnd 9: *Sk2p, yo, k2tog, yo, k5, yo, skp, yo; repeat from * to end.
Rnd 10: Knit.
Rnd 11: *K1, k2tog, yo, k1, yo, skp; repeat from * to end.
Rnd 12: Repeat Rnd 8.
Rnd 13: *Sk2p, yo, k3, yo; repeat from * to end.
Rnd 14: Knit.
Repeat Rnds 1–14 for Chevron Lace in the Round.

Flat

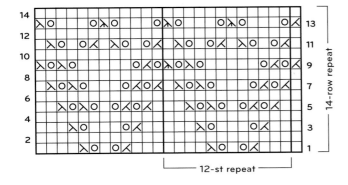

12-st repeat

14-row repeat

In the Round

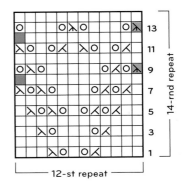

12-st repeat

14-rnd repeat

On Rnds 8 and 12 only, end 1 st before beginning-of-rnd marker; reposition beginning-of-rnd marker to before final st of rnd.

On first repeat of Rnd 9 and 13 only, work sk2p on what was last st of Rnds 8 and 12 and first 2 sts of Rnds 9 and 13; beginning-of-rnd marker should be before this sk2p.

ARROWHEADS

FLAT

(multiple of 12 sts + 1; 8-row repeat)

Row 1 (RS): *P1, k3, skp, yo, p1, yo, k2tog, k3; repeat from * to last st, p1.

Row 2 and all WS Rows: K1, *p5, k1; repeat from * to end.

Row 3: *P1, k2, skp, yo, k1, p1, k1, yo, k2tog, k2; repeat from * to last st, p1.

Row 5: *P1, k1, skp, yo, k2, p1, k2, yo, k2tog, k1; repeat from * to last st, p1.

Row 7: *P1, skp, yo, k3, p1, k3, yo, k2tog; repeat from * to last st, p1.

Row 8: Repeat Row 2.

Repeat Rows 1–8 for Arrowheads Flat.

IN THE ROUND

(multiple of 12 sts; 8-rnd repeat)

Rnd 1: *P1, k3, skp, yo, p1, yo, k2tog, k3; repeat from * to end.

Rnd 2 and all Even-Numbered Rnds: *P1, k5; repeat from * to end.

Rnd 3: *P1, k2, skp, yo, k1, p1, k1, yo, k2tog, k2; repeat from * to end.

Rnd 5: *P1, k1, skp, yo, k2, p1, k2, yo, k2tog, k1; repeat from * to end.

Rnd 7: *P1, skp, yo, k3, p1, k3, yo, k2tog; repeat from * to end.

Rnd 8: Repeat Rnd 2.

Repeat Rnds 1–8 for Arrowheads in the Round.

Flat

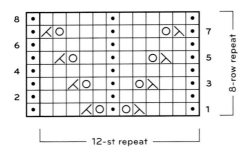

In the Round

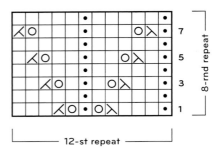

NESTED FANS

FLAT

(multiple of 9 sts + 2; 4-row repeat)

Row 1 (RS): K2, *yo, k2, skp, k2tog, k2, yo, k1; repeat from * to end.
Row 2 and all WS Rows: Purl.
Row 3: K1, *yo, k2, skp, k2tog, k2, yo, k1; repeat from * to last st, k1.
Row 4: Purl.
Repeat Rows 1–4 for Nested Fans Flat.

IN THE ROUND

(multiple of 9 sts; 4-rnd repeat)

Rnd 1: *K1, yo, k2, skp, k2tog, k2, yo; repeat from * to end.
Rnd 2 and all Even-Numbered Rnds: Knit.
Rnd 3: *Yo, k2, skp, k2tog, k2, yo, k1; repeat from * to end.
Rnd 4: Knit.
Repeat Rnds 1–4 for Nested Fans in the Round.

Flat

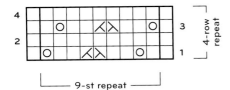

In the Round

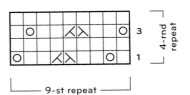

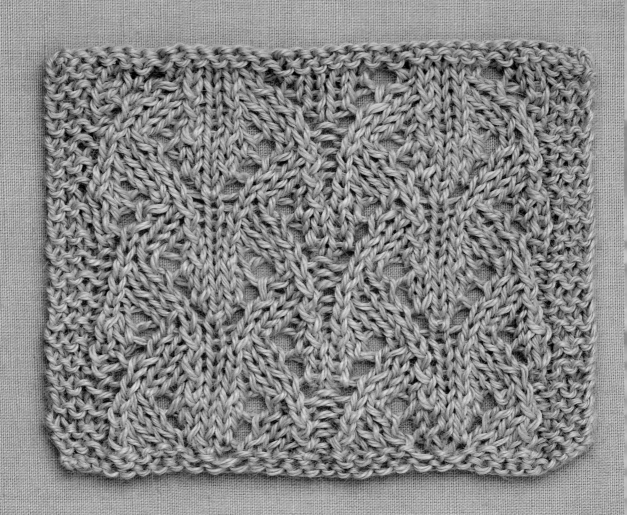

AMPHORA LACE

FLAT

(multiple of 12 sts + 1; 12-row repeat)

Row 1 (RS): *P1, skp, k3, yo, k1, yo, k3, k2tog; repeat from * to last st, p1.
Row 2 and all WS Rows: K1, *p11, k1; repeat from * to end.
Row 3: *P1, skp, k2, yo, k3, yo, k2, k2tog; repeat from * to last st, p1.
Row 5: *P1, skp, k1, yo, k5, yo, k1, k2tog; repeat from * to last st, p1.
Row 7: *P1, yo, k3, k2tog, k1, skp, k3, yo; repeat from * to last st, p1.
Row 9: *P1, k1, yo, k2, k2tog, k1, skp, k2, yo, k1; repeat from * to last st, p1.
Row 11: *P1, k2, yo, k1, k2tog, k1, skp, k1, yo, k2; repeat from * to last st, p1.
Row 12: Repeat Row 2.
Repeat Rows 1–12 for Amphora Lace Flat.

IN THE ROUND

(multiple of 12 sts; 12-rnd repeat)

Rnd 1: *P1, skp, k3, yo, k1, yo, k3, k2tog; repeat from * to end.
Rnd 2 and all Even-Numbered Rnds: *P1, k11; repeat from * to end.
Rnd 3: *P1, skp, k2, yo, k3, yo, k2, k2tog; repeat from * to end.
Rnd 5: *P1, skp, k1, yo, k5, yo, k1, k2tog; repeat from * to end.
Rnd 7: *P1, yo, k3, k2tog, k1, skp, k3, yo; repeat from * to end.
Rnd 9: *P1, k1, yo, k2, k2tog, k1, skp, k2, yo, k1; repeat from * to end.
Rnd 11: *P1, k2, yo, k1, k2tog, k1, skp, k1, yo, k2; repeat from * to end.
Rnd 12: Repeat Rnd 2.
Repeat Rnds 1–12 for Amphora Lace in the Round.

Flat

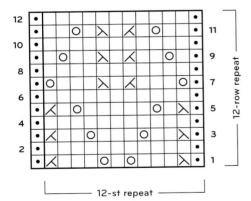

In the Round

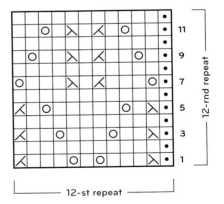

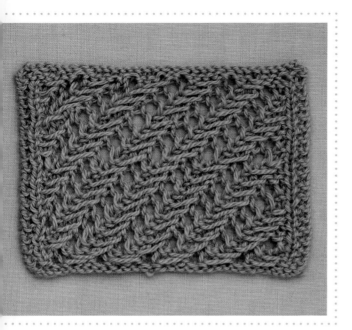

RIPPLES

FLAT

(multiple of 5 sts + 2; 10-row repeat)

Row 1 (RS): K1, *p1, slip 2 wyif, p2tog, yo; repeat from * to last st, k1.
Row 2 and all WS Rows: Purl.
Row 3: K1, *slip 2 wyif, p2tog, yo, p1; repeat from * to last st, k1.
Row 5: K1, *slip 1 wyif, p2tog, yo, p1, slip 1 wyif; repeat from * to last st, k1.
Row 7: K1, *p2tog, yo, p1, slip 2 wyif; repeat from * last st, k1.
Row 9: K1, p1, *p1, slip 2 wyif, p2tog, yo; repeat from * to last 5 sts, p1, slip 2 wyif, p1, k1.
Row 10: Purl.
Repeat Rows 1–10 for Ripples Flat.

IN THE ROUND

(multiple of 5 sts; 10-rnd repeat)

Rnd 1: *Slip 1 wyif, p2tog, yo, p1, slip 1 wyif; repeat from * to end.
Rnd 2 and all Even-Numbered Rnds: Knit.
Rnd 3: *P2tog, yo, p1, slip 2 wyif; repeat from * to end.
Rnd 5: *Yo, p1, slip 2 wyif, p2tog; repeat from * to end.
Rnd 7: *P1, slip 2 wyif, p2tog, yo; repeat from * to end.
Rnd 9: *Slip 2 wyif, p2tog, yo, p1; repeat from * to end.
Rnd 10: Knit.
Repeat Rnds 1–10 for Ripples in the Round.

Flat

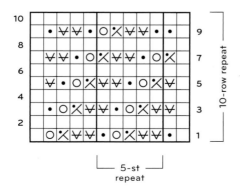

In the Round

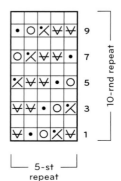

LITTLE FROGS

FLAT

(multiple of 8 sts + 1; 8-row repeat)

Row 1 (RS): *K1, skp, k1, [yo, k1] twice, k2tog; repeat from * to last st, k1.
Row 2 and all WS Rows: Purl.
Row 3: *K1, skp, yo, k3, yo, k2tog; repeat from * to last st, k1.
Row 5: *K1, yo, k1, k2tog, k1, skp, k1, yo; repeat from * to last st, k1.
Row 7: *K2, yo, k2tog, k1, skp, yo, k1; repeat from * to last st, k1.
Row 8: Purl.
Repeat Rows 1-8 for Little Frogs Flat.

IN THE ROUND

(multiple of 8 sts; 8-rnd repeat)

Rnd 1: *K1, skp, k1, [yo, k1] twice, k2tog; repeat from * to end.
Rnd 2 and all Even-Numbered Rnds: Knit.
Rnd 3: *K1, skp, yo, k3, yo, k2tog; repeat from * to end.
Rnd 5: *K1, yo, k1, k2tog, k1, skp, k1, yo; repeat from * to end.
Rnd 7: *K2, yo, k2tog, k1, skp, yo, k1; repeat from * to end.
Rnd 8: Knit.
Repeat Rnds 1-8 for Little Frogs in the Round.

Flat

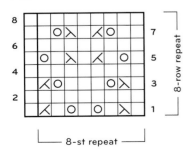

In the Round

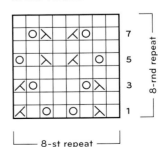

KABUKI LACE

FLAT

(multiple of 11 sts + 2; 16-row repeat)

Row 1 (RS): *P2, yo, k3, k2tog, k4; repeat from * to last 2 sts, p2.

Row 2: K2, *p4, p2tog, p2, yo, p1, k2; repeat from * to end.

Row 3: *P2, k2, yo, k1, k2tog, k4; repeat from * to last 2 sts, p2.

Row 4: K2, *p4, p2tog, yo, p3, k2; repeat from * to end.

Row 5: *P2, k1, yo, k6, k2tog; repeat from * to last 2 sts, p2.

Row 6: K2, *p2tog, p5, yo, p2, k2; repeat from * to end.

Row 7: *P2, k3, yo, k4, k2tog; repeat from * to last 2 sts, p2.

Row 8: K2, *p2tog, p3, yo, p4, k2; repeat from * to end.

Row 9: *P2, yo, k4, skp, k3; repeat from * to last 2 sts, p2.

Row 10: K2, *p2, spp, p4, yo, p1, k2; repeat from * to end.

Row 11: *P2, k2, yo, k4, skp, k1; repeat from * to last 2 sts, p2.

Row 12: K2, *spp, p4, yo, p3, k2; repeat from * to end.

Row 13: *P2, k4, skp, k3, yo; repeat from * to last 2 sts, p2.

Row 14: K2, *p1, yo, p2, spp, p4, k2; repeat from * to end.

Row 15: *P2, k4, skp, k1, yo, k2; repeat from * to last 2 sts, p2.

Row 16: K2, *p3, yo, spp, p4, k2; repeat from * to end.

Repeat Rows 1–16 for Kabuki Lace Flat.

Flat

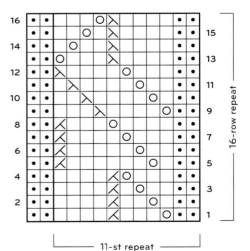

IN THE ROUND

(multiple of 11 sts; 16-rnd repeat)

Rnd 1: *P1, yo, k3, k2tog, k4, p1; repeat from * to end.

Rnd 2: *P1, k1, yo, k2, k2tog, k4, p1; repeat from * to end.

Rnd 3: *P1, k2, yo, k1, k2tog, k4, p1; repeat from * to end.

Rnd 4: *P1, k3, yo, k2tog, k4, p1; repeat from * to end.

Rnd 5: *P1, k1, yo, k6, k2tog, p1; repeat from * to end.

Rnd 6: *P1, k2, yo, k5, k2tog, p1; repeat from * to end.

Rnd 7: *P1, k3, yo, k4, k2tog, p1; repeat from * to end.

Rnd 8: *P1, k4, yo, k3, k2tog, p1; repeat from * to end.

Rnd 9: *P1, yo, k4, skp, k3, p1; repeat from * to end.

Rnd 10: *P1, k1, yo, k4, skp, k2, p1; repeat from * to end.

Rnd 11: *P1, k2, yo, k4, skp, k1, p1; repeat from * to end.

Rnd 12: *P1, k3, yo, k4, skp, p1; repeat from * to end.

Rnd 13: *P1, k4, skp, k3, yo, p1; repeat from * to end.

Rnd 14: *P1, k4, skp, k2, yo, k1, p1; repeat from * to end.

Rnd 15: *P1, k4, skp, k1, yo, k2, p1; repeat from * to end.

Rnd 16: *P1, k4, skp, yo, k3, p1; repeat from * to end.

Repeat Rnds 1–16 for Kabuki Lace in the Round.

In the Round

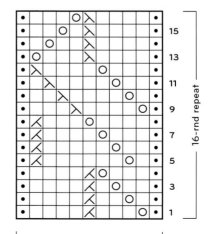

11-st repeat

16-rnd repeat

TRAVELING FERN

BOTTOM-UP FLAT

(multiple of 16 sts; 12-row repeat)

Row 1 (RS): *K9, yo, k1, yo, k3, sk2p; repeat from * to end.
Row 2 and all WS Rows: Purl.
Row 3: *K10, yo, k1, yo, k2, sk2p; repeat from * to end.
Row 5: *K3tog, k4, yo, k1, yo, k3, [yo, k1] twice, sk2p; repeat from * to end.
Row 7: *K3tog, k3, yo, k1, yo, k9; repeat from * to end.
Row 9: *K3tog, k2, yo, k1, yo, k10; repeat from * to end.
Row 11: *K3tog, [k1, yo] twice, k3, yo, k1, yo, k4, sk2p; repeat from * to end.
Row 12: Purl.
Repeat Rows 1–12 for Traveling Fern Bottom-Up Flat.

BOTTOM-UP IN THE ROUND

(multiple of 16 sts; 12-rnd repeat)

Rnd 1: *K9, yo, k1, yo, k3, sk2p; repeat from * to end.
Rnd 2 and all Even-Numbered Rnds: Knit.
Rnd 3: *K10, yo, k1, yo, k2, sk2p; repeat from * to end.
Rnd 5: *K3tog, k4, yo, k1, yo, k3, [yo, k1] twice, sk2p; repeat from * to end.
Rnd 7: *K3tog, k3, yo, k1, yo, k9; repeat from * to end.
Rnd 9: *K3tog, k2, yo, k1, yo, k10; repeat from * to end.
Rnd 11: *K3tog, [k1, yo] twice, k3, yo, k1, yo, k4, sk2p; repeat from * to end.
Rnd 12: Knit.
Repeat Rnds 1–12 for Traveling Fern Bottom-Up in the Round.

Bottom-Up Flat and in the Round

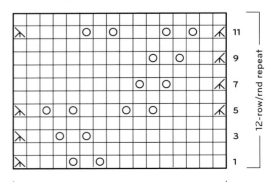

TOP-DOWN FLAT
(multiple of 16 sts; 12-row repeat)

Row 1 (RS): *Sk2p, k4, yo, k1, yo, k3, [yo, k1] twice, k3tog; repeat from * to end.
Row 2 and all WS Rows: Purl.
Row 3: *K10, yo, k1, yo, k2, k3tog; repeat from * to end.
Row 5: *K9, yo, k1, yo, k3, k3tog; repeat from * to end.
Row 7: *Sk2p, [k1, yo] twice, k3, yo, k1, yo, k4, k3tog; repeat from * to end.
Row 9: *Sk2p, k2, yo, k1, yo, k10; repeat from * to end.
Row 11: *Sk2p, k3, yo, k1, yo, k9; repeat from * to end.
Row 12: Purl.
Repeat Rows 1–12 for Traveling Fern Top-Down Flat.

TOP-DOWN IN THE ROUND
(multiple of 16 sts; 12-rnd repeat)

Rnd 1 (RS): *Sk2p, k4, yo, k1, yo, k3, yo, k1, yo, k1, k3tog; repeat from * to end.
Rnd 2 and all Even-Numbered Rnds: Knit.
Rnd 3: *K10, yo, k1, yo, k2, k3tog; repeat from * to end.
Rnd 5: *K8, yo, k1, yo, k3, k3tog; repeat from * to end.
Rnd 7: *Sk2p, [k1, yo] twice, k3, yo, k1, yo, k4, k3tog; repeat from * to end.
Rnd 9: *Sk2p, k2, yo, k1, yo, k10; repeat from * to end.
Rnd 11: *Sk2p, k3, yo, k1, yo, k8; repeat from * to end.
Rnd 12: Knit.
Repeat Rnds 1–12 for Traveling Fern Top-Down in the Round.

Top-Down Flat and in the Round

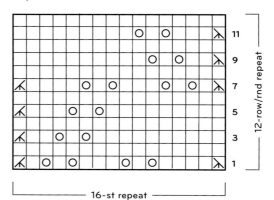

16-st repeat

12-row/rnd repeat

CHECKS

FLAT (REVERSIBLE)

(multiple of 6 sts; 12-row repeat)

Row 1: *K3, yo, s2kp2, yo; repeat from * to end.
Rows 2-6: *K3, p3; repeat from * to end.
Row 7: *Yo, s2kp2, yo, k3; repeat from * to end.
Rows 8-12: *P3, k3; repeat from * to end.
Repeat Rows 1–12 for Checks Flat.

IN THE ROUND (REVERSIBLE)

(multiple of 6 sts; 12-rnd repeat)

Rnd 1: *K3, yo, s2kp2, yo; repeat from * to end.
Rnds 2-6: *K3, p3; repeat from * to end.
Rnd 7: *Yo, s2kp2, yo, k3; repeat from * to end
Rnds 8-12: *P3, k3; repeat from * to end.
Repeat Rnds 1–12 for Checks in the Round.

Flat and in the Round

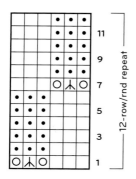

GOTHIC LEAVES

FLAT

(multiple of 8 sts + 1; 14-row repeat)

Row 1 (RS): *K1, yo, k2tog, k3, skp, yo; repeat from * to last st, k1.

Row 2 and all WS Rows: Purl.

Row 3: *K2, yo, k2tog, k1, skp, yo, k1; repeat from * to last st, k1.

Row 5: *K3, yo, s2kp2, yo, k2; repeat from * to last st, k1.

Rows 7, 9, 11, and 13: *K1, k2tog, k1, [yo, k1] twice, skp; repeat from * to last st, k1.

Row 14: Purl.

Repeat Rows 1–14 for Gothic Leaves Flat.

IN THE ROUND

(multiple of 8 sts; 14-rnd repeat)

Rnd 1: *K1, yo, k2tog, k3, skp, yo; repeat from * to end.

Rnd 2 and all Even-Numbered Rnds: Knit.

Rnd 3: *K2, yo, k2tog, k1, skp, yo, k1; repeat from * to end.

Rnd 5: *K3, yo, s2kp2, yo, k2; repeat from * to end.

Rnds 7, 9, 11, and 13: *K1, k2tog, k1, [yo, k1] twice, skp; repeat from * to end.

Rnd 14: Knit.

Repeat Rnds 1–14 for Gothic Leaves in the Round.

Flat

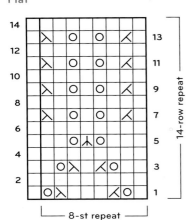

8-st repeat

14-row repeat

In the Round

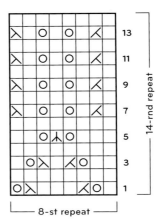

8-st repeat

14-rnd repeat

LACE

207

FIR CONE LACE

BOTTOM-UP IN THE ROUND

(multiple of 10 sts; 16-rnd repeat)

Rnd 1: *K1, yo, k3, sk2p, k3, yo; repeat from * to end.

Rnd 2: Knit.

Rnds 3-6: Repeat Rnds 1 and 2.

Rnd 7: Repeat Rnd 1.

Rnd 8: Knit to last st, reposition beginning-of-rnd marker to before last st.

Rnd 9: *Sk2p, k3, yo, k1, yo, k3; repeat from * to end.

Rnds 10-15: Repeat Rnds 8 and 9.

Rnd 16: Knit.

Repeat Rnds 1-16 for Fir Cone Lace Bottom-Up in the Round.

BOTTOM-UP FLAT

(multiple of 10 sts + 1; 16-row repeat)

Row 1 (RS): K1, *yo, k3, sk2p, k3, yo, k1; repeat from * to end.

Row 2 and all WS Rows: Purl.

Rows 3, 5, and 7: Repeat Row 1.

Rows 9, 11, 13, and 15: K2tog, *k3, yo, k1, yo, k3, sk2p; repeat from * to last 9 sts, k3, yo, k1, yo, k3, ssk.

Row 16: Purl.

Repeat Rows 1-16 for Fir Cone Lace Bottom-Up Flat.

Bottom-Up in the Round

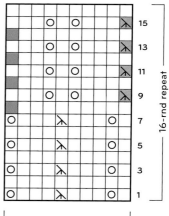

10-st repeat

16-rnd repeat

On Rnds 8, 10, 12, and 14 only, end rnd 1 st before beginning-of-rnd marker; reposition beginning-of-rnd marker to before final st of rnd.

On first repeat of Rnd 9, 11, 13, and 15 only, work sk2p on what was last st of Rnds 8, 10, 12, and 14 and first 2 sts of Rnds 9, 11, 13, and 15; beginning-of-rnd marker should be before this sk2p.

Bottom-Up Flat

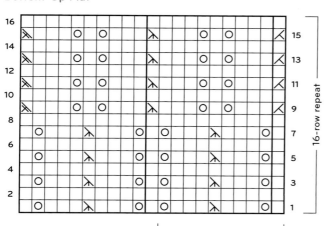

10-st repeat

16-row repeat

TOP-DOWN FLAT

(multiple of 10 sts + 1; 16-row repeat)

Row 1 (RS): Ssk, *k3, yo, k1, yo, k3, s2kp; repeat from * to last 9 sts, k3, yo, k1, yo, k3, k2tog.
Row 2 and all WS Rows: Purl.
Rows 3, 5, and 7: Repeat Row 1.
Rows 9, 11, 13, and 15: K1, *yo, k3, s2kp, k3, yo, k1; repeat from * to end.
Row 16: Purl.
Repeat Rows 1–16 for Fir Cone Lace Top-Down Flat.

TOP-DOWN IN THE ROUND

(multiple of 10 sts; 16-rnd repeat)

Rnd 1: *Sk2p, k3, yo, k1, yo, k3; repeat from * to end.
Rnd 2: Knit to last st, reposition beginning-of-rnd marker to before last st.
Rnds 3-6: Repeat Rnds 1 and 2.
Rnd 7: Repeat Rnd 1.
Rnd 8: Knit.
Rnd 9: *K1, yo, k3, s2kp, k3, yo; repeat from * to end.
Rnds 10-15: Repeat Rnds 8 and 9.
Rnd 16: Repeat Rnd 2.
Repeat Rnds 1–16 for Fir Cone Lace Top-Down in the Round.

Top-Down Flat

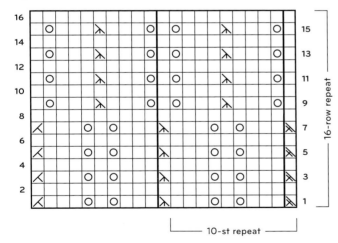

Top-Down in the Round

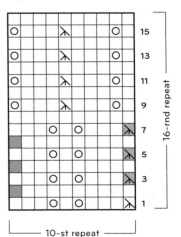

On Rnds 2, 4, and 6 only, end rnd 1 st before beginning-of-rnd marker; reposition beginning-of-rnd marker to before final st of rnd.

On first repeat of Rnd 3, 5, and 7 only, work sk2p on what was last st of Rnds 2, 3, and 6 and first 2 sts of Rnds 3, 5, and 7; beginning-of-rnd marker should be before this sk2p.

WAVE CRESTS

FLAT

(multiple of 12 sts + 1; 12-row repeat)

Row 1 (RS): Knit.
Rows 2-4: Knit.
Row 5: *K1, [k2tog] twice, [yo, k1] 3 times, yo, [ssk] twice; repeat from * to last st, k1.
Row 6: Purl.
Rows 7-12: Repeat Rows 5 and 6.
Repeat Rows 1-12 for Wave Crests Flat.

IN THE ROUND

(multiple of 12 sts; 12-rnd repeat)

Rnd 1: Knit.
Rnd 2: Purl.
Rnds 3 and 4: Repeat Rnds 1 and 2.
Rnd 5: *K1, [k2tog] twice, [yo, k1] 3 times, yo, [ssk] twice; repeat from * to end.
Rnd 6: Knit.
Rnds 7-12: Repeat Rnds 5 and 6.
Repeat Rnds 1-12 for Wave Crests in the Round.

Flat

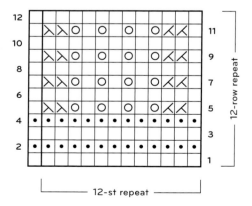

In the Round

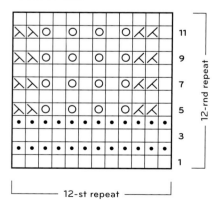

FALLING LEAVES LACE

FALLING LEAVES LACE

BOTTOM-UP FLAT

(multiple of 10 sts + 1; 16-row repeat)

Row 1 (RS): K1, *yo, k3, sk2p, k3, yo, k1; repeat from * to end.

Row 2 and all WS Rows: Purl.

Row 3: K1, *k1, yo, k2, sk2p, k2, yo, k2; repeat from * to end.

Row 5: K1, *k2, yo, k1, sk2p, k1, yo, k3; repeat from * to end.

Row 7: K1, *k3, yo, sk2p, yo, k4; repeat from * to end.

Row 9: K2tog, *k3, yo, k1, yo, k3, sk2p; repeat from * to last 9 sts, k3, yo, k1, yo, k3, skp.

Row 11: K2tog, *k2, yo, k3, yo, k2, sk2p; repeat from * to last 9 sts, k2, yo, k3, yo, k2, skp.

Row 13: K2tog, *k1, yo, k5, yo, k1, sk2p; repeat from * to last 9 sts, k1, yo, k5, yo, k1, skp.

Row 15: K2tog, *yo, k7, yo, sk2p; repeat from * to last 9 sts, yo, k7, yo, skp.

Row 16: Purl.

Repeat Rows 1–16 for Falling Leaves Lace Bottom-Up Flat.

BOTTOM-UP IN THE ROUND

(multiple of 10 sts; 16-rnd repeat)

Rnd 1: *K1, yo, k3, sk2p, k3, yo; repeat from * to end.

Rnd 2: Knit.

Rnd 3: *K2, yo, k2, sk2p, k2, yo, k1; repeat from * to end.

Rnd 4: Knit.

Rnd 5: *K3, yo, k1, sk2p, k1, yo, k2; repeat from * to end.

Rnd 6: Knit.

Rnd 7: *K4, yo, sk2p, yo, k3; repeat from * to end.

Rnd 8: Knit to last st, reposition beginning-of-rnd marker to before last st.

Rnd 9: *Sk2p, k3, yo, k1, yo, k3; repeat from * to end.

Rnd 10: Repeat Rnd 8.

Rnd 11: *Sk2p, k2, yo, k3, yo, k2; repeat from * to end.

Rnd 12: Repeat Rnd 8.

Rnd 13: *Sk2p, k1, yo, k5, yo, k1; repeat from * to end.

Rnd 14: Repeat Rnd 8.

Rnd 15: *Sk2p, yo, k7, yo; repeat from * to end.

Rnd 16: Knit.

Repeat Rnds 1–16 for Falling Leaves Lace Bottom-Up in the Round.

Bottom-Up Flat

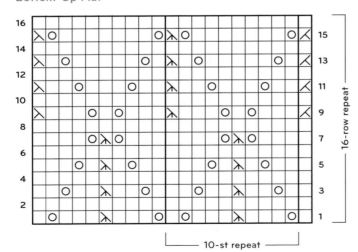

Bottom-Up in the Round

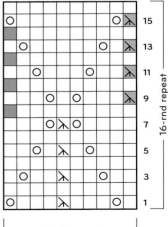

On Rnds 8, 10, 12, and 14 only, end rnd 1 st before beginning-of-rnd marker; reposition beginning-of-rnd marker to before final st of rnd.

On first repeat of Rnds 9, 11, 13, and 15 only, work sk2p on what was last st of Rnds 8, 10, 12, and 14, and first 2 sts of Rnds 9, 11, 13, and 15; beginning-of-rnd marker should be before this sk2p.

TOP-DOWN FLAT

(multiple of 10 sts + 1; 16-row repeat)

Row 1 (RS): Skp, *yo, k7, yo, sk2p; repeat from * to last 9 sts, yo, k7, yo, k2tog.
Row 2 and all WS Rows: Purl.
Row 3: Skp, *k1, yo, k5, yo, k1, sk2p; repeat from * to last 9 sts, k1, yo, k5, yo, k1, k2tog.
Row 5: Skp, *k2, yo, k3, yo, k2, sk2p; repeat from * to last 9 sts, k2, yo, k3, yo, k2, k2tog.
Row 7: Skp, *k3, yo, k1, yo, k3, sk2p; repeat from * to last 9 sts, k3, yo, k1, yo, k3, k2tog.
Row 9: K1, *k3, yo, sk2p, yo, k4; repeat from * to end.
Row 11: K1, *k2, yo, k1, sk2p, k1, yo, k3; repeat from * to end.
Row 13: K1, *k1, yo, k2, sk2p, k2, yo, k2; repeat from * to end.
Row 15: K1, *yo, k3, sk2p, k3, yo, k1; repeat from * to end.
Row 16: Purl.
Repeat Rows 1–16 for Falling Leaves Lace Top-Down Flat.

TOP-DOWN IN THE ROUND

(multiple of 10 sts; 16-rnd repeat)

Rnd 1: Knit to last st, reposition beginning-of-rnd marker to before last st.
Rnd 2: *Sk2p, yo, k7, yo; repeat from * to end.
Rnd 3: Repeat Rnd 1.
Rnd 4: *Sk2p, k1, yo, k5, yo, k1; repeat from * to end.
Rnd 5: Repeat Rnd 1.
Rnd 6: *Sk2p, k2, yo, k3, yo, k2; repeat from * to end.
Rnd 7: Repeat Rnd 1.
Rnd 8: *Sk2p, k3, yo, k1, yo, k3; repeat from * to end.
Rnd 9: Knit.
Rnd 10: *K4, yo, sk2p, yo, k3; repeat from * to end.
Rnd 11: Knit.
Rnd 12: *K3, yo, k1, sk2p, k1, yo, k2; repeat from * to end.
Rnd 13: Knit.
Rnd 14: *K2, yo, k2, sk2p, k2, yo, k1; repeat from * to end.
Rnd 15: Knit.
Rnd 16: *K1, yo, k3, sk2p, k3, yo; repeat from * to end.
Repeat Rnds 1–16 for Falling Leaves Lace Top-Down in the Round.

Top-Down Flat

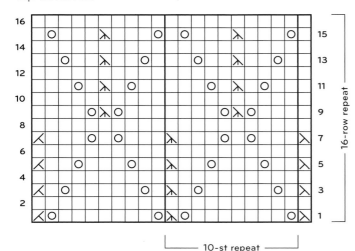

16-row repeat

10-st repeat

Top-Down in the Round

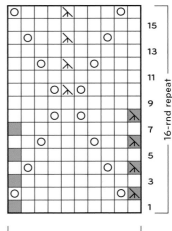

16-rnd repeat

10-st repeat

On Rnds 1, 3, 5, and 7 only, end rnd 1 st before beginning-of-rnd marker; reposition beginning-of-rnd marker to before final st of rnd.

On first repeat of Rnds 2, 4, 6, and 8 only, work sk2p on what was last st of Rnds 1, 3, 5, and 7, and first 2 sts of Rnds 2, 4, 6, and 8; beginning-of-rnd marker should be before this sk2p.

CHECKERBOARD MESH PULLOVER

In this pullover, I incorporated a lace motif that runs down the center front. Since there are 50 stitches that comprise the motif in each of the sizes, it's easy to substitute another lace pattern if you'd like—either try to find another stitch pattern with a multiple of 2, 5, 10, or 25, or do a little bit of math. Simply take the number of stitches for the front, subtract the central panel stitches from that number, and then divide the leftover stitches by 2. This will give you the number of stitches that you will need to work on either side of the panel.

STITCH PATTERN

Checkerboard Mesh in the Round
(see page 178 for chart)
(multiple of 10 sts; 20-rnd repeat)

Rnd 1: *Yo, ssk, k1, [k2tog, yo] twice, k3; repeat from * to end.

Rnd 2 and all Even-Numbered Rnds: Knit.

Rnd 3: *Ssk, yo, ssk, k1, k2tog, yo, k3, yo; repeat from * to end.

Rnd 5: *[Yo, ssk] twice, k4, yo, ssk; repeat from * to end.

Rnd 7: *Ssk, [yo, ssk] twice, k2, yo, ssk, yo; repeat from * to end.

Rnd 9: Repeat Rnd 5.

Rnd 11: Repeat Rnd 3.

Rnd 13: Repeat Rnd 1.

Rnd 15: *K2, [k2tog, yo] 3 times, k2; repeat from * to end.

Rnd 17: *K1, [k2tog, yo] 4 times, k1; repeat from * to end.

Rnd 19: Repeat Rnd 15.

Rnd 20: Knit.

Repeat Rnds 1–20 for Checkerboard Mesh in the Round.

NOTE

This Pullover is worked in one piece from the top down to the underarms, then the Sleeves are put on waste yarn while the Body is worked to the bottom edge. Finally, the Sleeves are picked up and worked down to the cuff.

YOKE

Using shorter circ needle, CO 128 (128, 132, 132, 134, 134, 138) sts. Join for working in the rnd, being careful not to twist sts; pm (color A) for beginning of rnd. Purl 1 rnd, knit 1 rnd, purl 1 rnd.

Next Rnd: K14 (14, 14, 14, 14, 13, 13, 13) for Right Sleeve, pm, k50 (50, 52, 52, 52, 54, 54, 56) for Front, pm, k14 (14, 14, 14, 14, 13, 13, 13) for Left Sleeve, pm, k50 (50, 52, 52, 52, 54, 54, 56) for Back.

Shape Raglan

Note: Change to longer circ needle when necessary for number of sts on needle.

Increase Rnd: [K1, yo, work to 1 st before next marker, yo, k1, sm] 4 times—136 (136, 140, 140, 140, 142, 142, 146) sts. Knit 1 rnd.

SIZES

XX-Small (X-Small, Small, Medium, Large, 1X-Large, 2X-Large, 3X-Large)

FINISHED MEASUREMENTS

31 ¾ (33 ¾, 36 ¼, 38 ½, 41 ¾, 44 ¼, 47 ¾, 49 ¾)" [80.5, (85.5, 92, 98, 106, 112.5, 121.5, 126.5) cm] chest

YARN

Blue Sky Alpacas Melange (100% baby alpaca; 110 yards / 50 grams): 7 (8, 8, 9, 10, 10, 11, 12) hanks #800 Cornflower

NEEDLES

One 24" (60 cm) long circular (circ) needle size US 4 (3.5 mm)

One 29" (70 cm) long or longer circular needle size US 4 (3.5 mm)

One set of five double-pointed needles (dpn) size US 4 (3.5 mm)

Change needle size if necessary to obtain correct gauge.

NOTIONS

Stitch markers in 2 colors; ⅔ yard ¼" (.65 cm) wide ribbon (optional)

GAUGE

26 sts and 30 rows = 4" (10 cm) in Stockinette stitch (St st)

20 sts and 30 rows = 4" (10 cm) in Checkerboard Mesh Pattern

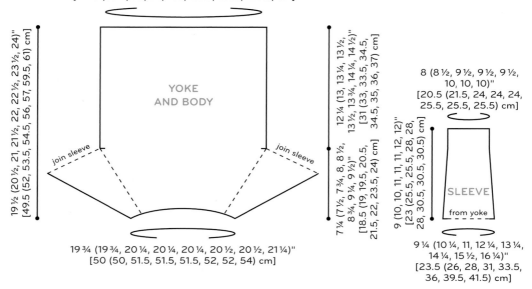

31¾ (33¾, 36¼, 38½, 41¾, 44¼, 47¾, 49¾)"
[80.5 (85.5, 92, 98, 106, 112.5, 121.5, 126.5) cm]

YOKE
AND BODY

19½ (20½, 21, 21½, 22, 22½, 23½, 24)"
[49.5 (52, 53.5, 54.5, 56, 57, 59.5, 61) cm]

join sleeve

join sleeve

12¼ (13, 13¼, 13½,
13½, 13¾, 14¼, 14½)"
[31 (33, 33.5, 34.5,
34.5, 35, 36, 37) cm]

7¼ (7½, 7¾, 8, 8½,
8¾, 9¼, 9½)"
[18.5 (19, 19.5, 20.5,
21.5, 22, 23.5, 24) cm]

9 (10, 10, 11, 11, 12, 12)"
[23 (25.5, 25.5, 28, 28,
28, 30.5, 30.5) cm]

19¾ (19¾, 20¼, 20¼, 20¼, 20½, 20½, 21¼)"
[50 (50, 51.5, 51.5, 51.5, 52, 52, 54) cm]

8 (8½, 9½, 9½, 9½,
10, 10, 10)"
[20.5 (21.5, 24, 24, 24,
25.5, 25.5, 25.5) cm]

SLEEVE
from yoke

9¼ (10¼, 11, 12¼, 13¼,
14¼, 15½, 16¼)"
[23.5 (26, 28, 31, 33.5,
36, 39.5, 41.5) cm]

Repeat Increase Rnd once—144 (144, 148, 148, 148, 150, 150, 154) sts.

Next Rnd: Knit to marker, k2 (2, 3, 3, 3, 4, 4, 5), pm (color B) work Checkerboard Mesh across next 50 sts, pm (color B), knit to end.

Next Rnd: Continuing to work Checkerboard Mesh between color B markers, and St st on remaining sts, repeat Increase Rnd every other rnd 20 (21, 22, 23, 25, 26, 27, 28) times—304 (312, 324, 332, 348, 358, 366, 378) sts [58 (60, 62, 64, 68, 69, 71, 73) sts each Sleeve; 94 (96, 100, 102, 106, 110, 112, 116) sts each for Front and Back]. *Note:* End with an odd-numbered rnd of Checkerboard Mesh.

BODY

Join Back and Front: Transfer next 58 (60, 62, 64, 68, 69, 71, 73) sts to waste yarn for Right Sleeve, removing markers, CO 1 (3, 5, 8, 11, 13, 18, 19) st(s) for underarm, reposition color A marker for new beginning of rnd, CO 1 (3, 5, 8, 11, 13, 18, 19) st(s) for underarm, work across Front to next marker, transfer next 58 (60, 62, 64, 68, 69, 71, 73) sts to waste yarn for Left Sleeve, removing markers, CO 2 (6, 10, 16, 22, 26, 36, 38) sts for underarm, knit across Back—192 (204, 220, 236, 256, 272, 296, 308) sts. Continue in pattern as established until piece measures 12¼ (13, 13¼, 13½, 13½, 13¾,

14¼, 14½)" [31 (33, 33.5, 34.5, 34.5, 35, 36, 37) cm] from underarm, ending with a knit rnd. Purl 2 rnds, knit 2 rnds, purl 2 rnds. BO all sts.

SLEEVES

Transfer Sleeve sts to dpns. With RS facing, rejoin yarn at center underarm; pick up and knit 1 (3, 5, 8, 9, 12, 15, 16) st(s) evenly from sts CO for underarm, knit to end, pick up and knit 1 (3, 5, 8, 9, 12, 15, 16) st(s) evenly from sts CO for underarm—60 (66, 72, 80, 86, 93, 101, 105) sts. Join for working in the rnd; pm for beginning of rnd. Begin St st; work even for 1".

Shape Sleeves

Decrease Rnd: Decrease 2 sts this rnd, then every 15 (13, 13, 7, 5, 4, 4, 3) rnds 3 (4, 4, 8, 11, 13, 17, 19) times, as follows: K1, k2tog, knit to last 3 sts, ssk, k1—52 (56, 62, 62, 62, 65, 65, 65) sts remain. Work even until piece measures 8½ (9½, 9½, 10½, 10½, 10½, 11½, 11½)" [21.5 (24, 24, 26.5, 26.5, 26.5, 29, 29) cm] from underarm. Purl 2 rnds, knit 2 rnds, purl 2 rnds. BO all sts.

FINISHING

Block as desired.

Optional: For a firmer boatneck, sew a length of ribbon along inside of Back neck edge.

COLORWORK

This section contains stitch patterns that employ two or more colors. Some of the patterns utilize slipped stitches to show off the interplay of color, while others rely on dip stitches for the simple exchange of colors from row to row or round to round. When there are patterns requiring Color A and Color B, and Color A is the lighter of the two, I recommend swatching it both ways, switching light for dark and dark for light, to see how different the pattern can look.

When working colorwork stitch patterns in the round, you're essentially working in spirals, so in some cases you may see a jog where one round ends and the new one begins. This will be less noticeable if color changes happen a few stitches away from the beginning or end of the round. When color changes happen on the first or last stitch of the round (like in the Afghan Stitch pattern on page 221, which is essentially a stripe pattern), refer to the Knitting Two Colors Together tutorial on page 282 to minimize the appearance of a jog in color.

AFGHAN STITCH

FLAT

(multiple of 12 sts + 3 in 2 colors; 4-row repeat)

Note: After cast on, pattern begins with a WS row. You may use any number of colors for this pattern. Change colors on RS rows.
Using A, cast on.
Row 1 (WS): Using A, knit.
Row 2: Using B, k1, ssk, *k9, s2kp2; repeat from * to last 12 sts, k9, k2tog, k1.
Row 3: Using B, k1, *p1, k4, [k1, yo, k1] in next st, k4; repeat from * to last 2 sts, p1, k1.
Rows 4 and 5: Using A, repeat Rows 1 and 2.
Repeat Rows 2–5 for Afghan Stitch Flat.

IN THE ROUND

(multiple of 12 sts in 2 colors; 4-rnd repeat)

Note: You may use any number of colors for this pattern. Change colors on odd-numbered rows.
Using A, cast on.
Rnd 1: Using A, purl.
Rnd 2: Using B, *k9, s2kp2; repeat from * to end.
Rnd 3: Using B, *p4, [p1, yo, p1] in next st, p4, k1; repeat from * to end, remove beginning-of-rnd marker, slip 1, replace marker.
Rnds 4 and 5: Using A, repeat Rnds 2 and 3.
Repeat Rnds 2–5 for Afghan Stitch in the Round.

Flat

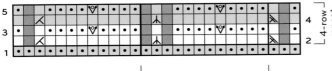

12-st repeat

Note: Flat chart begins with a WS row after casting on.

In the Round

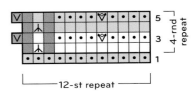

12-st repeat

V̌ [P1, yo, p1] in next st on RS, [k1, yo, k1] in next st on WS.

V At end of Rnds 3 and 5 only, remove beginning-of-rnd marker, slip 1, pm. Beginning of rnd will not shift.

TWO-COLOR LOOP STITCH

FLAT

(odd number of sts in 2 colors; 8-row repeat)

Row 1 (RS): Using A, knit.
Row 2: Using A, purl.
Rows 3 and 4: Using B, k1, *slip 1 wyib, k1; repeat from * to end.
Row 5: Using B, knit.
Row 6: Using B, purl.
Row 7: Using A, k2, slip 1 wyib, *k1, slip 1 wyib; repeat from * to last 2 sts, k2.
Row 8: Using A, p1, k1, *slip 1 wyib, k1; repeat from * to last st, p1.
Repeat Rows 1–8 for Two-Color Loop Stitch Flat.

IN THE ROUND

(even number of sts in 2 colors; 8-rnd repeat)

Rnds 1 and 2: Using A, knit.
Rnd 3: Using B, *slip 1 wyib, k1; repeat from * to end.
Rnd 4: Using B, *slip 1 wyif, p1; repeat from * to end.
Rnds 5 and 6: Using B, knit.
Rnd 7: Using A, *k1, slip 1 wyib; repeat from * to end.
Rnd 8: Using A, *p1, slip 1 wyif; repeat from * to end.
Repeat Rnds 1–8 for Two-Color Loop Stitch in the Round.

BIRD'S EYE

FLAT

(even number of sts in 2 colors; 4-row repeat)

Row 1 (RS): Using A, *slip 1, k1; repeat from * to end.
Row 2: Using A, purl.
Row 3: Using B, *k1, slip 1; repeat from * to end.
Row 4: Using B, purl.
Repeat Rows 1–4 for Bird's Eye Flat.

IN THE ROUND

(even number of sts in 2 colors; 4-rnd repeat)

Rnd 1: Using A, *slip 1, k1; repeat from * to end.
Rnd 2: Using A, knit.
Rnd 3: Using B, *k1, slip 1; repeat from * to end.
Rnd 4: Using B, knit.
Repeat Rnds 1–4 for Bird's Eye in the Round.

THORN PATTERN

FLAT

(multiple of 4 sts + 1 in 2 colors; 8-row repeat)

Note: Do not count sts after Rows 1, 2, 5, and 6; original st count is restored on Rows 3 and 7.

Row 1 (RS): Using A, k2, *[k1, yo, k1] in next st, k3; repeat from * to last 3 sts, [k1, yo, k1] in next st, k2.

Row 2: Using B, p2, *slip 3 wyif, p3; repeat from * to last 5 sts, slip 3 wyif, p2.

Row 3: Using B, k1, *k2tog, slip 1 wyib, ssk, k1; repeat from * to end.

Row 4: Using A, p4, *slip 1 wyif, p3; repeat from * to last st, p1.

Row 5: Using A, k4, *[k1, yo, k1] in next st, k3; repeat from * to last st, k1.

Row 6: Using B, p4, *slip 3 wyif, p3; repeat from * to last st, p1.

Row 7: Using B, k3, *k2tog, slip 1 wyib, ssk, k1; repeat from * to last 2 sts, k2.

Row 8: Using A, p2, *slip 1 wyif, p3; repeat from * to last 3 sts, slip 1 wyif, p2.

Repeat Rows 1–8 for Thorn Pattern Flat.

IN THE ROUND

(multiple of 4 sts in 2 colors; 8-rnd repeat)

Note: Do not count sts after Rnds 1, 2, 5, and 6; original st count is restored on Rnds 3 and 7.

Rnd 1 (RS): Using A, *k1, [k1, yo, k1] in next st, k2; repeat from * to end.

Rnd 2: Using B, *k1, slip 3 wyib, k2; repeat from * to end.

Rnd 3: Using B, *k2tog, slip 1 wyib, ssk, k1; repeat from * to end.

Rnd 4: Using A, *k3, slip 1 wyib; repeat from * to end.

Rnd 5: Using A, *k3, [k1, yo, k1] in next st; repeat from * to end.

Rnd 6: Using B, *k3, slip 3 wyib; repeat from * to end.

Rnd 7: Using B, remove beginning-of-rnd marker, slip 1, replace marker, *k1, k2tog, slip 1 wyib, ssk; repeat from * to end, reposition beginning-of-rnd marker to before ssk.

Rnd 8: Using A, *slip 1 wyib, k3; repeat from * to last 3 sts, slip 1, k2.

Repeat Rnds 1–8 for Thorn Pattern in the Round.

Flat

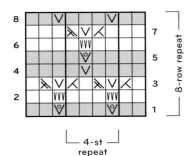

8-row repeat

4-st repeat

In the Round

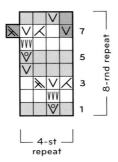

8-rnd repeat

4-st repeat

[⋁] [K1, yo, k1] in next st on RS, [p1, yo, p1] in next st on WS.

[⋁⋁⋁] Slip 3 wyif

[V] On first repeat of Rnd 7 only, remove beginning-of-rnd marker, slip 1, reposition beginning-of-rnd marker to after this slipped st; omit this st on remaining repeats.

[⋊] On final repeat of Rnd 7 only, work final ssk, then reposition beginning-of-rnd marker to before this ssk.

[ ] On first repeat of Rnd 8 only, skip this st (it was worked in final ssk on Rnd 7); on following repeats, work as knit st.

SWEDISH WEAVE

FLAT

(odd number of sts in 2 colors; 2-row repeat)

Note: Color B is never worked; it is simply brought to front or back between the needles while Color A is knit. For best results, keep Color B loose.

Row 1 (RS): K1 using A, then bring B across st in front of work, *bring B to back between needles and k1 using A with B in back, bring B to front between needles and k1 using A with B in front; repeat from * to end.

Row 2: P1 using A, then bring B across st in front of work, *bring B to back between needles and p1 using A with B in back, bring B to front between needles and p1 using A with B in front; repeat from * to end.

Repeat Rows 1 and 2 for Swedish Weave Flat.

IN THE ROUND

(odd number of sts in 2 colors; 2-rnd repeat)

Note: Color B is never worked; it is simply brought to front or back between the needles while Color A is knit. For best results, keep Color B loose.

Rnd 1: K1 using A, then bring B across st in front of work, *bring B to back between needles and k1 using A with B in back, bring B to front between needles and k1 using A with B in front; repeat from * to end.

Rnd 2: Bring B to back between needles and k1 using A with B in back, *bring B to front between needles and k1 using A with B in front, bring B to back between needles and k1 using A with B in back; repeat from * to end.

Repeat Rnds 1 and 2 for Swedish Weave in the Round.

FLECKED TWEED

FLAT

(multiple of 4 sts + 3 in 2 colors; 4-row repeat)

Note: Pattern begins with a WS row.
Row 1 (WS): Using A, p1, *slip 1 wyib, p3; repeat from * to last 2 sts, slip 1 wyib, p1.
Row 2: Using A, k1, *slip 1 wyib, k3; repeat from * to last 2 sts, slip 1 wyib, k1.
Row 3: Using B, p3, *slip 1 wyib, p3; repeat from * to end.
Row 4: Using B, *k3, slip 1 wyib; repeat from * to last 3 sts, k3.
Repeat Rows 1–4 for Flecked Tweed Flat.

IN THE ROUND

(multiple of 4 sts in 2 colors; 4-rnd repeat)

Rnd 1: Using A, *k1, slip 1 wyif, k2; repeat from * to end.
Rnd 2: Using A, *k1, slip 1 wyib, k2; repeat from * to end.
Rnd 3: Using B, *k3, slip 1 wyif; repeat from * to end.
Rnd 4: Using B, *k3, slip 1 wyib; repeat from * to end.
Repeat Rnds 1–4 for Flecked Tweed in the Round.

Flat

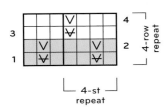

Note: Chart begins with a WS row.

In the Round

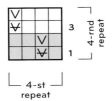

TWO-COLOR STAR STITCH

FLAT

(multiple of 3 sts in 2 colors; 4-row repeat)

Note: Pattern begins with a WS row.
Row 1 (WS): Using A, purl.
Row 2: Using A, k2, *yo, k3, pass first of 3 knit sts over second and third sts; repeat from * to last st, k1.
Row 3: Using B, purl.
Row 4: Using B, k1, *k3, pass first of 3 knit sts over second and third sts, yo; repeat from * to last 2 sts, k2.
Repeat Rows 1–4 for Two-Color Star Stitch Flat.

IN THE ROUND

(multiple of 3 sts in 2 colors; 4-rnd repeat)

Note: Beginning of rnd will shift 1 st to the left with every repeat of Rnds 2–5.
Rnd 1: Using A, knit.
Rnd 2: Using A, *yo, k3, pass first of 3 knit sts over second and third sts; repeat from * to end.
Rnd 3: Using B, knit.
Rnd 4: Using B, remove beginning-of-rnd marker, slip 2, replace marker, *yo, k3, pass first of 3 knit sts over second and third sts; repeat from * to end.
Rnd 5: Using A, knit to last st, reposition beginning-of-rnd marker to before last st.
Repeat Rnds 2–5 for Two-Color Star Stitch in the Round.

Flat

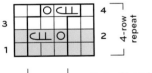

L 3-st ⌐
repeat

Note: Chart begins with a WS row.

In the Round

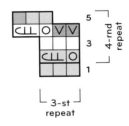

L 3-st ⌐
repeat

| CLL | K3, pass first of 3 knit sts over second and third sts. |

 At beginning of Rnd 4 only, remove beginning-of-rnd marker, slip 2, replace beginning-of-rnd marker; omit these sts on following repeats.

At end of Rnd 5 only, reposition beginning-of-rnd marker to before last st; the st will be worked with first 2 sts of Rnd 2.

DIP STITCH TWEED

FLAT

(multiple of 4 sts + 3 in 2 colors; 4-row repeat)

Dip 1: Insert needle into st below next st on left-hand needle and pull up a loop, knit next st on left-hand needle, pass loop over.
Row 1 (RS): Using B, knit.
Row 2: Using B, purl.
Row 3: Using A, *k3, dip 1; repeat from * to last 3 sts, k3.
Row 4: Using A, purl.
Row 5: Using B, k1, *dip 1, k3; repeat from * to last 2 sts, dip 1, k1.
Row 6: Using B, purl.
Repeat Rows 3–6 for Dip Stitch Tweed Flat.

IN THE ROUND

(multiple of 4 sts in 2 colors; 4-rnd repeat)

Dip 1: Insert needle into st below next st on left-hand needle and pull up a loop, knit next st on left-hand needle, pass loop over.
Rnds 1 and 2: Using B, knit.
Rnd 3: Using A, *k3, dip 1; repeat from * to end.
Rnd 4: Using A, knit.
Rnd 5: Using B, *k1, dip 1, k2; repeat from * to end.
Rnd 6: Using B, knit.
Repeat Rnds 3–6 for Dip Stitch Tweed in the Round.

Flat

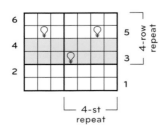

4-st repeat

In the Round

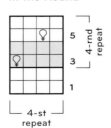

4-st repeat

> **Dip 1:** Insert needle into st below next st on left-hand needle and pull up a loop, knit next st on left-hand needle, pass loop over.

TWO-COLOR HURDLES

FLAT

(multiple of 4 sts + 3 in 2 colors; 4-row repeat)

Note: Pattern begins with a WS row. Slip all sts knitwise.

Row 1 (WS): Using A, knit.

Row 2: Using B, *k3, slip 1 wyib; repeat from * to last 3 sts, k3.

Row 3: Using B, k3, *slip 1 wyif, k3; repeat from * to end.

Row 4: Using A, k1, *slip 1 wyib, k3; repeat from * to last 2 sts, slip 1 wyib, k1.

Row 5: Using A, k1, *slip 1 wyif, k3; repeat from * to last 2 sts, slip 1 wyif, k1.

Repeat Rows 2–5 for Two-Color Hurdles Flat.

IN THE ROUND

(multiple of 4 sts in 2 colors; 4-rnd repeat)

Note: Slip all sts knitwise wyib.

Rnd 1: Using A, purl.

Rnd 2: Using B, *k2, slip 1, k1; repeat from * to end.

Rnd 3: Using B, *p2, slip 1, p1; repeat from * to end.

Rnd 4: Using A, *slip 1, k3; repeat from * to end.

Rnd 5: Using A, *slip 1, p3; repeat from * to end.

Repeat Rnds 2–5 for Two-Color Hurdles in the Round.

Flat

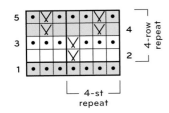

Note: Chart begins with a WS row.

|Y| Slip 1 knitwise wyib on RS, slip 1 knitwise wyif on WS.

In the Round

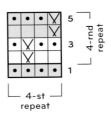

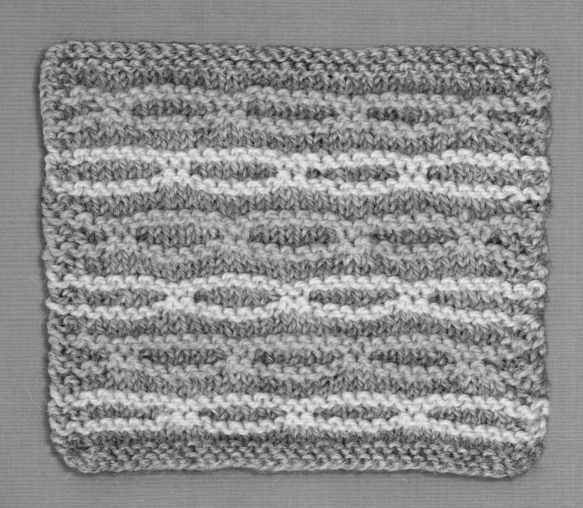

CHAINS

(multiple of 8 sts + 6 in 3 colors; 16-row repeat)

Row 1 (RS): Using A, knit.
Row 2: Using A, purl.
Rows 3 and 4: Using B, knit.
Row 5: Using A, *k6, slip 2 wyib; repeat from * to last 6 sts, k6.
Row 6: Using A, p6, *slip 2 wyif, p6; repeat from * to end.
Row 7: Using B, repeat Row 5.
Row 8: Using B, knit.
Rows 9 and 10: Using A, repeat Rows 1 and 2.
Rows 11 and 12: Using C, knit.
Row 13: Using A, k2, *slip 2 wyib, k6; repeat from * to last 4 sts, slip 2 wyib, k2.
Row 14: Using A, p2, *slip 2 wyif, p6; repeat from * to last 4 sts, slip 2 wyif, p2.
Row 15: Using C, repeat Row 13.
Row 16: Using C, knit.
Repeat Rows 1–16 for Chains Flat.

IN THE ROUND

(multiple of 8 sts in 3 colors; 16-rnd repeat)

Rnds 1 and 2: Using A, knit.
Rnd 3: Using B, knit.
Rnd 4: Using B, purl.
Rnds 5 and 6: Using A, *k6, slip 2 wyib; repeat from * to end.
Rnd 7: Using B, repeat Rnd 5.
Rnd 8: Using B, purl.
Rnds 9 and 10: Using A, knit.
Rnd 11: Using C, knit.
Rnd 12: Using C, purl.
Rnds 13 and 14: Using A, *k2, slip 2 wyib, k4; repeat from * to end.
Rnd 15: Using C, repeat Rnd 13.
Rnd 16: Using C, purl.
Repeat Rnds 1–16 for Chains in the Round.

Flat

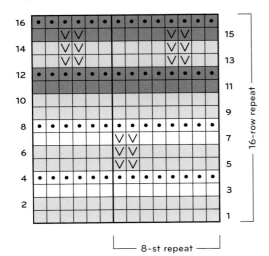

In the Round

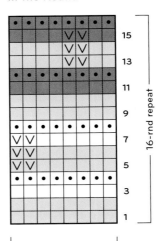

TRIANGLE CHECK

FLAT

(multiple of 6 sts + 3 in 2 colors; 8-row repeat)

Row 1 (RS): Using A, k1, *slip 1 wyib, k5; repeat from * to last 2 sts, slip 1 wyib, k1.

Row 2: Using A, p1, *slip 1 wyif, p5; repeat from * to last 2 sts, slip 1 wyif, p1.

Row 3: Using B, k3, *slip 3 wyib, k3; repeat from * to end.

Row 4: Using B, *p3, slip 3 wyif; repeat from * to last 3 sts, p3.

Row 5: Using A, k1, slip 2 wyib, *k3, slip 3 wyib; repeat from * to last 6 sts, k3, slip 2 wyib, k1.

Row 6: Using A, p1, slip 2 wyif, p3, *slip 3 wyif, p3; repeat from * to last 3 sts, slip 2 wyif, p1.

Row 7: Using B, k4, *slip 1 wyib, k5; repeat from * to last 5 sts, slip 1 wyib, k4.

Row 8: Using B, p4, *slip 1 wyif, p5; repeat from * to last 5 sts, slip 1 wyif, p4.

Repeat Rows 1–8 for Triangle Check Flat.

IN THE ROUND

(multiple of 6 sts in 2 colors; 8-rnd repeat)

Rnds 1 and 2: *Using A, k1, slip 1 wyib, k4; repeat from * to end.

Rnds 3 and 4: *Using B, k3, slip 3 wyib; repeat from * to end.

Rnds 5 and 6: *Using A, slip 3 wyib, k3; repeat from * to end.

Rnds 7 and 8: *Using B, *k4, slip 1 wyib, k1; repeat from * to end.

Repeat Rnds 1–8 for Triangle Check in the Round.

Flat

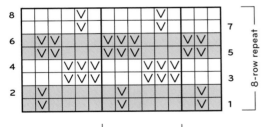

In the Round

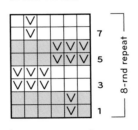

Note: To convert this pattern for working top down, simply work A instead of B, and B instead of A.

LADDER STITCH

FLAT

(multiple of 6 sts + 5 in 2 colors; 4-row repeat)

Row 1 (RS): Using A, k2, *slip 1 wyib, k5; repeat from * to last 3 sts, slip 1 wyib, k2.
Row 2: Using A, p2, *slip 1 wyif, p5; repeat from * to last 3 sts, slip 1 wyif, p2.
Row 3: Using B, *k5, slip 1 wyib; repeat from * to last 5 sts, k5.
Row 4: Using B, p5, *slip 1 wyif, p5; repeat from * to end.
Repeat Rows 1–4 for Ladder Stitch Flat.

IN THE ROUND

(multiple of 6 sts in 2 colors; 4-rnd repeat)

Rnds 1 and 2: Using A, *k4, slip 1 wyib, k1; repeat from * to end.
Rnds 3 and 4: Using B, *k1, slip 1 wyib, k4; repeat from * to end.
Repeat Rnds 1–4 for Ladder Stitch in the Round.

Flat

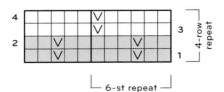

In the Round

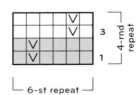

HOUNDSTOOTH CHECK

FLAT

(multiple of 4 sts in 2 colors; 4-row repeat)

Row 1 (RS): Knit 1 with A, *knit 1 with B, k3 with A; repeat from * to last 3 sts, k1 with B, k2 with A.

Row 2: *P3 with B, p1 with A; repeat from * to end.

Row 3: *K3 with B, k1 with A; repeat from * to end.

Row 4: P1 with A, *p1 with B, p3 with A; repeat from * to last 3 sts, p1 with B, p2 with A.
Repeat Rows 1–4 for Houndstooth Check Flat.

IN THE ROUND

(multiple of 4 sts in 2 colors; 4-rnd repeat)

Rnd 1: *K1 with A, k1 with B, k2 with A; repeat from * to end.

Rnd 2: *K1 with A, k3 with B; repeat from * to end.

Rnd 3: *K3 with B, k1 with A; repeat from * to end.

Rnd 4: *K2 with A, k1 with B, k1 with A; repeat from * to end.
Repeat Rnds 1–4 for Houndstooth Check in the Round.

Flat and in the Round

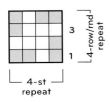

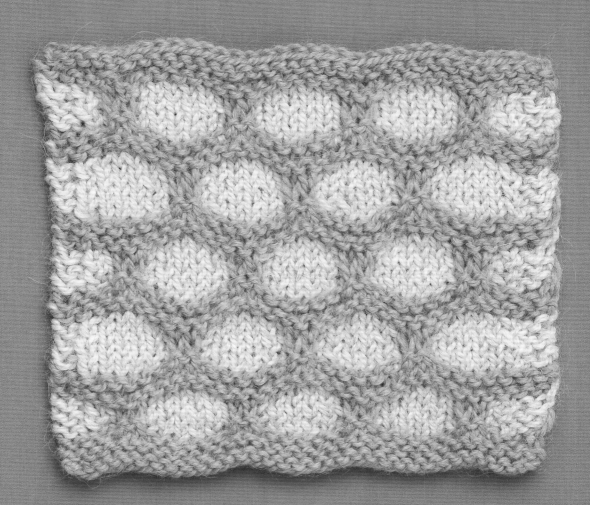

HEXAGONS

FLAT

(multiple of 8 sts + 6 in 2 colors; 20-row repeat)

Row 1 (RS): Using A, knit.
Row 2: Repeat Row 1.
Row 3: Using B, k2, *slip 2 wyib, k6; repeat from * to last 4 sts, slip 2 wyib, k2.
Row 4: Using B, p2, *slip 2 wyif, p6; repeat from * to last 4 sts, slip 2 wyif, p2.
Rows 5-8: Repeat Rows 3 and 4.
Rows 9-12: Using A, knit.
Row 13: Using B, *k6, slip 2 wyib; repeat from * to last 6 sts, k6.
Row 14: Using B, p6, *slip 2 wyif, p6; repeat from * to end.
Rows 15-18: Repeat Rows 13 and 14.
Rows 19 and 20: Using A, knit.
Repeat Rows 1–20 for Hexagons Flat.

IN THE ROUND

(multiple of 8 sts in 2 colors; 20-rnd repeat)

Rnd 1: Using A, knit.
Rnd 2: Using A, purl.
Rnds 3-8: Using B, *slip 2 wyib, k6; repeat from * to end.
Rnd 9: Using A, knit.
Rnd 10: Using A, purl.
Rnds 11 and 12: Repeat Rnds 9 and 10.
Rnds 13-18: Using B, *k4, slip 2 wyib, k2; repeat from * to end.
Rnd 19: Using A, knit.
Rnd 20: Using A, purl.
Repeat Rnds 1–20 for Hexagons in the Round.

Flat

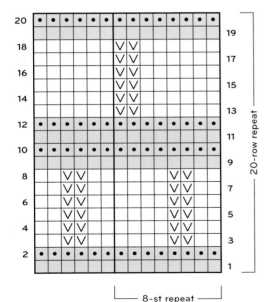

In the Round

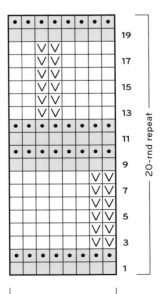

CHAINS MITTS

This fun colorwork pattern will give you an opportunity to experiment with how three colors can work together.

STITCH PATTERN

Chains in the Round
(see page 233 for chart)
(multiple of 8 sts in 3 colors; 16-rnd repeat)

Rnds 1 and 2: Using MC, knit.

Rnd 3: Using A, knit.

Rnd 4: Using A, purl.

Rows 5 and 6: Using MC, *k6, slip 2 wyib; repeat from * to end.

Rnd 7: Using A, repeat Rnd 5.

Row 8: Using A, purl.

Rnds 9 and 10: Using MC, knit.

Rnds 11 and 12: Using B, repeat Rnds 3 and 4.

Rnds 13 and 14: Using MC, *k2, slip 2 wyib, k4; repeat from * to end.

Rnd 15: Using B, repeat Rnd 13.

Rnd 16: Using B, purl.

Repeat Rnds 1-16 for Chains in the Round.

MITTS

Forearm

Using MC, CO 40 (48, 56) sts. Do not join. Knit 3 rows.

Next Row (WS): K4, purl to last 4 sts, knit to end.

Next Row: Knit to end. Join for working in the rnd, being careful not to twist sts; pm for beginning of rnd.

Next Rnd: Change to Chains in the Round; work Rnds 1-16 twice, then Rnds 1-8 once. Break A and B.

Continuing in MC, knit 2 rnds.

Shape Wrist

Decrease Rnd: Decrease 2 sts this rnd, then every other rnd 0 (1, 2) time(s) as follows: K1, k2tog, knit to last 3 sts, ssk, k1—38 (44, 50) sts remain. Knit 1 rnd.

Next Rnd: Knit to last 3 sts, ssk, k1—37 (43, 49) sts remain.

Shape Thumb Gusset

Increase Rnd 1: K18 (21, 24) pm, M1-l, k1, M1-r, pm, knit to end—39 (45, 51) sts. Knit 2 rnds.

Increase Rnd 2: Increase 2 sts this rnd, then every 3 rnds until you have 13 (13, 17) sts between markers, as follows: Knit to marker, sm, M1-l, knit to marker, M1-r, sm, knit to end—49 (55, 65) sts.

Next Rnd: Knit to first marker, remove marker, transfer next 13 (13, 17) sts to waste yarn, remove marker, using Backward Loop CO (see Special Techniques, page 282), CO 1 st over gap, knit to end—37 (43, 49) sts remain.

Work even in St st until piece measures 1½ (2, 2½)" [4 (5, 6.5) cm] from sts on waste yarn. Purl 1 rnd. Knit 1 rnd. Purl 1 rnd. BO all sts.

Thumb

Transfer 13 (13, 17) sts from waste yarn to dpns. Rejoin yarn; pick up and knit 1 st from st CO over gap—14 (14, 18) sts. Join for working in the rnd; pm for beginning of rnd. Knit 5 (5, 7) rnds. Purl 1 rnd. Knit 1 rnd. Purl 1 rnd. BO all sts.

SIZES
Adult Small (Average, Large)

FINISHED MEASUREMENTS
Approximately 7 (8, 9)" [18 (20.5, 23) cm] forearm circumference

Approximately 6 ¼ (7 ¼, 8 ¼)" [16 (18.5, 21) cm] hand circumference

Approximately 9 (9 ½, 10 ¾)" [23 (24, 27.5) cm] tall

YARN USED
Blue Sky Alpacas Melange (100% baby alpaca; 110 yards / 50 grams): 2 hanks #813 Pomegranate (MC); 1 hank each #807 Dijon (A) and #806 Salsa (B)

NEEDLES
One set of five double-pointed needles (dpn) size US 4 (3.5 mm)

Change needle size if necessary to obtain correct gauge.

NOTIONS
Stitch marker; waste yarn

GAUGE
24 sts and 36 rows = 4" (10 cm) in Stockinette stitch (St st)

COLORWORK

HEMS
AND
EDGINGS

In most cases, you'll find that the hems and edgings in this chapter flow from the knitting, so you won't have to pick up and knit stitches. There will be times, however, when you'll want to add on an edging after the work is completed. If you're sure that you want to add an edging later, cast on provisionally for a seamless project, or go ahead and cast on as you normally would and pick up and knit stitches in the proper multiple after you decide what you want to do. If you're adding an edge to an already completed part of a garment (say a neckline or a hem), just pay attention to which direction you'll be working before you select which version of the stitch pattern to use.

When selecting a hem or edging for a project, think about the drape and fiber content of the yarn (or yarns) you're using. If you have a yarn with considerable drape, ruffles and lacy edgings will work really well. But if you're using a chunky or heavy yarn, ruffles may not be the best choice. Also keep in mind that folded-under hems will obviously be thicker with chunky yarn.

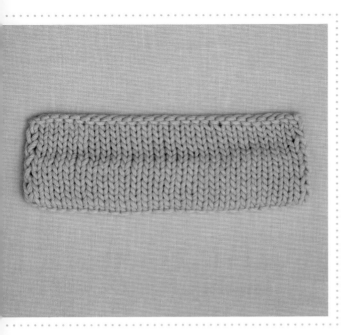

PURL RIDGE HEM

BOTTOM-UP FLAT

(any number of sts and rows)

CO using smaller needles. Work in St st (knit RS rows, purl WS rows) for approximately 1 to 1 1/2" (2.5 to 4 cm), ending with a RS row.
Turning Row (WS): Change to larger needles. Knit.
Change to working pattern.
Finishing: After project or pieces are complete, fold hem to WS at Turning Row and sew to WS, being careful not to let sts show on RS.

BOTTOM-UP IN THE ROUND

(any number of sts and rnds)

CO using smaller needle. Join for working in the rnd. Work in St st (knit every rnd) for approximately 1 to 1 1/2" (2.5 to 4 cm).
Turning Rnd: Change to larger needle. Purl. Change to working pattern.
Finishing: After project or pieces are complete, fold hem to WS at Turning Rnd and sew to WS, being careful not to let sts show on RS.

TOP-DOWN FLAT

(any number of sts and rows)

Turning Row (WS): Knit.
Change to smaller needle and work in St st (knit RS rows, purl WS rows) for approximately 1 to 1 1/2" (2.5 to 4 cm). Do not BO sts.
Finishing: After piece is complete, fold hem to WS at Turning Row and sew live sts to WS, being careful not to let sts show on RS.

TOP-DOWN IN THE ROUND

(any number of sts and rnds)

Turning Rnd: Purl.
Change to smaller needle and work in St st (knit every rnd) for approximately 1 to 1 1/2" (2.5 to 4 cm). Do not BO sts.
Finishing: After piece is complete, fold hem to WS at Turning Rnd and sew live sts to WS, being careful not to let sts show on RS.

PICOT HEM

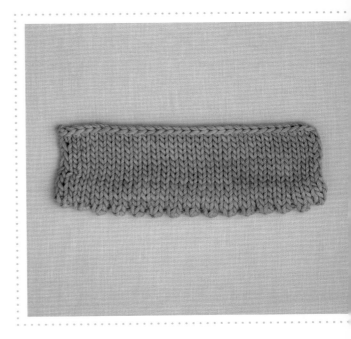

BOTTOM-UP FLAT

(odd number of sts; any number of rows)

CO an odd number of sts using smaller needles. Work in St st (knit RS rows, purl WS rows) for approximately 1 to 1 1/2" (2.5 to 4 cm), ending with a WS row.

Turning Row (RS): Change to larger needles. K1, *yo, k2tog; repeat from * to end. Change to working pattern.
Finishing: After project or pieces are complete, fold hem to WS at Turning Row and sew to WS, being careful not to let sts show on RS.

BOTTOM-UP IN THE ROUND

(even number of sts; any number of rnds)

CO an even number of sts using smaller needle. Join for working in the rnd. Work in St st (knit every rnd) for approximately 1 to 1 1/2" (2.5 to 4 cm).

Turning Rnd: Change to larger needles. *Yo, k2tog; repeat from * to end. Continue in working pattern.
Finishing: After project or pieces are complete, fold hem to WS at Turning Rnd and sew to WS, being careful not to let sts show on RS.

TOP-DOWN FLAT

(odd number of sts; any number of rows)

Turning Row (RS): K1, *yo, k2tog; repeat from * to end.
Change to smaller needles. Work in St st (knit RS rows, purl WS rows) for approximately 1 to 1 1/2" (2.5 to 4 cm). Do not BO sts.
Finishing: After piece is complete, fold hem to WS at Turning Row and sew live sts to WS, being careful not to let sts show on RS.

TOP-DOWN IN THE ROUND

(even number of sts; any number of rnds)

Turning Rnd: *Yo, k2tog; repeat from * to end. Change to smaller needles. Work in St st (knit every rnd) for approximately 1 to 1 1/2" (2.5 to 4 cm). Do not BO sts.
Finishing: After piece is complete, fold hem to WS at Turning Rnd and sew live sts to WS, being careful not to let sts show on RS.

FEATHER EDGING

FLAT

(multiple of 7 sts + 1; 2-row repeat)

Note: Pattern begins with a WS row.
Row 1 (WS): Purl.
Row 2: *K1, yo, k1, ssk, k2tog, k1, yo; repeat from * to last st, k1.
Repeat Rows 1 and 2 to desired depth, ending with Row 1.
Change to working pattern if working bottom-up; BO all sts in pattern if working top-down.

IN THE ROUND

(multiple of 7 sts; 2-rnd repeat)

Rnd 1: Knit.
Rnd 2: *Yo, k1, ssk, k2tog, k1, yo, k1; repeat from * to end.
Repeat Rnds 1 and 2 to desired depth, ending with Rnd 1.
Change to working pattern if working bottom-up; BO all sts in pattern if working top-down.

Flat

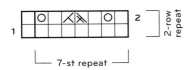

Note: Chart begins with a WS row.

In the Round

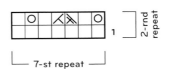

WAVES EDGING

BOTTOM-UP FLAT

(multiple of 18 sts + 2; 4-row repeat)

Row 1 (RS): Knit.
Row 2: Purl.
Row 3: K1, *[k2tog] 3 times, [yo, k1] 6 times, [k2tog] 3 times; repeat from * to last st, k1.
Row 4: Knit.
Repeat Rows 1–4 to desired depth. Change to working pattern.

BOTTOM-UP IN THE ROUND

(multiple of 18 sts; 4-rnd repeat)

Rnds 1 and 2: Knit.
Rnd 3: *[K2tog] 3 times, *[yo, k1] 6 times, [k2tog] 3 times; repeat from * to end.
Rnd 4: Purl.
Repeat Rnds 1–4 to desired depth. Change to working pattern.

Bottom-Up Flat

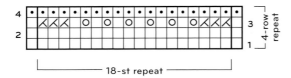

Bottom-Up in the Round

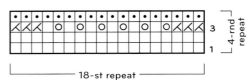

TOP-DOWN FLAT

(multiple of 18 sts + 2; 4-row repeat)

Note: Pattern begins with a WS row.
Row 1 (WS): Knit.
Row 2: K1, *[ssk] 3 times, [k1, yo] 6 times, [ssk] 3 times; repeat from * to last st, k1.
Row 3: Purl.
Row 4: Knit.
Repeat Rows 1–4 to desired depth.
BO all sts.

TOP-DOWN IN THE ROUND

(multiple of 18 sts; 4-rnd repeat)

Rnd 1: Purl.
Rnd 2: *[Ssk] 3 times, [k1, yo] 6 times, [ssk] 3 times; repeat from * to end.
Rnds 3 and 4: Knit.
Repeat Rnds 1–4 to desired depth.
BO all sts.

Top-Down Flat

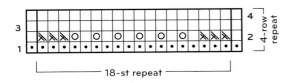

Note: Chart begins with a WS row.

Top-Down in the Round

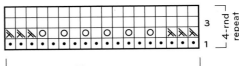

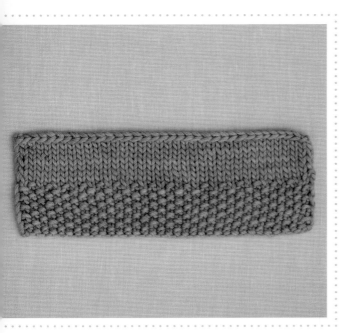
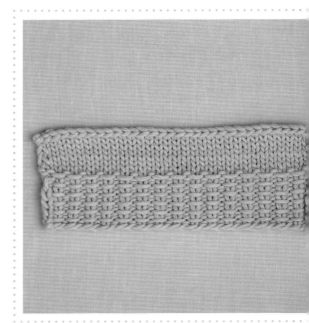

SEED STITCH EDGING

FLAT

(even number of sts; any number of rows)

Row 1 (RS): *K1, p1; repeat from * to end.
Row 2: Knit the purl sts and purl the knit sts as they face you.
Repeat Row 2 to desired depth.
Change to working pattern if working bottom-up; BO all sts in pattern if working top-down.

IN THE ROUND

(odd number of sts; any number of rnds)

Rnd 1: K1, *p1, k1; repeat from * to end.
Rnd 2: Knit the purl sts and purl the knit sts as they face you.
Repeat Rnd 2 to desired depth.
Change to working pattern if working bottom-up; BO all sts in pattern if working top-down.

MOCK RIB EDGING

FLAT

(odd number of sts; 2-row repeat)

Note: Pattern begins with a WS row.
Row 1 (WS): K1, *p1, k1; repeat from * to end.
Row 2: *P1, slip 1 wyif; repeat from * to last st, p1.
Repeat Rows 1 and 2 to desired depth.
Change to working pattern if working bottom-up; BO all sts in pattern if working top-down.

IN THE ROUND

(even number of sts; 2-rnd repeat)

Rnd 1: *K1, p1; repeat from * to end.
Rnd 2: *Slip 1 wyif, p1; repeat from * to end.
Repeat Rnds 1 and 2 to desired depth.
Change to working pattern if working bottom-up; BO all sts in pattern if working top-down.

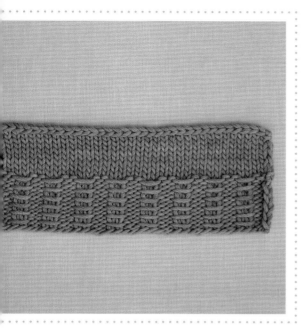

DOUBLE MOCK RIB EDGING

FLAT

(multiple of 4 sts + 2; 2-row repeat)

Note: Pattern begins with a WS row.
Row 1 (WS): K2, *p2, k2; repeat from * to end.
Row 2: *P2, slip 2 wyif; repeat from * to last 2 sts, p2.
Repeat Rows 1 and 2 to desired depth.
Change to working pattern if working bottom-up; BO all sts in pattern if working top-down.

IN THE ROUND

(multiple of 4 sts; 2-rnd repeat)

Rnd 1: *P2, k2; repeat from * to end.
Rnd 2: *P2, slip 2 wyif; repeat from * to end.
Repeat Rnds 1 and 2 to desired depth.
Change to working pattern if working bottom-up; BO all sts in pattern if working top-down.

GARTER DITCH EDGING

FLAT

(multiple of 5 sts + 1; 2-row repeat)

Row 1 (RS): P1, *k4, p1; repeat from * to end.
Row 2: Purl.
Repeat Rows 1 and 2 to desired depth.
Change to working pattern if working bottom-up; BO all sts in pattern if working top-down.

IN THE ROUND

(multiple of 5 sts; 2-rnd repeat)

Rnd 1: *K4, p1; repeat from * to end.
Rnd 2: Knit.
Repeat Rnds 1 and 2 to desired depth.
Change to working pattern if working bottom-up; BO all sts in pattern if working top-down.

HERRINGBONE EYELET EDGING

FLAT

(multple of 12 sts + 1; 2-row repeat)

Note: Pattern begins with a WS row.
Row 1 (WS): Purl.
Row 2: *K1, yo, k4, sk2p, k4, yo; repeat from * to last st, k1.
Repeat Rows 1 and 2 to desired depth.
Change to working pattern if working bottom-up; BO all sts in pattern if working top-down.

IN THE ROUND

(multiple of 12 sts; 2-rnd repeat)

Rnd 1: Knit.
Rnd 2: *Yo, k4, sk2p, k4, yo, k1; repeat from * to end.
Repeat Rnds 1 and 2 to desired depth.
Change to working pattern if working bottom-up; BO all sts in pattern if working top-down.

Flat

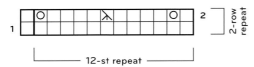

Note: Chart begins with a WS row.

In the Round

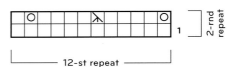

KICK PLEAT EDGING

KICK PLEAT EDGING

BOTTOM-UP FLAT

(begins with multiple of 7 sts + 4, ends with multiple of 4 sts + 4; 14 rows)

Row 1 (RS): *K4, p3; repeat from * to last 4 sts, k4.
Row 2 and all WS Rows: Knit the knit sts and purl the purl sts as they face you.
Row 3: Repeat Row 1.
Row 5: *K4, p2tog, p1; repeat from * to last 4 sts, k4.
Row 7: Repeat Row 2.
Row 9: *K4, p2tog; repeat from * to last 4 sts, k4.
Row 11: Repeat Row 2.
Row 13: *K3, k2tog; repeat from * to last 4 sts, k4.
Row 14: Purl.
Change to working pattern.

BOTTOM-UP IN THE ROUND

(begins with multiple of 7 sts, ends with multiple of 4 sts; 14 rnds)

Rnds 1 and 3: *K4, p3; repeat from * to end.
Rnd 2 and all Even-Numbered Rnds: Knit the knit sts and purl the purl sts as they face you.
Rnd 5: *K4, p2tog, p1; repeat from * to end.
Rnd 7: Repeat Rnd 2.
Rnd 9: *K4, p2tog; repeat from * to end.
Rnd 11: Repeat Rnd 2.
Rnd 13: *K3, k2tog; repeat from * to end.
Rnd 14: Knit.
Change to working pattern.

Bottom-Up Flat

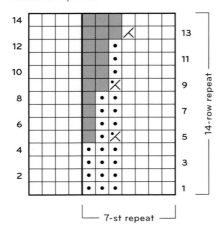

7-st repeat

Bottom-Up in the Round

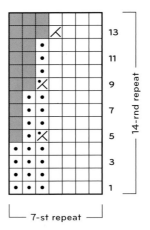

7-st repeat

TOP-DOWN FLAT

(begins with multiple of 4 sts + 4, ends with multiple of 7 sts + 4; 14 rows)

Row 1 (RS): *K4, M1-p-r; repeat from * to last 4 sts, k4.

Row 2 and all WS Rows: Knit the knit sts and purl the purl sts as they face you.

Row 3: Repeat Row 2.

Row 5: *K4, p1, M1-p-r; repeat from * to last 4 sts, k4.

Row 7: Repeat Row 2.

Row 9: *K4, p2, M1-p-r; repeat from * to last 4 sts, k4.

Row 11: Repeat Row 2.

Rows 13 and 14: Repeat Row 2.
BO all sts.

TOP-DOWN IN THE ROUND

(begins with multiple of 4 sts, ends with multiple of 7 sts; 14 rnds)

Rnd 1: *K4, M1-p-r; repeat from * to end.

Rnd 2 and all Even-Numbered Rnds: Knit the knit sts and purl the purl sts as they face you.

Rnd 3: Repeat Rnd 2.

Rnd 5: *K4, p1, M1-p-r; repeat from * to end.

Rnd 7: Repeat Rnd 2.

Rnd 9: *K4, p2, M1-p-r; repeat from * to end.

Rnd 11: Repeat Rnd 2.

Rnds 13 and 14: Repeat Rnd 2.
BO all sts.

Top-Down Flat

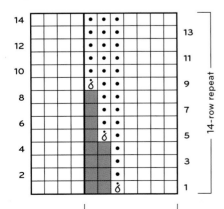

4-st repeat
at beginning;
7-st repeat at end

Top-Down in the Round

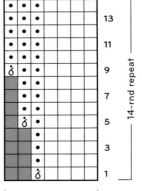

4-st repeat
at beginning;
7-st repeat at end

EYELET RUFFLE

BOTTOM-UP FLAT

(begins with multiple of 4 sts + 2, ends with
even number of sts; odd number of rows)

Note: St count is halved on Decrease Row.
Cast on twice the number of sts needed for
working pattern.
Row 1 (RS): K1, *skp, [yo] twice, k2tog; repeat
from * to last st, k1.
Row 2: P1, *p1, [p1, k1] in double yo, p1; repeat
from * to last st, p1.
Repeat Rows 1 and 2 to desired depth, ending
with a WS row.
Decrease Row (RS): *K2tog; repeat from * to
end.
Change to working pattern.

BOTTOM-UP IN THE ROUND

(begins with multiple of 4 sts, ends with even
number of sts; odd number of rnds)

Note: St count is halved on Decrease Rnd.
Cast on twice the number of sts needed for
working pattern.
Rnd 1: *Skp, [yo] twice, k2tog; repeat from *
to end.
Rnd 2: *K1, [p1, k1] in double yo, k1; repeat
from * to end.
Repeat Rnds 1 and 2 to desired depth.
Decrease Rnd: K2tog around.
Change to working pattern.

Bottom-Up Flat

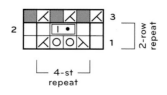

I • P1, k1 into double yo.

Bottom-Up in the Round

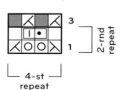

TOP-DOWN FLAT

(begins with even number of sts, ends with
multiple of 4 sts; odd number of rows)

Note: Pattern begins with a WS row. St count is
doubled on Row 1.

Row 1 (WS): *P1-f/b; repeat from * to end.

Row 2: K1, *skp, [yo] twice, k2tog; repeat
from * to last st, k1.

Row 3: P1, *p1, [p1, k1] in double yo, p1; repeat
from * to last st, p1.

Repeat Rows 2 and 3 to desired length.

BO all sts.

TOP-DOWN IN THE ROUND

(begins with even number of sts, ends with
multiple of 4 sts; odd number of rnds)

Note: St count is doubled on Rnd 1.

Rnd 1: *K1-f/b; repeat from * to end.

Rnd 2: *Skp, [yo] twice, k2tog; repeat from *
to end.

Rnd 3: *K1, [p1, k1] in double yo, k1; repeat
from * to end.

Repeat Rnds 2 and 3 to desired depth.

BO all sts.

Top-Down Flat

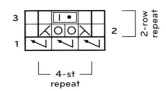

Top-Down in the Round

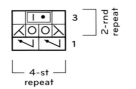

Note: Chart begins with a WS row.

P1, k1 into double yo.

K1-f/b on RS, p1-f/b on WS.

GARTER RIDGE RUFFLE

BOTTOM-UP FLAT

(any number of sts; 11 rows)

Note: Pattern begins with a WS row. St count is halved on Row 11.
CO twice the number of sts needed for working pattern.
Row 1 (WS): Knit.
Rows 2-4: Knit.
Row 5: Purl.
Rows 6-9: Repeat Rows 4 and 5.
Row 10: Knit.
Row 11: *K2tog; repeat from * to end.
Change to working pattern.

BOTTOM-UP IN THE ROUND

(any number of sts; 11 rnds)

Note: St count is halved on Rnd 11.
CO twice the number of sts needed for working pattern. Join for working in the rnd.
Rnd 1: Purl.
Rnd 2: Knit.
Rnd 3: Purl.
Rnds 4-10: Knit.
Rnd 11: *P2tog; repeat from * to end.
Change to working pattern.

TOP-DOWN FLAT

(any number of sts; 11 rows)

Note: Pattern begins with a WS row. St count is doubled on Row 2.
Row 1 (WS): Purl.
Row 2: *K1-f/b; repeat from * to end.
Row 3: Purl.
Row 4: Knit.
Rows 5-8: Repeat Rows 3 and 4.
Rows 9-11: Knit.
BO all sts.

TOP-DOWN IN THE ROUND

(any number of sts; 11 rnds)

Note: St count is doubled on Rnd 2.
Rnd 1: Knit.
Rnd 2: *K1-f/b; repeat from * to end.
Rnds 3-8: Knit.
Rnd 9: Purl.
Rnd 10: Knit.
Rnd 11: Purl.
BO all sts.

MOCK CABLE RIB EDGING

MOCK CABLE RIB EDGING

BOTTOM-UP FLAT

(multiple of 4 sts + 2; 18 rows)

Row 1 (RS): *P2, k2; repeat from * to last 2 sts, p2.

Rows 2-5 and all WS Rows: Knit the knit sts and purl the purl sts as they face you; purl all yos.

Row 7: *P2, k2tog, yo; repeat from * to last 2 sts, p2.

Row 9: *P2, yo, skp; repeat from * to last 2 sts, p2.

Rows 11 and 13: Repeat Rows 7 and 9.

Rows 15, 17, and 18: Repeat Row 2.

Change to working pattern.

BOTTOM-UP IN THE ROUND

(multiple of 4 sts; 18 rnds)

Rnds 1-6 and all Even-Numbered Rnds: *K2, p2; repeat from * to end.

Rnd 7: *K2tog, yo, p2; repeat from * to end.

Rnd 9: *Yo, skp, p2; repeat from * to end.

Rnds 11 and 13: Repeat Rnds 7 and 9.

Rnds 15, 17, and 18: Repeat Rnd 1.

Change to working pattern.

Bottom-Up Flat

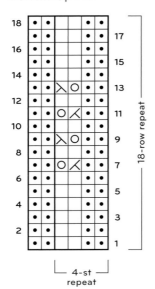

Bottom-Up in the Round

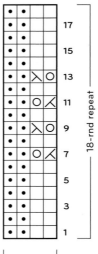

TOP-DOWN FLAT

(multiple of 4 sts + 2; 18 rows)

Note: Pattern begins with a WS row.

Row 1 and all WS Rows (WS): K2, *p2, k2; repeat from * to end.

Rows 2 and 4: Knit the knit sts and purl the purl sts as they face you.

Row 6: *P2, skp, yo; repeat from * to last 2 sts, p2.

Row 8: *P2, yo, k2tog; repeat from * to last 2 sts, p2.

Rows 10 and 12: Repeat Rows 6 and 8.

Rows 14, 16, and 18: Repeat Row 2.

BO all sts in pattern.

TOP-DOWN IN THE ROUND

(multiple of 4 sts; 18 rnds)

Rnds 1–6 and all Even-Numbered Rnds: *K2, p2; repeat from * to end.

Rnd 7: *Skp, yo, p2; repeat from * to end.

Rnd 9: *Yo, k2tog, p2; repeat from * to end.

Rnds 11 and 13: Repeat Rnds 7 and 9.

Rnds 15, 17, and 18: Repeat Rnd 1.

BO all sts in pattern.

Top-Down Flat

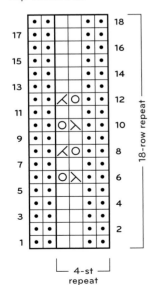

Top-Down in the Round

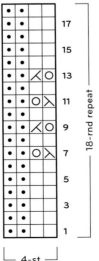

Note: Chart begins with a WS row.

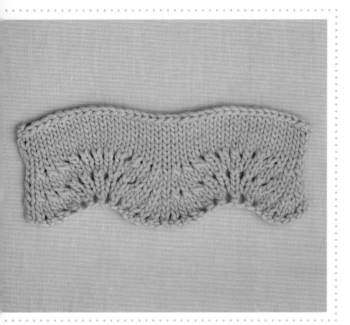

MADEIRA
SHELL EDGING

BOTTOM-UP FLAT

(multiple of 18 sts + 1; 4-row repeat)

Row 1 (RS): *K1, [k2tog] 3 times, [yo, k1] 5 times, yo, [ssk] 3 times; repeat from * to last st, k1.
Row 2: Purl.
Row 3: Knit.
Row 4: Purl.
Repeat Rows 1–4 to desired depth.
Change to working pattern.

BOTTOM-UP IN THE ROUND

(multiple of 18 sts; 4-rnd repeat)

Rnd 1: *K1, [k2tog] 3 times, [yo, k1] 5 times, yo, [ssk] 3 times; repeat from * to end.
Rnds 2-4: Knit.
Repeat Rnds 1–4 to desired depth.
Change to working pattern.

Bottom-Up Flat

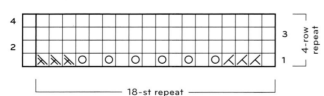

Bottom-Up in the Round

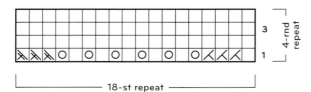

TOP-DOWN FLAT

(multiple of 18 sts + 1; 4-row repeat)

Row 1: *K1, [ssk] 3 times, [yo, k1] 5 times, yo, [k2tog] 3 times; repeat from * to last st, k1.
Row 2: Purl.
Row 3: Knit.
Row 4: Purl.
Repeat Rows 1–4 to desired depth, ending with Row 1.
BO all sts.

TOP-DOWN IN THE ROUND

(multiple of 18 sts; 4-rnd repeat)

Rnd 1: *K1, [ssk] 3 times, [yo, k1] 5 times, yo, [k2tog] 3 times; repeat from * to end.
Rnds 2-4: Knit.
Repeat Rnds 1–4 to desired depth, ending with Rnd 1.
BO all sts.

Top-Down Flat

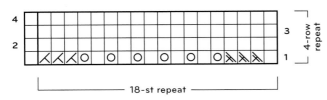

18-st repeat

Top-Down in the Round

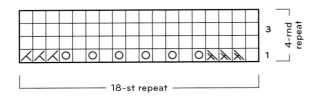

18-st repeat

FRILLY
RUFFLE

BOTTOM-UP FLAT

(any number of sts and rows)

Note: St count is halved on Decrease Row.
CO twice the number of sts needed for working
pattern. Work in St st (knit RS rows, purl WS
rows) to desired depth, ending with a WS row.
Decrease Row (RS): *K2tog; repeat from *
to end.
Change to working pattern.

BOTTOM-UP IN THE ROUND

(any number of sts and rnds)

Note: St count is halved on Decrease Rnd.
CO twice the number of sts needed for working
pattern. Join for working in the rnd. Work in
St st (knit every rnd) to desired depth.
Decrease Rnd: *K2tog; repeat from * to end.
Change to working pattern.

TOP-DOWN FLAT

(any number of sts and rows)

Note: St count is doubled on Increase Row.
Increase Row (RS): *K1–f/b; repeat from *
to end.
Work in St st, beginning with a purl row, to
desired depth. BO all sts.

TOP-DOWN IN THE ROUND

(any number of sts and rnds)

Note: St count is doubled on Increase Rnd.
Increase Rnd: *K1–f/b; repeat from * to end.
Work in St st (knit every rnd) to desired depth.
BO all sts.

ARBOR LACE EDGING

ARBOR LACE EDGING

BOTTOM-UP FLAT

(multiple of 11 sts; 10 or more rows)

Row 1 (RS): *Ssk, [k1-tbl] 3 times, yo, k1, yo, [k1-tbl] 3 times, k2tog; repeat from * to end.
Row 2: Purl.
Row 3: *Ssk, [k1-tbl] twice, yo, k1, yo, ssk, yo, [k1-tbl] twice, k2tog; repeat from * to end.
Row 4: Purl.
Row 5: *Ssk, k1-tbl, yo, k1, [yo, ssk] twice, yo, k1-tbl, k2tog; repeat from * to end.
Row 6: Purl.
Row 7: *Ssk, yo, k1, [yo, ssk] 3 times, yo, k2tog; repeat from * to end.
Row 8: Purl.
Row 9: *K1, p1, k7, p1, k1; repeat from * to end.
Row 10: *P1, k1, p7, k1, p1; repeat from * to end.
Repeat Rows 9 and 10 to desired length.
Change to working pattern.

BOTTOM-UP IN THE ROUND

(multiple of 11 sts; 9 or more rnds)

Rnd 1: *Ssk, [k1-tbl] 3 times, yo, k1, yo, [k1-tbl] 3 times, k2tog; repeat from * to end.
Rnd 2: Knit.
Rnd 3: *Ssk, [k1-tbl] twice, yo, k1, yo, ssk, yo, [k1-tbl] twice, k2tog; repeat from * to end.
Rnd 4: Knit.
Rnd 5: *Ssk, k1-tbl, yo, k1, [yo, ssk] twice, yo, k1-tbl, k2tog; repeat from * to end.
Rnd 6: Knit.
Rnd 7: *Ssk, yo, k1, [yo, ssk] 3 times, yo, k2tog; repeat from * to end.
Rnd 8: Knit.
Rnd 9: *K1, p1, k7, p1, k1; repeat from * to end.
Repeat Rnd 9 to desired length.
Change to working pattern.

Bottom-Up Flat

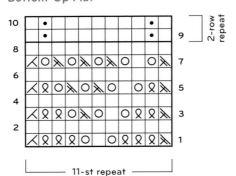

Bottom-Up in the Round

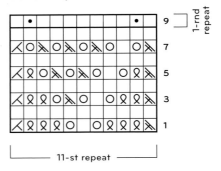

TOP-DOWN FLAT

(multiple of 11 sts; 10 or more rows)

Row 1 (RS): *K1, p1, k7, p1, k1; repeat from * to end.

Row 2: *P1, k1, p7, k1, p1; repeat from * to end. Repeat Rows 1 and 2 to desired length, ending with Row 2, before working lace as follows:

Row 3 (RS): *K2tog, yo, [ssk, yo] 3 times, k1, yo, ssk; repeat from * to end.

Row 4: Purl.

Row 5: *K2tog, k1-tbl, yo, [ssk, yo] twice, k1, yo, k1-tbl, ssk; repeat from * to end.

Row 6: Purl.

Row 7: *K2tog, [k1-tbl] twice, yo, ssk, yo, k1, yo, [k1-tbl] twice, ssk; repeat from * to end.

Row 8: Purl.

Row 9: *K2tog, [k1-tbl] 3 times, yo, k1, yo, [k1-tbl] 3 times, ssk; repeat from * to end.

Row 10: Purl.

BO all sts.

TOP-DOWN IN THE ROUND

(multiple of 11 sts; 9 or more rnds)

Rnd 1: *K1, p1, k7, p1, k1; repeat from * to end. Repeat Rnd 1 to desired length, before working lace as follows:

Rnd 2: *K2tog, yo, [ssk, yo] 3 times, k1, yo, ssk; repeat from * to end.

Rnd 3: Knit.

Rnd 4: *K2tog, k1-tbl, yo, [ssk, yo] twice, k1, yo, k1-tbl, ssk; repeat from * to end.

Rnd 5: Knit.

Rnd 6: *K2tog, [k1-tbl] twice, yo, ssk, yo, k1, yo, [k1-tbl] twice, ssk; repeat from * to end.

Rnd 7: Knit.

Rnd 8: *K2tog, [k1-tbl] 3 times, yo, k1, yo, [k1-tbl] 3 times, ssk; repeat from * to end.

Rnd 9: Knit.

BO all sts.

Top-Down Flat

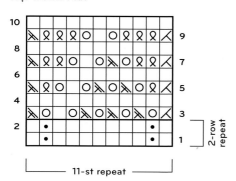

Top-Down in the Round

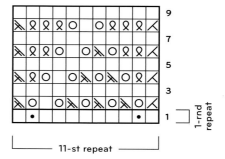

RUFFLE EDGE SCARF

Here's an example of a pattern where we're adding an edging to an already-knit item. The scarf is worked from end to end with shaping that happens on one edge only to give it an effortless, elongated shape. Then, stitches are picked up along the shaped edge and a light frill is worked for some added fun.

SCARF

Using larger needle, CO 4 sts.

Shape First Half

Row 1 (Increase Row) (RS): K2, k1-f/b, k1—5 sts.

Row 2 and all WS Rows: Slip 1, purl to last 3 sts, k3 [edge sts, keep in Garter st (knit every row)].

Row 3: Knit.

Row 5 (Increase Row): Knit to last 2 sts, k1-f/b, k1—6 sts.

Row 7: Knit.

Row 9 (Increase Row): Knit to last 2 sts, k1-f/b, k1—7 sts.

Continue to shape first half of Scarf as established, working an Increase Row every fourth row, until you have 56 sts, ending with an Increase Row. Work even for 3 rows.

Shape Second Half

Row 1 (Decrease Row): Knit to last 3 sts, k2tog, k1—55 sts remain.

Row 3: Knit.

Row 5 (Decrease Row): Knit to last 3 sts, k2tog, k1—54 sts remain.

Continue to shape second half of Scarf as established, working a Decrease Row every fourth row, until you have 4 sts, ending with a Decrease Row. Work even for 1 row. BO all sts knitwise.

FINISHING

Ruffle

With RS facing, using smaller needle and beginning at CO edge, pick up and knit approximately 3 sts out of every 4 rows along right-hand (slipped) edge. Purl 1 row.

Increase Row (RS): *K1-f/b; repeat from * to end, doubling your original st count. Work 9 rows in St st, beginning with a purl row. BO all sts; allow edge to roll slightly.

FINISHING

Block as desired.

FINISHED MEASUREMENTS

Approximately 9 ¼" (23.5 cm) wide at widest point x 59" (150 cm) long along straight edge

YARN

Blue Sky Alpacas Alpaca Silk (50% alpaca / 50% silk; 146 yards / 50 grams): 3 hanks #147 Crabapple

NEEDLES

One 29" (70 cm) long circular (circ) needle size US 5 (3.75 mm)

One 32" (80 cm) long or longer circular (circ) needle US 4 (3.5mm)

Change needle size if necessary to obtain correct gauge.

GAUGE

24 sts and 28 rows = 4" (10 cm) in Stockinette stitch (St st), using larger needle

APPENDIX

If you would like to try your hand at incorporating stitch patterns into basic designs, these "From Scratch" formulas are a great place to start. The patterns here are guidelines you can follow to either recreate garments that are similar to the ones shown in the photos, or design garments with your own creative fingerprint. Designing these types of projects is easy and fun, and it's also a great way to practice swapping out stitch patterns.

FROM-SCRATCH PROJECT 1

LACE STOLE

To create your own version of this lace stole, you can use any of the flat stitch patterns in this book. Simply select three stitch patterns (or more if you like) and separate the motifs using panels of Garter or Stockinette stitch.

Before you begin, decide on your finished measurements. Here are some typical dimensions to get you started:

Stole: 16" x 70" (40.5 x 178 cm)
Skinny Scarf: 4" x 54" (10 x 137 cm)
Basic Scarf: 10" x 42" (25.5 x 106.5 cm)
    or 15" x 45" (38 x 114.5 cm)
Muffler: 12" x 54" (30.5 x 137 cm)

Choose your stitch pattern or patterns and plot them out on a piece of paper, making note of the necessary multiples of stitches. I suggest swatching all three stitch patterns at once, casting on the appropriate multiple of stitches for each pattern and separating them with a small panel of Garter stitch. Also, don't forget to add a nonrolling border at your cast-on and bind-off edges, and on either side of the swatch.

Work your 4" (10 cm) gauge swatch, bind off, and block it. Measure the swatch and decide if you like the way the stitch patterns look together. When you're happy with your swatch, cast on enough stitches for your desired measurements, including stitches for a nonrolling edge (you may find it helpful to place markers to separate motifs and borders). Work your project to your desired length, keeping in mind your swatch measurement after blocking (i.e., your scarf will grow), and just before you've hit the right length, add a nonrolling edge. If you prefer, you could bind off stitches and then pick up and knit stitches on each side, adding a border from chapter 8 after the fact.

The stole shown below is 15" x 60" (38 x 152.5 cm). I cast on 77 sts and used a combination of Amphora Lace Flat (page 198) and Easy Lace Flat (page 188). Notice that there is a row of eyelets separating the sections and that panels of Stockinette Stitch are set in between the three panels of Easy Lace. This stole took four hanks of Blue Sky Alpacas Alpaca Silk in Peridot #148. The gauge is 21 sts and 32 rows to 4" (10 cm) on size US 4 (3.5 mm) needles in Amphora Lace, before blocking.

SLOUCH CAP

You can knit a top-down cap using just about any stitch pattern you like. As you add stitches to the eight sections that comprise the crown, the trick is to figure out how to make your chosen stitch pattern elegantly flow into the final stitch count. Use the Basic Top-Down In-the-Round Cap Formula below to design your own cap; if you would like to create a cable cap just like the one on page 277, read through the notes at the end of the formula.

BASIC TOP-DOWN IN-THE-ROUND CAP FORMULA

You'll need a set of double-pointed needles (dpn), 8 stitch markers, and a 12"-16" (30-40 cm) –long circular needle (optional).

Knit a gauge swatch in your stitch pattern and fill in the blanks below.

Stitches per inch (from your swatch): _____ (A).

Goal head circumference for brim: _____(B). (Negative ease is required for a close-fitting cap. Subtract an inch or two for best fit. For a slouchier version, use the actual head circumference).

Stitches per section: $(A \times B) \div 8 =$ _____ rounded to a whole number (C).

Using dpn, CO 8 sts.

Rnd 1: K1-f/b into each stitch—16 sts. Divide sts among 3 needles.

Rnd 2: Knit.

Rnd 3: *K1, k1-f/b; rep from * to end—24 sts. **Note:** you may use any type of increase you want so that the following stitches appear as you want them to.

Rnd 4: Knit, placing markers after every third st—8 markers, including beginning of rnd marker.

Shape Crown

Note: Change to circular needle if desired to accommodate number of sts on needles (optional).

*K1-f/b, work to marker, sm; repeat from * to end—32 sts. Knit 1 rnd. Repeat the last 2 rnds until the stitch count per section equals C. Work even until the cap measures your desired depth to the beginning of the ribbing. You may need to increase or decrease a stitch or two to accommodate your desired ribbing multiple. Work the ribbing to your desired finished length. BO all sts loosely in pattern. Thread CO tail through CO sts at crown and pull tight. Fasten off. Block as desired.

For the top-down cap shown at right, I followed the Top-Down Cap Formula using the Hugs and Kisses Cables (page 153). The trick to making the crown look planned and neat is to separate the stitches into eight sections at the crown and add stitches to each section every other round. Keeping in mind my goal stitches for my intended circumference (96 stitches with a total of 12 stitches in each section) and knowing that the Hugs and Kisses Cables requires a multiple of eight stitches, I added stitches and planned to keep the center eight stitches in Stockinette, while maintaining two stitches on either side in Reverse Stockinette. Once I reached my goal, I started working the cables in each section until the cap measured about 2" (5 cm) less than my desired length. Using smaller needles, I changed to a rib pattern that matched the cables and Reverse Stockinette Stitch until it was time to bind off. I used two hanks of Blue Sky Alpacas Worsted Hand Dyes in Putty #2015 and US 9 (5.5 mm) circular needles for the main Body of the cap. My gauge was 18 sts and 24 rows to 4" (10 cm) in Hugs and Kisses Cables.

PLEATED MITTENS

If you are using yarn in the same weight as the mittens shown at right, it's easy to swap out the pleats for an in-the-round stitch pattern of your choice. You'll have to pay attention to your stitch count and adjust it after you complete the cuff, but from there on out you can follow the pattern as written. And if you want to go rogue and work a pair of mittens without referring to a specific pattern, here is a basic formula:

1. Swatch any stitch patterns you plan to use. Measure the circumference of your palm (or the recipient's).

2. Using double-pointed needles, cast on enough stitches to equal your hand measurement, rounding to a number that will accommodate your chosen stitch pattern. If you're concerned that it will be too loose, go down a needle size for this portion of the mitten.

3. Place a marker, join in the round, and work a couple rounds of Stockinette stitch or your selected stitch pattern.

4. Work to where you want to start your thumb gusset. Place a marker, increase 1 stitch, place a marker and work to the end. Work 2 rounds.

5. Work to the first marker and slip it, increase 1 stitch, knit to the second marker, increase 1 stitch, slip the marker and work to the end. You will have 3 gusset stitches. Work 2 rounds.

6. Continue working an increase round as in Step 5 and working 2 rounds even until the gusset measures about 3" (7.5 cm) wide for an adult and about 2 1/2" (6.5 cm) for a child. If the height of the gusset doesn't reach the place on your hand where the thumb separates from your palm, work a few extra rounds without increasing. Typical gusset heights are 2-2 1/2" (5-6.5 cm) for an adult. For children, aim for 1 3/4-2" (4.5-5 cm).

7. On the next round, work to the marker separating the gusset stitches. Transfer the gusset stitches onto waste yarn. Using the Backward Loop Cast-On method (page 282), cast on 1 stitch and work to the end. (If you are working a stitch pattern on your mitten and this extra stitch affects it, you can omit it.)

8. Continue working the body of the mitten in the round until it reaches about 1 1/2" (4 cm) from the end of your fingers.

CLOSING THE MITTEN TOP AND FINISHING THE THUMB

Count your stitches and separate them into 4 or 5 sections, depending upon your stitch count. Place markers to separate each section. On the next round, *k2tog, work to next marker, slip marker; repeat from * to last section, k2tog, work to end. You will have decreased 4 or 5 sts. **Note:** You can use any type of decrease you desire—k2tog for a right-leaning decrease or ssk for a left-leaning one. Work 1 round even. Continue working decreases right after each marker every other round until you have 8 or 10 sts left. Cut yarn; thread tail through remaining stitches; pull tight and fasten off.

For the thumb, place the reserved stitches onto 3 dpns and pick up and knit 1 stitch over the gap. Join yarn and work in the round until the thumb measures to the middle of the thumbnail or about 1 1/2-2" (4-5 cm) for adults and about 1-1 1/2" (2.5-4 cm) for children. Count your total stitches and try to separate them into 3 or 4 equal portions by placing markers. Work decreases as you did with the top of the mitten every other round until you have just a few stitches left. Cut yarn; thread tail through remaining stitches; pull tight and fasten off.

If you want to re-create the mitts shown at right, you'll need two hanks of Blue Sky Alpacas Alpaca Silk in Papaya #143. I used double-pointed needles in size US 4 (3.5 mm) and had a gauge of 24 sts and 34 rows to 4" (10 cm) in Stockinette stitch. For the cuff, I started out with Seed stitch for 3 rounds, then changed to Pleats in the Round (page 74) for 2 repeats. After that, I just followed the Mittens formula at left. Pay attention to your stitch counts and the multiples required for your stitch patterns as you go, and make stealth decreases or increases to accommodate when necessary. I promise, no one will notice!

ABBREVIATIONS

1/1 LT-p Slip 1 stitch to cable needle, hold to front, p1, k1-tbl from cable needle.

1/1 RT-p Slip 1 stitch to cable needle, hold to back, k1-tbl, p1 from cable needle.

1/2 LC Slip 1 stitch to cable needle, hold to front, k2, k1 from cable needle.

1/2 LC-p Slip 1 stitch to cable needle, hold to front, p2, k1 from cable needle.

1/2 RC Slip 2 stitches to cable needle, hold to back, k1, k2 from cable needle.

1/2 RC-p Slip 2 stitches to cable needle, hold to back, k1, p2 from cable needle.

1/3 LC-p Slip 1 stitch to cable needle, hold to front, p3, k1 from cable needle.

1/3 RC-p Slip 3 stitches to cable needle, hold to back, k1, p3 from cable needle.

2/1 LC-p Slip 2 stitches to cable needle, hold to front, p1, k2 from cable needle.

2/1 RC-p Slip 1 stitch to cable needle, hold to back, k2, p1 from cable needle.

BO Bind off.

C4B Slip 2 stitches to cable needle, hold to back, k2, k2 from cable needle.

C4F Slip 2 stitches to cable needle, hold to front, k2, k2 from cable needle.

C6B Slip 3 stitches to cable needle, hold to back, k3, k3 from cable needle.

C6F Slip 3 stitches to cable needle, hold to front, k3, k3 from cable needle.

C8F Slip 4 stitches to cable needle, hold to front, k4, k4 from cable needle.

Circ Circular

Cn Cable needle

CO Cast on

Dpn Double-pointed needle(s)

K1b Knit into stitch below next stitch on left-hand needle dropping stitch from left-hand needle.

K1-f/b Knit into front loop and back loop of same stitch—1 stitch increased.

K1-tbl Knit 1 stitch through back loop.

K2tog (right-slanting decrease) Knit 2 stitches together—1 stitch decreased.

K3tog (right-slanting decrease) Knit 3 stitches together—2 stitches decreased.

K Knit

LC (Left Cross) Insert needle from back to front between first and second stitches on left-hand needle and knit the second stitch. Knit into back of second stitch, then into front of first stitch; slip both from left-hand needle together.

LI (right-slanting lifted increase) Knit into stitch in row below next stitch on left-hand needle—1 stitch increased.

LLI (left-slanting lifted increase) On right-side rows, with left-hand needle, pick up left leg of stitch 2 stitches below last stitch on right-hand needle; knit picked-up stitch through back loop. On wrong-side rows, purl into purl bump below first stitch on left-hand needle, working into bump from top down—1 stitch increased.

M1-l (make 1-left slanting)
With tip of left-hand needle inserted from front to back, lift strand between 2 needles onto left-hand needle; knit strand through back loop—1 stitch increased.

M1-p-r (make 1 purlwise-right slanting)
With tip of left-hand needle inserted from back to front, lift strand between 2 needles onto left-

hand needle; purl strand through front loop—1 stitch increased.

M1-r (make 1-right slanting) With tip of left-hand needle inserted from back to front, lift strand between 2 needles onto left-hand needle; knit strand through front loop—1 stitch increased.

P1b Purl into stitch below next stitch on left-hand needle, dropping stitch from left-hand needle.

P1-f/b (worked on a wrong-side row) Purl into front loop, then back loop of same stitch—1 stitch increased.

P1-f/b/f Purl into front loop, back loop, then front loop of same stitch—2 stitches increased.

P1-tbl Purl one stitch trhough back loop.

P2sp (left-slanting decrease) P2tog, slip resulting stitch purlwise back to left-hand needle, pass second stitch on left-hand needle over first, slip resulting stitch back to right-hand needle—2 stitches decreased.

P2tog (right-slanting decrease) Purl 2 stitches together—1 stitch decreased.

P3tog (right-slanting decrease) Purl 3 stitches together—2 stitches decreased.

Pm Place marker

P Purl

Psso (pass slipped stitch over) Pass slipped stitch on right-hand needle over stitch(es) indicated in the instructions, as in binding off.

Rev Reverse

Rnd(s) Round(s)

RC (right cross) On right-side rows, insert tip of right-hand needle into front of second stitch, bringing tip to front of work between second and first stitches, knit stitch, knit first stitch through front loop, slip both stitches from left-hand needle together. On wrong-side rows, purl into front of second stitch, then purl into front of first stitch, slip both stitches from left-hand needle together.

RLI (right-slanting lifted increase) On right-side rows, with right-hand needle, pick up right side of stitch below next stitch on left-hand needle, and place it on left-hand needle; knit the picked-up stitch through front loop—1 stitch increased. On wrong-side rows, with left-hand needle, pick up second purl bump below last stitch on right-hand needle, picking up from bottom up; purl picked-up stitch—1 stitch increased.

RS Right side

RT (right twist) K2tog, but do not drop stitches from left-hand needle; insert right-hand needle between 2 stitches just worked and knit first stitch again, slip both stitches from left-hand needle together.

S2kp2 (centered decrease) Slip next 2 stitches together to right-hand needle as if to knit 2 together, k1, pass the 2 slipped stitches over—2 stitches decreased.

Skp (slip, knit, pass; left-slanting decrease) Slip next stitch knitwise to right-hand needle, k1, pass slipped stitch over knit stitch—1 stitch decreased.

Sk2p (left-slanting decrease) Slip next stitch knitwise to right-hand needle, k2tog, pass slipped stitch over stitch from k2tog—2 stitches decreased.

Sm Slip marker

Spp (slip, purl, pass, worked on a wrong-side row; left-slanting decrease) Slip next stitch purlwise to right-hand needle, p1, pass slipped stitch over purl stitch—1 stitch increased.

Ssk (slip, slip, knit, left-slanting decrease) Slip next 2 stitches to right-hand needle one at a time as if to knit; return them to left-hand needle one at a time in their new orientation; knit them together through back loops.

Ssp (slip, slip, purl, worked on a wrong-side row; left-slanting decrease) Slip next 2 stitches to right-hand needle one at a time as if to knit; return them to left-hand needle one at a time in their new orientation; purl them together through back loops.

St(s) Stitch(es)

St st Stockinette stitch

T3R (twist 3 right) Knit into third stitch on left-hand needle, then second, then first, slip all 3 stitches from left-hand needle together.

Tbl Through the back loop

Tog Together

WS Wrong side

Wyib With yarn in back

Wyif With yarn in front

Yo Yarnover

SPECIAL TECHNIQUES

Backward Loop CO Make a slip knot and place it on the right-hand needle (first st CO), *wind yarn around thumb clockwise, insert right-hand needle into the front of the loop on thumb, remove thumb and tighten st on needle; repeat from * for remaining sts to be CO, or for casting on at the end of a row in progress.

Kitchener Stitch Using a tapestry needle, thread a length of yarn approximately 4 times the length of the section to be joined. Hold the pieces wrong sides together, with the needles holding the sts parallel, both ends pointing to the right. Working from right to left, insert tapestry needle into first st on front needle as if to purl, pull yarn through, leaving st on needle; insert tapestry needle into first st on back needle as if to knit, pull yarn through, leaving st on needle; *insert tapestry needle into first st on front needle as if to knit, pull yarn through, remove st from needle; insert tapestry needle into next st on front needle as if to purl, pull yarn through, leave st on needle; insert tapestry needle into first st on back needle as if to purl, pull yarn through, remove st from needle; insert tapestry needle into next st on back needle as if to knit, pull yarn through, leave st on needle. Repeat from *, working 3 or 4 sts at a time, then go back and adjust tension. When 1 st remains on each needle, cut yarn and pass through last 2 sts to fasten off.

Knitting Two Colors Together When making color changes at the beginning of a round, knit the first stitch of the next round with both colors—the old one and the new one—then drop the old one and continue knitting. Once you've worked several rounds or the whole item, use the end of a tapestry needle to tease out the yarn ends so the old color is on the right-hand side of knit-stitch "v" and the new color is to the left. This makes the color change look like it is in the middle of a stitch instead of a jog.

KEY

☐	Knit on RS, purl on WS.	⅄	S2kp2
☐	In color charts, work using color A.	⩃	K4tog
☐	In color charts, work using color B.	I ȣ	On RS, [k1-tbl, k1] into double yo; on WS, [p1, p1-tbl] into double yo.
☐	In color charts, work using color C.	• I	[K1, p1] into double yo.
•	Purl on RS, knit on WS.	I •	[P1, k1] into double yo.
ȣ	K1-tbl on RS, p1-tbl on WS.	RT	RT
ȣ	P1-tbl on RS, k1-tbl on WS.	RC	RC
O	Yo	LC	LC
V	Slip 1 wyib on RS, slip 1 wyif on WS.	1/1 RT-p	1/1 RT-p
⩔	Slip 1 wyif on RS, slip 1 wyib on WS.	1/1 LT-p	1/1 LT-p
☐	No stitch	T3R	T3R
ठ	M1-l	1/2 RC	1/2 RC
ठ	M1-r	1/2 LC	1/2 LC
ठ	M1-p-r	1/2 RC-p	1/2 RC-p
V	Ll	1/2 LC-p	1/2 LC-p
⟍	K1-f/b on RS, p1-f/b on WS.	2/1 RC-p	2/1 RC-p
ⱴ	[K1, yo, k1] in next st on RS, [p1, yo, p1] in next st on WS.	2/1 LC-p	2/1 LC-p
ⱴ	[P1, yo, p1] in next st on RS, [k1, yo, k1] in next st on WS.	ȣ ȣ	Slip 2 sts to cn, hold to front, k1-tbl, slip last st from cn back to left-hand needle, p, k1-tbl from cn.
⟱	P1-f/b/f	C4B	C4B
Ч	LLI	C4F	C4F
Г	RLI		Slip 2 sts to cn, hold to back, k2tog, yo, p2 from cn.
⟋	K2tog on RS, p2tog on WS.		Slip 2 sts to cn, hold to front, p2, yo, ssk from cn.
⟋	P2tog on RS, k2tog on WS.	1/3 RC-p	1/3 RC-p
⟍	Skp on RS, spp on WS.	1/3 LC-p	1/3 LC-p
⟍	Spp on WS.	C6B	C6B
⟍	Ssk on RS, ssp on WS.	C6F	C6F
⟋	K3tog on RS, p3tog on WS.	C8F	C8F
⟋	P3tog on RS, k3tog on WS.		
⟍	Sk2p on RS, p2sp on WS.		

STITCH MULTIPLE INDEX

If you are knitting a project and want to substitute one stitch pattern for another, the simplest way to go about it is to pick a stitch pattern that has the same multiple of stitches as the one written in the original pattern. In this section, you will find all of the stitch patterns from this book organized by the multiple of stitches they require.

STITCH MULTIPLE INDEX

285

ACKNOWLEDGMENTS

In the years that I've been knitting and designing, many people have inspired me.

First, I have to hand it to Barbara Walker, whose Treasury stitch dictionaries have delighted me and provided me with hours of inspiration. Ditto to the handful of authors and editors who have culled stitch patterns originating from all parts of the world and eras gone by into volumes and volumes of patterns that I—and you—can use.

I am grateful for my cheerful, capable, and incredibly quick-witted editor, Liana Allday, whose support has never wavered. Sue McCain, my technical editor, has been by my side from day one and I will always be happy to know her. She loves creating charts. In a way, I like to think that this book is sort of a sideways gift to her. (Although now I'm hoping I haven't cured her of her passion!) And, of course, Anna Christian: She has been the graphic-design brain behind all of my books and this one, I believe, is just beautiful. Thanks also to Robin Melanson, who provided another set of eyes, making sure that the text is as technically correct as possible.

It is no coincidence that all the swatches and patterns in this book are made from Blue Sky Alpacas yarns. I have admired their range of colors for years and it was an honor to be able to use their beautiful fibers in this book.

As always, I give my husband and daughter all my appreciation. They have never looked at me while I'm knitting and declared that I should be doing something else. They've always known what was up, even though I never had to say it.

The craft of knitting has given me so many gifts. I would never have imagined that knitting that first teeny-tiny strawberry cap for my teeny-tiny infant daughter would have come to this. The crafting community, and specifically the knitting community, has given me joy and freedom that I never thought I would have. Thank you to all of you.

Now, go and knit!

Wendy.

Wendy Bernard is a knitwear designer based in Southern California. She is the author of the Custom Knits series and is the creator of the popular blog Knit and Tonic (knitandtonic.net). Her knitwear patterns have been published online by Knitty and Stitch Diva Studios, in the magazines *Interweave Knits* and *Knitscene*, in the books *No Sheep for You*, *Brave New Knits*, and *My Grandmother's Knitting* (STC), and in a DVD series teaching top-down knitting techniques.